"The Christian church's first theologian, sec t re-
mains the most accurate and penetrating d y of
God is man fully alive.' Matt Heard has taken that brief sentence and expanded it
into this marvelous book, telling by story and observation, and using vigorous language (there is not a dull sentence in what he writes), to get us to embrace what has
been given to us."

—EUGENE H. PETERSON, translator of *The Message*

"Matt Heard is a fresh new voice with a literally life-changing message. *Life with a
Capital L* is a call to each of us to embrace our own humanity—just as God does.
Here's a book that will deepen your walk with God and elevate your life to the level
of Life."

—MARK BATTERSON, author of *The Grave Robber* and *All In*

"This is Praise with a capital P for *Life with a Capital L*. 'What does it mean to be
alive?' and 'What does it mean to be human?' are two of the most important questions any human being can ask. They are questions that all Christians share with all
of humanity. Matt Heard reflects on them with a warmth and honesty that will be
welcomed by all who ask the questions."

—JOHN ORTBERG, author of *The Life You've Always Wanted*

"For years, I've treasured St. Irenaeus's words, 'The glory of God is man fully alive.'
The quote rests on a shelf above my computer, and hardly a day goes by that I don't
ask God to help me live out that enigmatic statement. Well, I now have a book to
guide me. My friend, Matt Heard, writes winsomely and compellingly, answering
that quiet aching so many people have—yes, even Christians—that there must be
more to life. Trust me, the book you hold in your hands will awaken in you a deep
desire to be all that God intended. I highly recommend *Life with a Capital L!*"

—JONI EARECKSON TADA, Joni and Friends International Disability Center

"The problem of pain may be one of the greatest challenges to faith in God, but the
problem of pleasure can be more precarious. Disappointment in pleasure gives rise
to emptiness, and sometimes not just for a moment but for life. Yet God created us

for a purpose, and as Matt Heard writes, for so much more than we often recognize. Matt challenges us to look deeper into the mirror and to God who knows us fully and loves us intimately. *Life with a Capital L* is rich in encouragement, illustration, scriptural insight, and pastoral wisdom, and offers readers fresh insight and lasting hope."

—RAVI ZACHARIAS, author and speaker

"I know Matt Heard to be a thoughtful, humble follower of Christ. Those qualities are evident in *Life with a Capital L*. This book is a clear and powerful call to rediscover the depth and breadth of Life as God intended—to embrace the longing we all have to really Live as humans made in God's image."

—JIM DALY, president of Focus on the Family

"Matt goes to the heart of our need for Jesus. He makes us hope for heaven in a way that marks the everyday. He's a pastor, a leader, and a friend, and none of that is lost in these words."

—JENNIE ALLEN, author of *Restless* and founder of IF: Gathering

"Your world can be full of color, adventure, and discovery—Life with a capital L. Let Matt guide you on a journey to your full humanity—empowered, equipped, and inspired by the One who created you to live abundantly. Read this book and get ready to come alive in new ways!"

—LEE STROBEL, best-selling author of *The Case for Christ* and professor
    at Houston Baptist University

"This is what it's all about. Literally. Unless God's people understand what's in this book, we cannot be God's people. It's that important. Please read this book and rejoice that Matt Heard has written it!"

—ERIC METAXAS, *New York Times* best-selling author of *Bonhoeffer:*
    Pastor, Martyr, Prophet, Spy and *Miracles: What They Are, Why They*
    Happen, and How They Can Change Your Life

"Matt Heard's new book is a deep well of resource for the soul. In *Life with a Capital L*, we have an invaluable resource to live the abundant Life of God, a map toward cultural life around us, and a blessing to re-humanize our world. Matt's approach toward beauty grows my heart as an artist and nourishes my creativity. His stories stir within me a deeper longing to create, love, and worship—with passion—our Savior-artist who pours grace into my heart."

—MAKO FUJIMURA, artist, author, and culture-care catalyst

"Matt Heard is a master storyteller, and peeking through all his stories is the Life Giver. I was struck by the intellectual depth of this book, but even more I was embraced by the personal Savior revealing himself through its stories. This book helped me see God not just in its pages but in my everyday experiences. Matt Heard ushers me into the greater Life."

—DR. JOEL C. HUNTER, senior pastor of Northland, A Church Distributed

"An essential part of the gospel is often missed by Christians and left untold by churches: Christ didn't come to save us from our humanity but to return us to it! Matt Heard has skillfully preached and taught this for years, and now he skillfully articulates this truth through this book. Like me, I suspect readers will find themselves asking *What if? What if this is actually true?* and find their imaginations running wild with the Good News."

—JOHN STONESTREET, speaker and fellow at Chuck Colson Center
for Christian Worldview

"Life is a journey more than a destination. Matt Heard demonstrates and exemplifies this as one who seeks to be fully alive and longs for any who are interested to join him in that journey. This book is charged with all the stimulus and struggle that authentic human life must engage. Matt's artful portrait of Life is honest and hopeful, assured of God's love in Jesus Christ, but never glib or reductionist. This book awakens our thirst for Life as the real thing and nothing less."

—MARK LABBERTON, president of Fuller Theological Seminary

"Part Francis Schaeffer, part Max Lucado, and part Rick Steves, *Life with a Capital L* is one of those rare books that is both a page-turner and yet deeply contemplative. Matt Heard dives heart-first into Jesus's promise of a full Life and shows through biblical insight and hard-won experience how this promise is alive and well and meant for each of us. Matt's joyful engagement with art, music, food, conversation, travel, the Bible…and LIFE gives hope that God is actively restoring our humanity. Reading *Life with a Capital L* was a highlight of my year."

—JEFF MYERS, PhD, president of Summit Ministries

"*Life with a Capital L* will breathe new energy, new excitement, and new purpose into the life you are living. This is a challenge to all of us to go full tilt, be all in, and make it our ambition to embrace the fullness of what Life can and should be in relationship with Jesus. Being fully alive and fully human means we experience the eternal now. I'm fired up after reading this book!"

—BRAD LOMENICK, former president and key visionary of Catalyst, and author of *The Catalyst Leader*

"Matt Heard does not want to say something new but something old, only in a new, fresh way. And that he does well. Matt tells just the right story at just the right time. He writes with a pastor's heart and experience. He has read good books and learned from the masters. And he writes in a winsome, accessible style. His point is clear, compelling, and significant: we long for real Life, real Life can be ours, and real Life is available in Jesus Christ. This truth never grows old. Matt Heard knows this in his soul. This book is not simply about Life with a capital L. It actually conveys that Life."

—GERALD L. SITTSER, author of *A Grace Disguised, A Grace Revealed,* and *Water from a Deep Well,* and theology teacher at Whitworth University

"This book is Uplifting with a capital U. In it, Matt Heard pours out wise pastoral insights on being fully human."

—DON SWEETING, president of Reformed Theological Seminary in Orlando

"Many Christians have never considered that *abundant life* actually means becoming more human, not less. God's image lived out through us means we get to experience the fullness of what it means to be human, and to a skeptical world, that's Good News!"

—GABE LYONS, author of *The Next Christians*

"Loved Matt Heard's book on Life. I read it in one night and believe he squeezed the life out of the title. It's accented well with great personal stories; some of my all-time favorite quotes from Kierkegaard, Eliot, Pascal, and 'Babette's Feast'; and liberal use of appropriate Scripture. This book is the package."

—PEB JACKSON, Jackson Consulting Group

life

with a capital

life
with a capital

EMBRACING
YOUR
GOD-GIVEN
HUMANITY

matt heard

MULTNOMAH
BOOKS

LIFE WITH A CAPITAL L
PUBLISHED BY MULTNOMAH BOOKS
12265 Oracle Boulevard, Suite 200
Colorado Springs, CO 80291

Italics in Scripture quotations reflect the author's added emphasis.

Details in some anecdotes and stories have been changed to protect the identities of the persons involved.

Trade Paperback ISBN 978-1-60142-446-4
eBook ISBN 978-1-60142-447-1

Cover design by Kristopher K. Orr; cover image by Mmdi, Getty Images

Published in association with the literary agency of Alive Communications Inc., 7680 Goddard Street, Suite 200, Colorado Springs, Colorado 80920, www.alivecommunications.com.

Library of Congress Cataloging-in-Publication Data
Heard, Matt.
    Life with a capital L : embracing your God-given humanity / Matt Heard. — First Edition.
        pages cm
    Includes bibliographical references.
    ISBN 978-1-60142-446-4 — ISBN 978-1-60142-447-1 1. Life—Religious aspects—Christianity. 2. Christian life. 3. Christianity—Philosophy. I. Title.
    BV4509.5.H43 2014
    248.4—dc23
                                        2014024950

Printed in the United States of America
2015

10 9 8 7 6 5 4

SPECIAL SALES
Most WaterBrook Multnomah books are available at special quantity discounts when purchased in bulk by corporations, organizations, and special-interest groups. Custom imprinting or excerpting can also be done to fit special needs. For information, please e-mail SpecialMarkets@WaterBrookMultnomah.com or call 1-800-603-7051.

To Andrew, Joel, and Stephen:

As you pursue Christ's Life,
fight for your hearts, fight with your hearts,
and relish the gift and calling of being human.

contents

acknowledgments

This book was birthed not from the ink of a pen or keystrokes of a computer but from a journey enriched by Christ's Life in a caring and authentic community of companions. The contents of these pages have been nurtured by them.

First and foremost: Arlene, I could not have tackled this project without your loving support as well as your honest and encouraging first-reads. Most of all, thank you for your beautiful partnership in Life and for your extraordinary and Life-giving love for our sons. I'm humbly and forever grateful.

Andrew, Joel, and Stephen, our Band of Brothers never ceases to be Life-giving for my heart. Thank you for your grace-filled and loving encouragement for me to take the time and solitude to put on paper what I earnestly hope will be both a beacon and compass for your entire journey.

Mary Heard, Mom, not only did you give me life but you pointed me to Life. Awe-filled thanks to you and Dad for so consistently keeping your encouraging "chair" turned toward me.

Ken Petersen, I entered into this project humbled by the attentiveness of an incredible editor, and I finished it with a new friend. Thank you for convincing this first-time author to find his voice. Your belief in me, encouragement, honesty, and coaching have all been Life-giving.

Rick Christian, abundant thanks to you and Alive for patiently and persistently insisting that my spoken words find their place on the page in a lasting and Life-giving way. Your vision has truly been a gift.

Carie Freimuth, Allison O'Hara, Ashley Boyer, Laura Wright, and the rest of the great team at WaterBrook Multnomah, thank you for believing in this message.

Josh Ellis, Carrie Smith, Lynn Williams, thank you for your energetic help with research and paperwork, and, most of all, your encouragement.

Kent Eilers, Vernon Rainwater, and Allen Arnold, thank you for seeing the Life-giving potential of the manuscript. Even more significant, your companionship has fueled me along the way.

Thank you, Rick and Debbie, Jim and Jean, Peb and Sharon, Al and Susan, for breathing Life into my journey.

To the men and women of Woodmen Valley Chapel who bolstered me along the way, thank you for your affirmation and hunger for grace, truth, and Life.

Thank you to the community of Lost Valley Ranch, for being sounding boards and launching pads of Life with a capital L.

Thank you, Curt, Mary Em, Grace, Jerry, Mako, Max, Mac, Karen, Harv, Dan, Shirley, Luke, Tom, Kay, Cris, Steve, Patton, Lee, Frank, Brady, Jeff, Marty, Catherine, and Richard for your particular encouragement to stay the course with this vision and venture.

And my gratitude is great for the many other companions who have been and continue to be grace-giving "pipes" of Life to me.

Because of all of you, I can more deeply relish the path of Life and God's gift of being human. Thank you from my core.

There Is Life Everywhere by Nikolai Yaroshenko

There Is Life Everywhere

> It is not that they chose to die, but rather that they
> could no longer figure out how to live.
> —ROBERT KURSON

It was a moment that changed me, and I almost missed it. Touring the State Tretyakov Gallery in Moscow, I was rushing through a small room to catch up with some friends when the painting caught my eye. Russian artist Nikolai Yaroshenko had purposefully layered his oils on this canvas back in 1888. Five diverse prisoners—a soldier, a worker, a peasant, a mother, and a child—are huddled together, peering through the barred window of a halted prison railcar. The child reaches through the steel bars, feeding pigeons on the railway platform.

Even in the midst of an awful predicament, the five prisoners were making a choice to engage with something. With what?

Yaroshenko's title gave me the clue: *There Is Life Everywhere.*

Regardless of the day or the dilemma, we each have an opportunity to embrace something, not only the fact that our hearts are beating, but why they're beating. Yaroshenko beckons us to look beyond our immediate circumstances and seize the privilege of being human.

There Is Life Everywhere. With his title, Yaroshenko is making a statement. But with the deliberate, thoughtful strokes of his brush, he is also asking a question. A question posed to those who will turn down the volume of their circumstances and listen. A question addressed not only to our ears but our hearts: will we embrace the Life that's everywhere?

Like a well-aimed arrow, his question pierced the silent space of the gallery and penetrated my heart.

I sat down on the only bench in the room. Not only had I been rushing through my tour of the museum, I was just completing a season in which I'd been rushing through my life. Standing there, I realized I had been imprisoned by my busyness, difficulties, and burnout. Yes, hectic and challenging seasons in our lives are unavoidable, and they can even be invigorating. But they can also turn deadly if we let the sound of the chaos drown out the question Yaroshenko is asking.

～ ～ ～

Life. People define it in many ways. Is it merely when our cells are reproducing and our hearts are beating? We know there's more to being fully human than that. And we all have our ideas about what that element of "more" should include:

Some fulfilling relationships.

An enjoyable family.

The attainment of a particular bank account balance.

A gratifying career.

The accumulation of enough stuff.

A particular level of health and fitness.

The absence of disease and difficulty.

Plenty of exciting vacations.

Enough fun along the way to keep at bay the ache that's deep within our souls.

I sit back and look at that list. Is that it? Is that life? A cycle of well-crafted circumstances? Really?

Deep down, my objection comes in the form of a persistent suspicion, even a deafening hunch, that there's more to the dance and drama of my life on this planet than air in my lungs and even circumstances to my liking.

Take the characters in Yaroshenko's painting. Most of us think that a prison trip to Siberia would be a surefire snuffer of any kind of life worth experiencing. We'd think that humanity could never thrive in the context of conditions so inhumane. But Yaroshenko didn't think so. Even in less-than-ideal circumstances, he envisioned a type of life that's within reach.

～ ～ ～

Yaroshenko's painting was actually inspired by a short story written by Leo Tolstoy three years earlier. In "What Men Live By," Tolstoy, a follower of Christ, begins by quoting 1 John 3:14: "We know that we have passed from death to life, because we love our brothers. Anyone who does not love remains in death." Those words refer-ence a central theme of Jesus's teaching, one that goes to the core of why he came: to usher us into a new way of being human.

Before each of us is the choice to remain in a realm Jesus calls *death* or to allow him to transition us into the realm of *life*. "I tell you the truth, whoever hears my word and believes him who sent me has eternal life and will not be condemned; he has crossed over from death to life" (John 5:24). So many people miss this—that Jesus is referring to something that happens right here and now.

Yaroshenko's "life" that can be found "everywhere" is this life into which Jesus invites us. Today.

It's a way of doing life that can be present in every nook and cranny of our days—from heart-breaks to hobbies, client meetings to birthday cel-ebrations, dinner parties to soup kitchens, funerals to vacations. From enduring an illness to enjoying concert tickets in the front row.

> In the midst of Monday morning realities, Jesus can breathe Life into our life.

And, yes, even in prison railcars.

I've started calling it *Life with a capital L.*

Everyone experiences heart-beating, lung-breathing life. Some are able to add to that existence some enjoyable relationships, a satisfying career, and maybe a level of financial success. Some will even add a bit of religiosity or maybe even spirituality to their repertoire. But not everyone experiences Life with a capital L.

For some, it will be a surprise to learn that Life with a capital L doesn't start by trying to be more spiritual. It starts with becoming more fully human under God's direction.

It doesn't come with a permanent, plastered-on smile, a get-out-of-jail-free card, or an exemption from pain. But it does come with Jesus Christ's assurance that he will put our feet on the path and get us Home.

In the midst of Monday morning realities that can range from busy to broken to beautiful, Jesus can breathe Life into our life. He can overcome the problem of a life consumed by merely existing. He can satisfy our yearning to actually Live.

❧ ❧ ❧

Go back with me to that museum in Moscow. It was only after staring at the paint-ing for a few minutes that I saw him. He, too, was inside the railcar.

A sixth prisoner.

In the shadowed background, he is silhouetted against the light of the barred window on the opposite side of the carriage. With an empty stare, he looks the other way, into a stark, gray sky. Missing out on the Life-filled moment unfolding behind him, he is lost in a sea of his own hopelessness.

It struck me. Yaroshenko wanted me to see him—this other guy on the opposite side of the railcar who was missing the Life. Because too often I'm that guy.

How many times in my journey have I moved to the other side of that railcar and stared out through prison bars of pain, disappointment, or just plain busyness? How often do I look in the opposite direction and miss out on Life? Those are questions I'm still asking, and they are changing me. Deeply and positively.

The ultimate question is not whether Life—with a capital L—is everywhere.

The question is whether I'll experience it.

reclaiming our humanity

L

Fully Human

Realizing Life While We Live It

> If the church is not a place where we not only learn
> something about what it means to be human but also a
> place where seeds of a fuller humanity are planted in
> us and watered, to grow, then all our hymns and
> prayers and preachments are vanity.
>
> —FREDERICK BUECHNER

A graveyard can be an effective setting for thinking about your life. Especially when the occupants are having a conversation with one another.

I was attentively perched on a chair in the century-old Greenwich House in the West Village of New York City. Within the past decade, it had been converted into the Barrow Street Theatre, a small, intimate off-Broadway venue. Along with less than two hundred other people sitting in the three-quarter-round space, I was witnessing a favorite story of mine and, over the years, thousands of others.

Our Town, Thornton Wilder's 1938 Pulitzer Prize–winning play, invites us into the everyday life of the fictional small town of Grover's Corners, New Hampshire, at the turn of the twentieth century. As the narration of Wilder's stage manager, being brilliantly portrayed that evening by David Cromer, explains to the audience, "This is the way we were—in our growing up and in our marrying, and in our living, and in our dying."[1]

Serving as a window into the extraordinary nature of ordinary living, the play opens by including us in the daily routines of a group of the town's residents, focusing in particular on two families—the Webbs and the Gibbs. Act 2 takes place three years later and centers around the romance and eventual marriage of Emily Webb and George Gibbs. The third and final act takes place nine years later in the cemetery on the hill overlooking the town.

A funeral procession is arriving at the burial site of Emily Webb, who has died way too young—in childbirth. As the ceremony is taking place, we listen to the occupants of the cemetery, residents of the town who have already died, talk in a detached manner with one another and with Emily, the newest arrival. Emily misses her life and longs to go back. She discovers from the other deceased occupants that it's possible but not advisable. Emily ignores their caution and chooses to relive one day from her youth—her twelfth birthday.

> Christ came to save us from our empty rebelliousness, not from our humanity.

During her experience of repeating that wonderful day, she notices details, moments, and nuances that she'd overlooked the first time around—when she was living. Overwhelmed by the way she and others missed the significance of those moments, she's ready to return to the cemetery.

Now realizing how "in the dark" living persons are, Emily turns to the stage manager and regretfully reflects on her journey by articulating a haunting realization.

"Do any human beings ever realize life while they live it—every, every minute?"

The stage manager quietly responds, "No." Then he modifies his answer with a couple of possible exceptions. "Saints and poets maybe—they do some."[2]

The theatre, filled with the palpable echo of Emily's piercing question, was frozen in reflection. Sitting next to me was a gentleman in his later middle years, dressed in a charcoal pinstripe suit and crisp shirt. From a brief comment I had overheard as he was taking his seat before the play began, I'd discovered he had rushed up from Wall Street that evening, just in time for the performance. Now, in this moment that was inviting each of us to evaluate whether we were truly experiencing our life while we were living it, his hand moved to his face to wipe away some tears. I understood. I was right there as well, wrestling with my own, probably similar, thoughts.

But not everyone was in that same place. One row in front of me, on the other side of the aisle, were three high school girls. I had noticed them previously and wondered if they were there just to fulfill a school assignment. My suspicion was affirmed because, in this same powerful moment that had brought tears to the businessman, these girls were giggling. Though struck by the contrast of their out-of-place chuckles to the response of the man next to me, I entered back into the final moments of the play—which culminated with a standing ovation.

❧ ❧ ❧

As I walked into the fresh air of a Manhattan May evening, I thought about those two divergent reactions I had witnessed. Obviously, I didn't know all the reasons for the executive's tears or the students' snickers, but because of what was ricocheting around in my own heart, I had a strong hunch. As I walked, I pondered.

A middle-aged businessman has lived long enough—as have I—to know what all of us discover sooner or later: life, at least in some ways, has a way of turning out to be less than what we expected when we were younger. That's something those teenage girls probably hadn't yet come to grips with—or didn't want to. When your entire life's ahead, you just want to assume all your dreams will be delivered to your doorstep.

But eventually life happens. It's a sobering moment when we recognize that we've not been realizing life while we're living it, that we've not been living full lives, that we haven't wholly engaged in the privilege of being human for the few precious years we have on this planet. It's difficult to face the truth—that we've just been going through the motions and playing around with our lives. As the poet Robert Abrahams once articulated,

> Some men die by shrapnel,
> And some go down in flames.
> But most men perish inch by inch
> In play at little games.[3]

Are we just playing little games?

Or are we realizing life while we live it? Are we each experiencing—truly—what it means to be a human being? Are we really living? Are we engaging our full humanity?

It's one thing to wake up and realize you've been asleep.

But it's another to wake up and actually start living.

~ ~ ~

To realize life while we live it involves more than merely trying to pay attention. Sure, if we're just the protoplasmic product of an evolutionary accident, that's all it will be. But most of us, deep down, sense there's more—we just can't quite put our finger on what it is.

Even though we might struggle to articulate it, what we're sensing is the dignity of a calling that is embedded in each of us—the calling to fully experience our humanity. When we're born, we instinctively embark upon that quest. Kids celebrate their fresh and flourishing humanity with abandon. But somewhere along the way, we become sleepy regarding our significance, and we wearily shift to survival mode. That might involve days of busyness or boredom, but either way, the ultimate result is an "empty way of life" (1 Peter 1:18).

What happened?

We have lost our ability to realize life while we are living it. We've lost touch with the day-in, day-out experience of being fully human. That realization is behind T. S. Eliot's words as he wistfully contemplates, "Where is the Life we have lost in living?"[4]

The stage manager in Wilder's play muses, "Every time a child is born into the world it's Nature's attempt to make a perfect human being. Well, we've seen Nature pushing and contriving for some time now. We all know she's interested in quantity; but I think she's interested in quality too."[5]

A quality human being is someone who is realizing life while he or she is living it. That requires fully embracing the privilege as well as the calling that's central to being human. It means grappling and fighting to engage with my full humanity. It means beginning a journey of exploring and unpacking what that looks like.

~ ~ ~

A natural first step is to ask a simple question: What is my humanity? Is it just a reference to being a part of this species called *Homo sapiens*? Obviously it's much more. So what does it mean to be human? What is a healthy human being? What distinguishes us from animals? *Webster's* defines *humanity* as "the quality or state of being human,"[6] but I need more than that when the alarm clock rings.

So here's a place to start: *My humanity is my capacity to embrace the significance of my existence—and yours—as images of God in his creation.*

The more willing and able I am to embrace my significance and yours, the fuller my humanity. The less I embrace that significance, the more dehumanized I'll be—existing but not living.

An animal's life is one of mere existence: eating, sleeping, finding shelter, seeking safety, having sex, producing offspring who will go through the same cycle. But God's Word is clear about the dignity and uniqueness of our humanity.[7] We are more than mere animals. Embracing my humanity means going beyond mere existence to the realm of engagement—engaging with the meaning behind my existence and the significance of the people, environments, and events around me.

~ ~ ~

Fully embracing my humanity will obviously be multifaceted. It will involve embracing the significance embedded in the two primary realms of my existence: the *physical* and the *spiritual*.

By *physical* I'm not just referring to my heart beating. Realizing life while I'm living it involves physical, tangible experiences of human life:

- *Relational:* my connections with family and friends
- *Sensual:* my enjoyment of the ability to see, hear, smell, touch, and taste
- *Healthful:* my body's fitness and wellness and my commitment to rest and recreate
- *Intellectual:* my rational growth in knowledge about my world
- *Emotional:* my ability to experience and express all my emotions in a healthy way
- *Creativity:* my capacity to be imaginative and generative
- *Vocational:* my ability to contribute to my world through my occupation
- *Material:* my financial health and ability to acquire food, shelter, and clothing
- *Cultural:* my service in society and care for my culture
- *Environmental:* my appreciation of and care for creation

Fully experiencing my humanity requires engagement with all of those, deeply.

But—and this is critical—for full humanity to be tasted, I need to experience my humanity in *spiritual* terms as well. In fact, my humanity shrivels up when I focus on only one or a combination of these physical arenas without paying attention to my spiritual side.

For example, if I experience only the *sensual* arena of life while neglecting my spirituality, I'll head down a path of hedonism. If I experience only the *vocational* dimension of my life without a spiritual component, workaholism will result. If my focus is only in the *relational* arena without a spiritual foundation, I can become codependent. If I am preoccupied only in the *emotional* realm, a dysfunctional self-absorption will follow. If my life is dominated by *material things,* you guessed it—stifling materialism will be the result.

❧ ❧ ❧

Carl, an incredibly successful entrepreneur, had developed and sold several companies, becoming very affluent in the process. For years he had no time or interest in spiritual things because they were irrelevant to him as he constructed his empire and accumulated a wealth of possessions and properties. That's until he had, in his words, "the conversation."

One day, his adult son opened up in a painfully honest way, telling his dad he was more like a machine that churned out money than a human who could give love. That led Carl into some serious soul-searching. He realized that God and spiritual conversations might just have some relevance. He had been pursuing his vocation with intentional excellence, been generative with ideas and businesses, become materially prosperous—but because he was only focusing on the physical side of his humanity and ignoring the spiritual, even though he was doing some very human things, he was ironically becoming *less* human in the process.

❧ ❧ ❧

In our life journey, the spiritual is what makes the physical significant. Most of us, including Christians, already suspect and even accentuate the importance of the spiritual realm. But some Christians emphasize it to the extent of having such a deep preoccupation with the spiritual that the physical experience of life is downplayed and even squelched.

And not only Christians, but many who come from any number of spiritualities—from Buddhism to Judaism to Hinduism to Islam to witchcraft to Christianity—all of which have some followers who want to distance themselves from the physical in order to become more spiritual.

But I especially want to focus on those of us in the Christian traditions who've let the pendulum swing so far to this other side. Somewhere along the way, Christians, in their emphasis on the spiritual, started viewing the physical as something we should downplay, distrust, and guard against. The outcome is a compartmental-ized existence that highlights and even worships spirituality while ignoring and even denouncing the physical aspects of life.

I got caught up in that perspective early in my journey, and the result is some-thing that tragically departs from what Scripture actually teaches.

Too many Christians believe that the physical realm is contrary to our relation-ship with God, that things in the physical realm are at best distractions and at worst sinful, that physical experiences in life can't help us get closer to God but instead lead us away from him.

In church history, gnosticism and docetism were a couple of ancient heresies that were rightly jettisoned. Gnosticism emphasized that the material world was evil, and to walk toward God, you had to shun the physical because the spiritual needed to be freed from the material. Docetism followed that logic by saying that Jesus only *appeared* to be human—he wasn't really. He couldn't have had a physical body be-cause all matter is evil.

> A fulfilled human is someone who is becoming fully human.

Sadly, even today, in Bible-based churches, some of us are naively flirting with similar trains of thought— that our walk with God only applies to the spiritual realm. Humanity isn't seen as something that is physical and spiritual, only physical. Consequently, our humanity becomes something negative, even to the point of being viewed as the enemy of spirituality.

The tragic result is too many people, by emphasizing their spirituality in isola-tion from the physical realm, are unknowingly dehumanizing themselves.

In essence, when I take this path, I end up thinking that to become truly spir-itual it's necessary to deemphasize and even overcome my humanity. In doing so, I confuse worldliness with being human, sinfulness with humanness, and dying to self with dying to my humanity.[8]

Again, this isn't what the Bible teaches, yet it's what many Christians believe. It contributes to a common perception about Christians, who, as some have observed, "are often weird where they should be normal and normal where they should be weird."

The credibility, uniqueness, and power of Christianity are rooted in its embrace of both the physical as well as the spiritual. Hear the words of famed twentieth-century theologian John Murray: "The highest reaches of true spirituality are dependent upon events that occurred in the realm of the physical and sensuous. A religion that can be indifferent to the bodily, to the physical, to the phenomenal, has no affinity with the Christian faith; it is a spurious religiosity that does not warrant the name 'spirituality.'"[9]

❧ ❧ ❧

Just the other day, my friend Wayne and I were talking about the damage he'd experienced as a result of his upbringing. We also were discussing this issue of God's designing our humanity to be a combination of the spiritual and the physical realms.

He grew up in a Christian home and fundamentalist church environment. He trusted Christ as a youth. But, he conveyed to me, for much of his life his understanding of following Christ revolved around the chilling notion that "God had saved me from my humanity."

He grew up thinking that the elements of the physical realm are, at most, sinful or, at least, a waste of time and needed to be ignored or shunned. So vocations that were not ministry-related were less than God's best (left out was the logical fallacy that if we all were in vocational ministry, this would be a pretty lopsided world, and civilization wouldn't last too long). Being passionate about anything in life was considered sinful excess and dangerous temptation—"moderation in all things" was what was valued. Feelings and emotions were distrusted.

Wayne picked up the notion that the more spiritual he became, the less involved he'd be with these "human" pursuits. In his words, his daily goal, "even as a young boy, was to spend as much time in a spiritual state as possible, and I tried to focus on Bible reading and prayer. But I never had the willpower or capacity to live that fully in just a spiritual state of being. I couldn't sustain my spiritual focus. I perceived that as failure, weakness, and sin."

Essentially, the version of Christianity he had been taught was that Christ was anti-humanity.

My heart sank as he told me this. Since when did Jesus come to dehumanize us? That's not at all good news. Christ came to save us from our empty rebelliousness, not from our humanity.

~ ~ ~

Then there's Sarah. Not only was she a long way from being a follower of Jesus, but to her, Christians seemed odd, irrelevant, and out of touch. She didn't consider herself to be religious in any way. A marketing executive and an artist, she was wholehearted about being generative with her life.

But in her early thirties she also realized that just devoting her energies to the physical side of the spectrum was leaving her less than fully human (my words, not hers—she termed it as "out of balance as a person"). She realized she needed a spiritual component to her life, but she didn't look to organized religion as an answer.

So the pursuit of soul harmony and peace through spiritual practices—meditation, deep-breathing exercises, nature trips, values clarification, and connecting to the unifying spiritual essence of the universe—all became part of her journey. She believed it helped get her into better balance as a person.

Even so, she still didn't feel it was enough. So she kept trying new things, new techniques for wholeness and balance and a fuller life—as she put it, "like an orphan looking for my parent."

~ ~ ~

All three of the people I've mentioned were on different paths of trying to be fulfilled human beings. Carl was pursuing the physical without the spiritual. Wayne pursued the spiritual without the physical. Sarah sensed the need to combine both the physical and the spiritual, but there was still something missing.

Here's what I began to discover: Sarah, contrary to what I would have thought years ago, was probably the closest to at least being on a path of experiencing full humanity. Yes, early on, Wayne's trust in Christ obviously equipped him better than the others for such a purpose, but while his future in heaven was secured, the "spirituality isolated in a vacuum" he had learned from his upbringing was hindering the fullness of his present-tense humanity.

Instead of the secularism of Carl or the religiosity of Wayne, both of which dehumanized them to various degrees, Sarah was trying to engage with her full humanity.

She just needed to meet Someone.

Sarah had a friend who made the introduction. She was a woman whom Sarah trusted and admired for being an authentic, "normal" person, so, as she later explained with a smile, she was surprised to find out her friend was a follower of Christ. In a conversation many months into their relationship, Sarah's friend challenged her that, if she was really wanting to be honest in her pursuit of being a "balanced person," she should not let religious caricatures keep her from finding out who Jesus really is.

The friend gave Sarah a copy of the gospel of John to read.

One evening, Sarah read half of the gospel in one sitting. Later she recalled three passages that had a particularly potent impact.

The first was in the second chapter, where Jesus turned water into wine. Of course she had heard of the miracle, but it was the occasion—a wedding—that struck her. Here was Jesus enhancing a celebration (I'll add, a very *human* celebration) in a very down-to-earth way.

The second, in the fourth chapter of John, was his conversation with the woman at the well. Sarah didn't quite understand what was going on with the "living water" thing, but she caught Jesus's genuine care for a woman who was obviously on some kind of quest for fulfillment.

The third passage she later recalled was the biggie. It was a statement Jesus made—and that her friend had underlined—in John 10. The context is Jesus explaining that he is the gate to a new way of living. He contrasts himself with other proposals and pursuits that offer to fulfill our lives but instead end up taking Life from us. In John 10:10, he promises, "I have come that they may have life, and have it to the full."

This verse is one of the most popular statements Jesus made. Early in my walk with Christ, like many others, I became so familiar with it I missed what it's really saying. Until I started paying closer attention to who's speaking and what he's saying:

- Jesus Christ—fully God and fully human[10]—was the image of true humanity, the incarnation of the perfectly spiritual with the perfectly physical. The first human since Adam who is fully alive.
- He has come to conform us to that image[11] and bring us into that Life.

So to Carl, Jesus—fully God—is saying that there is more to life than physical things; the physical, apart from the spiritual, is empty.

And Jesus—fully human—is saying that if Wayne desires to become like him, it requires more than just the pursuit of the spiritual.

And to Sarah, Jesus—fully God and fully human—is saying that he himself is what makes a balanced life possible: "I have come that they may have life, and have it to the full." Today Sarah credits that statement as being the one that launched her into a relationship with Christ, led her into a truly meaningful balance of the physical and spiritual, and introduced her to Life with a capital L.

And now to me and you, Jesus is saying he wants to do something in us that's far beyond merely increasing the octane level of our spirituality or religiosity.

❧ ❧ ❧

I need to emphasize something. Sarah didn't have the baggage a lot of church people have when they read that promise of Christ's in John 10. Over the years it's a verse that has been misused in Christian circles that emphasize the spiritual while seeking to disparage the physical. So they force their dualism (separating the physical from the spiritual) into that verse, and it becomes a promise only about spiritual life.

I've heard people talk about this "abundant life" that Jesus promises (other Bible versions, instead of "to the full," translate it "abundantly") as a sort of superspiritual existence that we must achieve if we really want to fully follow Christ. Actually, when bringing John 10:10 into this discussion, I wince at the thought of some Christians seeing my reference to this particular verse and jumping to the conclusion that they already know what I'm talking about—a superspiritual approach to life. (Many will even add the word *Christian* to the phrase—the abundant *Christian* life—underscoring their bias that it's only a different kind of *spiritual* life that Jesus is promising.)

Bottom line, Jesus is not about making us superspiritual but fully human. He's not only interested in our spirituality but our humanity as well. For some of us, this helps explain why we aren't interested in cultivating a spiritual journey that's irrelevant to the rest of our lives. For others of us—haunted by the guilt of failed spiritual disciplines—we're intrigued.

And for others, this whole discussion just makes us uncomfortable. "But doesn't Jesus care about my spirituality? Didn't he come to make us more spiritual?"

Of course, but what's the purpose of my spirituality? He didn't come to enhance my spirituality as an end in itself. If I'm experiencing deeper prayer times but not deeply relishing sunsets, if I'm involved in my church but not in my community, if I'm worshiping God but slandering people, if I'm saying "Amen!" to sermons more than I'm saying "Awesome!" to the privilege of being human and created in God's image, there is still an outcome of my spirituality that's missing.

When God brings me to life by his Spirit,[12] the purpose is to enable me to be reborn into a new way of being human—a return to my original purpose of appreciating and living out the privilege and responsibility of being part of the Creator's creation. My spirituality isn't something to be developed in a vacuum; it's not an isolated compartment of my life but a central part of being human. An engaged and healthy spirituality should breed an engaged and healthy humanity.[13]

~ ~ ~

This is a major reason the outcasts and party crowd, instead of the religious people, were drawn to Jesus. It's what made him so contagious. They were looking at Someone who modeled the real deal to them. They weren't interested in some sort of fabricated religiosity or irrelevant, compartmentalized spirituality. Instead, here was Someone who would do life with them (so much so that the religious crowd accused Jesus of being a drunkard and glutton[14]). Here was Someone who showed them what being fully human looked like and offered to lead them in the same way. They probably wouldn't have described it in terms of "fully human," but many could recognize a perfectly fulfilled human being when they saw one. Unbeknown to them, he was the first person, since Adam and Eve before the Fall, who was fully human.[15]

But Christ didn't become fully human only to *model* full humanity for the first time since Adam. He came to *repair* our broken humanity. As one early church father, Gregory of Nazianzus, summarized about Jesus, "That which he has not assumed he has not healed."[16] So what he has assumed—our full humanity—he heals. What Adam, along with all of us, forfeited through sin, Jesus came to restore: our full humanity. When Adam sinfully rebelled, he died spiritually. At that point, obviously his relationship with God was broken, and in the process something tragic also happened to his ability to fully experience his humanity.

The worst thing about sin is that it dehumanizes us—it is devastating on both a spiritual as well as a physical level. Sin hijacks our humanity from its original, fulfilling, and God-glorifying purpose. Ironically, sin does the opposite of what we desire—it lures us *away* from experiencing the fullness and freedom of being a human created in the image of God.

Jesus didn't just come to forgive my sin as an end in itself—it's not just about relieving my guilt but restoring God's glory to my humanity. His forgiveness is meant to free me to once again be fully human. My humanity actually needs to be unshackled from sin in order to be re-created into the new humanity Jesus came to restore.[17]

A fulfilled human is someone who is becoming fully human under the grace and guidance of Jesus.

~ ~ ~

So I head back to John 10:10 and dig deeper. In Christ's statement, the word translated as "to the full" or "abundant" in English is the Greek word *perissos,* which means "exceeding, going beyond the ordinary." He's talking about doing life in a way that goes beyond what is *normally experienced* by human beings, but not beyond what was *originally intended.*

He comes to us in our small, shriveled routines of daily life—in which we're not realizing life while we live it—with an offer to take us back to the original purpose we were made for. God's purpose for creating us hasn't changed; his original blueprint doesn't need to be improved or modified—but simply restored to us.

That's what Jesus came to do. Casting a powerful vision, he beckons us into a larger realm of living than what has become disappointingly normal because of the great loss of Life brought on by the Fall (which we'll discuss later).

Jesus is saying he wants to reclaim the originally intended, fully human version of you and me.

~ ~ ~

To be fully human, I must engage with life in *both* a physical and a spiritual way, and not just as two parallel, unrelated compartments. This is where the debilitating division between the sacred and the secular enters the picture.

Religion tends to idolize the spiritual, and secularism tends to idolize the physical. But the boundary between sacred and secular is fabricated. To be fully human is to take down that boundary and live our days in an integrated way on both a physical and spiritual level.

When were Adam and Eve "spiritual"?

Before the Fall, everything they did was equally spiritual. They weren't more spiritual when they were talking with God than when they were tending the soil or enjoying each other's love. They were perfectly spiritual in whatever they were doing, even without hymns or Sunday schools. Their relationship with God involved *all* of their humanity, the spiritual *and* the physical.

They didn't have to become less human in order to be closer to God.

Both the physical and the spiritual should fuel each other. The way I relate with God should enhance the enthusiasm and appreciation with which I applaud at a concert. The beauty and creativity I experience at the concert should deepen my grasp and worship of the beauty and creativity of God. From serving at a soup kitchen to enjoying a sports event to grieving more authentically to laughing more deeply to tasting chocolate to celebrating a milestone at work to reflecting about a historical event to conversing with a friend about life and God and a medical appointment—those should all be ways for me to engage with my humanity and with God at the same time.

Contrary to what many of us think, the more healthy we become in our spirituality, the more—not less—of our humanity we experience.

~ ~ ~

David has become a hero of mine in this journey. The second king of Israel, he was a man who fully engaged with his humanity—in both the spiritual and physical realms. He was a worshiper, warrior, poet, leader, dancer, teacher, party lover, businessman, hunter, actor, musician. He was passionate. He was reflective. He was prayerful. He was courageous. He knew heartbreaking failure firsthand. He also knew what God-glorifying victory tasted like. He experienced God's blessing, God's intimacy, God's discipline, God's grace. He was a man after God's own heart[18] and lived Life with a capital L.

David was a man's man, a human's human. He was the epitome of what God can do in and through a flawed but faithful human being.

Which is why twenty-six-year-old Michelangelo Buonarroti, at the beginning of the sixteenth century, devoted himself with such passion for three years to sculpt the colossal—in both size as well as cultural impact—*David*.

If you've ever had the privilege of seeing the historic seventeen-foot-high marble sculpture in Florence's Galleria dell'Accademia, you'll never forget it. It's the majestic dignity of our humanity on display.

What deepens the impact is the path you take in order to approach the masterpiece. As soon as you enter the long hall, the massive figure at the other end grabs your gaze. As you make your way toward him, many overlook what's on the sides of the corridor: four sculptures of four slaves that are "non finito"—unfinished. Michelangelo had begun work on them in 1519 for the tomb of Julius II, but a combination of busyness and changing plans left them incomplete. They were found in the artist's studio in Florence when he died in 1564.

The rough, partial sculptures are labeled *The Four Prisoners,* partly because they depicted slaves, but also because they seem to be imprisoned in the marble, still trying to break free. Art historians convey that they illustrate Michelangelo's sculpting philosophy as one of freeing form from matter. He once wrote to a colleague, "I mean by sculpture what is done by removing."

> The worst thing about sin is that it dehumanizes us. Sin hijacks our humanity from its original, fulfilling, and God-glorifying purpose.

Michelangelo fashioned the epic figure by applying his vision to the marble and removing that which hindered the statue of David from becoming what he was meant to be. To see the completed, magnificent human form framed by four non finito others seeking to become like him is to catch a striking vision of what God is up to with fallen, imprisoned humanity.

That includes you. And me.

❧ ❧ ❧

When I begin to experience Life with a capital L, the gospel begins to actually inspire me as well as inform me. I begin to see that the gospel is not an optional, sidebar method for just making us more religious or spiritual. It's the vision and work of God to reclaim our full humanity. Jesus came to do battle for us, and his triumph is over the sinful fallenness that hinders us from becoming the human beings he originally intended for us to be.

The great hope for my humanity—and yours—is to allow Christ to breathe his vision into us and free us from what is holding us back from being fully human, to redeem us from the "empty way of life" (1 Peter 1:18) that keeps us from really living to his glory *and* realizing life while we live it.

Let the sculpting begin.

The Hunger of Being Human

It seems to me we can never give up longing
and wishing while we are thoroughly alive.
There are certain things we feel to be beautiful
and good, and we *must* hunger after them.

—George Eliot

Sure, sex and intimacy were important to her. But security was even higher on her list. And a desire to feel significant had gnawed at her as long as she could remember.

To her, a man was a primary way to have all that. And more.

So she got married. And she thought she had married *the* guy. The right guy who would satisfy her desires and complete her dreams. But when it turned out he wasn't the one, a python-like disappointment encircled her heart.

Failure was something she had never expected. But it was real. She had to move on, longings in tow. Then a second marriage proposal arrived, accompanied by a fragile hope that seemed to be rising from the ashes. "Surely this one will work out," she anticipated. But he hadn't. Neither had the third husband. Or the fourth. Or even the fifth.

Contrary to what she'd heard all her life, persistence had not paid off. Instead, plodding away—year after year through husband after husband—had actually numbed her heart instead of satisfying it. Over the years, she repeatedly had her hopeful optimism shattered. Disappointments piled up like rows of imprisoning bricks around her soul.

She hadn't given up on men. Yet. But her multiple failed marriages made her settle on just living with this current guy—no marrying this time. So what if none of her friends or family approved? She had too little hope and resolve left in her to be careless this time around. She sensed she was in dangerous territory—one more misstep and she feared she might never recover. More than her reputation was at stake. Her heart was about to die.

This morning had begun like most others—doing chores while the dull ache of her longings throbbed beneath the surface. As usual, she had waited until midday to head to the well outside the village to draw water. Yes, it was much hotter at this hour, but noon was the most likely time she could arrive alone, avoiding the contempt and condescension of all the gossiping women who had been there earlier in the morning.

As she approached the well, she was disappointed to see she wouldn't be alone after all. There was someone else there. As she got closer, she was dismayed to discover that the person was a man—and a Jew. In her world, men diminished women, and Jews despised her Samaritan race.

So she was shocked when he spoke to her.

❧ ❧ ❧

It's what makes you and me human. Longing. Desire. Ache. Yearning. Soul thirst. Heart hunger. Fashioning us in his image, God made us different from animals. Our longing for something greater than mere survival showcases that distinction.

It shows up in our capacity to yearn for companionship. For love. For resolution. For triumph. For purpose. For home. For what is yet to be. We're part of this vast fraternity called humanity, bound by an allegiance to something we rarely articulate but are constantly aware of.

I've got decades in my rearview mirror and hopefully a few more in my windshield. Throughout my journey, my constant reality has been the presence of persistent longings. Will I run out of highway before some of them are fulfilled? Referring to far more than a bucket list, that question is what fuels and frames my humanity. I long to experience what I'm supposed to experience and to be who I'm made to be as a human being.

Longings, whether they become fulfilled or not, are central to our identity. Your longings are what make you *you*. My longings are what make me *me*. But even though our longings are unique to each of us as human beings, they share a common

DNA—a desire for something greater in life. There's a reason we find it easy to sing along with U2, "But I still haven't found what I'm looking for."

I don't speak German, but a word that's become deeply helpful is one I learned from C. S. Lewis, the brilliant Oxford professor who wrote extensively about his journey from atheism to faith. Through his writings, he's profoundly mentored me about the nature and power of my longings. He used a powerful, nuanced German word to summarize it: *Sehnsucht* (pronounced ZEEN-zocht)—a deep, persistent longing.

> Where do I need to be compassionately cut with the scalpel of Jesus?

In 1977, two identical golden records were launched into space on NASA's unmanned probes *Voyager 1* and *Voyager 2*. Sent on a one-way trip into the galaxy, the images and audio on the discs were chosen to introduce Earth to any interstellar strangers that might happen upon it. The creative director of the project, Ann Druyan, teamed up with others to select the contents of the recording that would summarize humanity (no small task). For the significant final track, the music she chose was the cavatina from Beethoven's String Quartet no. 13, opus 130. The reason? In a 2009 interview, she explained that, when told this message from Earth would last a thousand million years, she immediately thought of "this great, beautiful, sad piece of music, on which Beethoven had written in the margin…the word *sehnsucht*.… Part of what we wanted to capture in the Voyager message was this great longing we feel."[1]

My longing is central to who I am as a human being. So if I'm going to figure out what it means to be fully human, I must—whether I can even pronounce the word or not—deal with my *Sehnsucht*. What is it I deeply desire? Why did I get up this morning? At what am I aiming with my life? What kept me awake last night? At a core level, what am I thirsty for?

Some of the same church people who might propose that our humanity is something we must shun for the sake of spirituality will also advise that our longings must likewise be suppressed. Yet my core longings are not bad—what I do with them can be sinful, but my longings themselves aren't. I can certainly try to fulfill those longings through inappropriate, destructive, or hedonistic pursuits, but the core longings themselves are the wiring God has placed within my humanity. Instead of minimizing them, I need to listen to them.

My longing connects me with my identity and purpose as a human being. As

Danish philosopher and theologian Søren Kierkegaard proposed: "Longing is the umbilical cord of the higher life."[2] My longing can serve as a connection, a sort of breadcrumb trail that I can follow as I'm orienting myself toward Home. In my deepest longings I can gain clues regarding who I am in the universe. As Lewis proposed, a man's physical hunger doesn't guarantee he'll get food, but it does indicate he "inhabits a world where eatable substances exist."[3] My longings for significance and security and shalom indicate that I'm wired to be able to experience those realities, but whether I will or not is another issue.

Line for line, your story or mine won't be identical to the story of the woman at that well in long-ago Samaria, but each of us can relate to her when it comes to our inventory of deep—and thwarted—yearnings. I might differ in the ways I try to address my longings (not too many of us have had five spouses), but the reality of the soul ache is something I can't ignore. You and I will vary in the ways, willingness, and abilities we have to articulate it, but just beneath the surface, gnawing at each of us are our longings for…

Significance… Truth… Beauty… Goodness…
Identity… Security… Shalom…

These longings are always lingering, but as powerful as they are, most of us are too focused on sheer survival, stress management, or superficial distractions to ever stop and actually evaluate them. This woman wasn't any different.

Until she met *him*.

❧ ❧ ❧

As my *Sehnsucht* companion by the well is drawing her water, the man asks her a simple question. "Will you give me a drink?"

She pushes back, asking why a Jewish man would even be speaking to a Samaritan woman.

He sticks with the deeper issue—the reason why he's been waiting for her in the first place—telling her if she knew who she was talking to, she would ask him for a gift from God; she would ask him for *living water*.[4] We now know the man's name was Jesus, the central figure in humanity's history, but at this moment he was in the process of simply yet profoundly revealing his care for this woman, her story, and, yes, her longings.

Initially, she doesn't get it. She doesn't yet understand that this man has actually been the One her thirst and longings have been pointing to her entire life.

Something quite similar is true today. Most see Jesus merely as a religious figurehead and perhaps a potential ticket to some sort of afterlife. We don't realize he comes to us—just as he came to her—as the One who can address our *Sehnsucht* like no other.

Here she's been earnestly longing for security, significance, self-esteem, and thinking that a man was going to be the key. Yet this new man she's just met is introducing the notion that what she really needs is something else. Something deeper. Something that only he could give her. Something he calls living water. The question is whether she'll actually engage with her thirst authentically enough to drink the water he's offering.

Such is the case with us.

~ ~ ~

But the problem I tend to have, like the woman at the well, is that I try to satisfy my Life-sized longings, my *Sehnsucht,* with trivial pursuits. We all do it: aim to fulfill our biggest longings with temporary distractions, short-term medications, and half-baked endeavors. Or perhaps we have given up on the possibility of our longing being addressed, and we settle for a life of mere existence. Or maybe we pursue a solution that fails, only to pursue it again and again. Like husbands and marriages.

Lewis, my *Sehnsucht* consultant, calls these misguided pursuits "mud pies."

> Indeed, if we consider the unblushing promises of reward and the staggering nature of the rewards promised in the Gospels, it would seem that Our Lord finds our desires not too strong, but too weak. We are half-hearted creatures, fooling about with drink and sex and ambition when infinite joy is offered us, like an ignorant child who wants to go on making mud pies in a slum because he cannot imagine what is meant by the offer of a holiday at the sea. We are far too easily pleased.[5]

It's a powerful moment in my journey as a human being when I finally stop being too easily pleased and admit that mud-pie pursuits aren't enough to address my deepest longings.

For this woman, her mud pies had to be exposed—exposed to her, not to Jesus. He already knew. So he asked her a question, "Go, call your husband and come back."

"I have no husband."

"The fact is, you have had five husbands, and the man you now have is not your husband."

She initially supposes he's just demonstrating his sleuthing or psychic skills. Today, when reading this story from John's gospel, judgmental people might opt for thinking his point is to shame her down guilt alley. He was doing none of that.

In his question, he was using words as a caring surgeon would use a scalpel. And instead of judging her for cohabitating with a man who wasn't her husband, he compassionately beckoned her to recognize her real longing. He was helping her see that a pursuit she had prioritized her entire adult life—men and marriage—was not her ultimate desire.

Incision made. Mud pie exposed. Healing begun.

It begs the question: Where do I need to be compassionately cut with the scalpel of Jesus? What endeavors of mine need to be exposed—pursuits upon which I'm relying to deliver more than they are capable of?

❧ ❧ ❧

We all have pursuits. Things for which we spend our time, money, and energy and upon which we hang our dreams and hopes.

Relationships. Work. Hobbies. Sports. Addictions. Eating. Art. Church. Politics. Stealing. Volunteering. Boyfriends. Girlfriends. Parenting. Fame. Religion. Drinking. Vacations. Shopping. Sex. Collecting. Making money. Spending money. Giving money. Success. Social causes. Selfish causes.

Good things, not so good things, they are all thrown in the pile.

What does the pursuit list of your life look like?

For me, there are a few pursuits and dreams I'll place at the top of my pile. Things I'm devoted to more than the rest. Many of those pursuits change with the ebb and flow of my life while other pursuits can remain constant for decades. At its core, a pursuit can be healthy, such as fortifying my marriage, or destructive, like my materialism going wild.

With each pursuit, whether I realize it or not, I'm treating it as a sort of restaurant where deeper hungers will hopefully be satisfied. Beneath the surface, we're actually saying, "I'm hungry for *X,* so I'll eat at this restaurant called *Y.*"

We turn to a particular pursuit to satisfy something we perceive is offered on its menu. For this woman, it could have been something like, "I'm hungry for *security,* so I'll eat at this restaurant called *marriage.*" For others it might be, "I'm thirsty for *significance,* so I'll drink at this pub called *career.*" Or "I want *pain relief,* so I'll head to this diner called *porn.*"

All these restaurants can initially be admirable and beautiful, or they can be rebellious, sinful, or even illegal from the start. Either way, when I try to extract from them more than they are capable of delivering, they all lead me down a futile and frustrating path of unfulfilled promises while leaving my actual longings unaddressed and unsatisfied.

It's rare for a person to go deeper and think about her longings and dreams like this, but that is exactly what Jesus is inviting this woman—and each of us—to do.

$$\sim \sim \sim$$

She was an older lady when I, as a young college student, met her. Her name was Miss Havisham, and she existed on the pages of Charles Dickens's masterpiece, *Great Expectations.* In her midfifties, she wore a tattered wedding dress every day and lived in a decaying mansion in which all the clocks were stopped at twenty minutes to nine. It had been at that moment, decades before, on her wedding day, when she'd received a letter from her fiancé. But instead of a love letter, it had been a letter of rejection, calling off the wedding.

As Dickens explains, "The day came, but not the bridegroom."

Afterward, Miss Havisham stopped all the clocks in her home at twenty minutes to nine because, at that moment, she had entered a prison of disappointment. The decomposed wedding cake remained encased in cobwebs on the table, and she had not left the house since. Her heart had continued beating, but she had stopped living.

As a college student, I pitied Miss Havisham, but I didn't identify with her like I do now. I didn't realize then how many bouts with disappointment I would encounter in my journey—in the form of failed pursuits at work, in relationships, with finances, the list goes on. I didn't comprehend the frequency of shattered dreams and unfulfilled longings and how, similar to Miss Havisham, I would experience the temptation to quit living while continuing to exist. I didn't understand, as a result, how often I would be tempted to ignore my longings and thereby numb my experience of what it means to be human.

> To ignore my longings is to numb my experience of what it means to be human.

Nor did I grasp how powerful those moments would prove to be.

That I would learn to intimately relate with a God who cares about the heartbreak and unfulfilled longings of human beings.

That my longings, instead of being a mere wish list, are mirrors of my soul— mirrors into which I can look and learn about the hunger I have to be fully human.

That my longings can serve as clues that can lead me to God and my heart's ultimate Home.

I didn't realize, as a result of responding to Christ's invitation to go deeper and process my longings—similar to the way he engaged with the woman by that well in Samaria—that I would learn more about what it means to be fully human in God's image.

And fully Alive.

3

The Depths of
Our Desire

And all the time your soul is craving
and longing for something else.
—Fyodor Dostoyevsky

To some, the idea of plunging underwater and sucking air through a tube to survive doesn't sound like a fun way to spend an afternoon at the beach. Scuba divers are thought by many to be just downright weird.

Well, I'm a diver and, in my weirdness, I've discovered a wonder that can't be found above the surface. Yes, you can see some cool things from the surface with a snorkel and a mask. But any diver will tell you that, deeper down, marvels await. When I submerge, I see a display of creatures and corals that have, for millennia, been reserved for the eyes of God alone.

When it comes to evaluating my longings, I typically remain in the shallows. So a worthwhile question is, Will I go deep enough to be able to engage with my true longings and celebrate them? Few of us ever do. Jesus invited the Samaritan woman to go deeper, and he does the same for you and me.

As a diver, to get deeper, I need to possess both *courage* and *expertise*. Courage to take the first plunge initially comes from within me, and expertise is given by people who know better than I. And as my expertise increases, so does my courage.

I'm starting to realize the same is true in my life—I bring the initial courage to go deeper and engage with my longings, and Jesus brings the expertise that can teach and liberate me to courageously engage with my longings in ways I've never before experienced.

As a result of the insight gained, I begin to realize I live my days swimming around on the surface with my pursuits and corresponding longings in tow. Then, for a few prioritized pursuits, I take them a bit deeper, going below the surface and devoting a bit or a lot more intensity to them (for the woman at the well, the number five, as in "five husbands," tells me plenty about her intensity level in her pursuit of marriage).

Sooner or later, the dragon of disappointment will rear its head and consume my energy and optimism. It might be because I've failed at something—or it might be because I've succeeded. (Actually the sooner I experience success in a pursuit, the quicker it's exposed as not being able to deliver to my heart what I thought it could; otherwise, I just keep following the siren call of empty promises that leads me further and further away from true contentment.) Either way, my intensity wanes. We all know too well what disillusionment feels like: "I thought this would be more satisfying than it is."

Then, with whatever pursuit has been failing us, we approach it from a different angle. "Yes, materialism will do it for me, but I just need to get a different, nicer car." "Yes, marriage is the answer, but I just need a new wife."

Sooner or later, disappointments mount, and my optimism becomes infected with doubt. Despair begins to take potshots at my soul. For the writer of Ecclesiastes, after trying all sorts of pleasure and acquiring piles of possessions, he reflected, "Yet when I surveyed all that my hands had done and what I had toiled to achieve, everything was meaningless, a chasing after the wind; nothing was gained under the sun" (Ecclesiastes 2:11).

For the woman by the well, she was now hesitating about marriage being able to address her heart's deepest aches, but she hadn't completely given up. So she's decided to just live with the current guy—no marriage yet. Her decision to come up with this unique option of only cohabitating is a radical move—remember this is first-century Palestine, not twenty-first-century Hollywood.

The commitment she's displaying to fulfill her heart is commendable but still misdirected.

❧ ❧ ❧

Once disappointment with a particular pursuit runs its course, a moment of decision presents itself. Do I swim back to the surface and find a different pursuit that I can try taking to a deeper level—another career, another relationship, another hobby, another vice—one that might deliver what the previous pursuits didn't? Or do I level off in despair and float along in numbed defeat?

The overall result: I either work myself into an exhausted frenzy—moving from pursuit to pursuit, restaurant to restaurant—looking for something or someone that will address the ache that's deep within me, or I finally give up and just start going through the motions with a sedated soul.

> When we live at the surface of our longings, we live a superficial gospel.

Sooner or later, the option of giving up—raising the white flag and merely existing instead of living—rears its head as a very real and likely option. It's why Henry David Thoreau concluded, "The mass of men lead lives of quiet desperation."[1]

Why? Because we're bitterly haunted by our disappointments. We become deafened to any hope of things changing. We become weary of the unresolved echo of our longings.

Starting over with another pursuit or just giving up. Neither alternative sounds great. This woman was about to discover there is a third option.

Jesus is inviting her to go deeper. To a deeper level of perceiving and experiencing as never before. Concerning her longings. Her pursuits. Her heart. Her journey. Her humanity.

In scuba diving, when you hit a depth of around one hundred feet, a condition called nitrogen narcosis can begin to develop. Because of the increased water pressure's impact, the gases in your body are dispersed differently, and the result is a sensation of intoxication coupled with fuzzy thinking and delayed responses. I've witnessed it in a friend while diving at a depth of 130 feet. Narcosis is not harmful by itself—the harm comes from decisions you make while experiencing it. Nor are the symptoms permanent; they are easily remedied by ascending to a shallower depth.

Now let me switch that around. When it comes to our longings, it's exactly the opposite. Spiritual narcosis—impaired understanding and consequent bad decisions regarding my life's pursuits—happens at the surface. Superficial pursuits intoxicate us in the moment but render us dazed and confused as human beings. The solution?

Go deeper.

I need to think more deeply and carefully about the longings beneath my pursuits. Why am I pursuing what I'm pursuing?

Christ is summoning this woman to a deeper place—away from shallow, superficial pursuits to a more substantive engagement with what he has to offer. We can summarize what he offers her as the gospel, but contrary to what a lot of religious people would have us believe, the gospel is not a religious ideology or a set of rules. It means "good news." I think it's safe to say that mere religiosity doesn't quite qualify as good news. But to someone who's dying of thirst on a daily basis, the promise of living water—now *that* is good news.

❧ ❧ ❧

Jesus is not only summoning this woman at the well. He's also summoning me to realize the gospel is about going deep regarding the longings of my humanity in the midst of my Mondays. Yes, it's about God the Son who became fully human, was crucified in my place, and raised again. But it's about him doing that in order to resurrect me into a new life and a new humanity, not just to introduce a new ideology and a new set of rules.

Christ beckons me to engage with the gospel, not as a religious person wanting a Christian label or a church person looking for something to do on a Sunday morning, but as a human being yearning to come alive.

Let me highlight a key truth that's becoming increasingly clear to me:

A superficial and therefore short-circuited engagement
with my longings leads to a superficial and therefore
short-circuited engagement with the gospel.

Could I ask you to read that again? It means that grappling with my longings is absolutely vital to my walk with God. When we live at the surface of our longings, we live a superficial gospel.

Sophie, in her forties, has gone to church all her life. She's committed to church activities and keeps busy. She knows the church's doctrine and follows the rules. It's a habit for her to attend church every Sunday, but in a way, she's playing a game called church, and it's oddly unrelated to the rest of her week and her life. Tragically, she lives her days divorced from both her longings as well as the heart of the gospel. But she still has the reputation of being a mature Christian. How?

As John Eldredge and Larry Crabb have pointed out, when church people opt for burying their longings and just getting on with life, they end up equating *pre-tending* with Christian *maturity*. Oh yes, there's one slight detail: "The only price we pay is a loss of soul, of communion with God, a loss of direction, and a loss of hope."[2]

That's a devastating price tag.

At their core, such superficial church environments might breed polished religious people but weird human beings. And the last time I checked, most normal people have a bit more interest in being authentically human than being religiously refined. I remember one unbelieving friend sarcastically commenting to me about some church people he'd been exposed to: "At least they're boring *and* superficial." Like saying of a football team's offensive line, "At least they're small *and* slow." It's a dismissive vote of no confidence.

Here's another realization that's taking root in my understanding:

> A more substantive engagement with my
> longings has to be accompanied by an authentic,
> substantive engagement with the gospel.

In other words, if I determine to go deeper with my longings but pair that with the superficial version of the gospel found in too many churches, I will find the gospel wanting. It will seem too superficial, too unengaged with what it means to be truly human.

A friend of mine was raised in church, but in his college and young adult years, he walked away from Christianity. The reason? As he began to seriously try to figure out who he was as a human being, the gospel he had grown up with seemed hollow. Only later did he realize that his hollow gospel wasn't the real gospel. When he finally sank his heart's teeth into the real teachings of Jesus, he finally trusted Christ for real—and began to really Live.

❧ ❧ ❧

So how do I go deeper with my longings? I'll first recognize there's a *difference* between my pursuits and my longings. As an example, a person might say "My longing is to be a concert pianist" or "a quarterback in the NFL." No, that's not a longing; it's a pursuit. Their longings are for the deeper benefits that becoming a concert pianist or pro football player will provide for their lives and hearts. Or so they assume.

While visiting France years ago, I ticked off a French waiter something fierce.

Sitting in a Parisian café, I was the stereotypical American trying out my cave man–level French and asked for a Coke. He brought me a bottle of Coke and a glass. I thanked him (*merci*—I had that word down solid), referenced my French-English dictionary, and when he came back by, I conveyed I also wanted a glass of water. He looked a bit irritated, took the bottle, and poured some Coke into my glass. *That's nice of him,* I thought.

A few minutes later, he came by my table, but *sans* (notice my fluency) water.

I asked him again for some water. He looked even further annoyed and poured some more Coke into my glass. That scenario repeated itself once more, with me reiterating my request for water. This time, *annoyed* doesn't do justice to our Frenchman. He swept up my Coke bottle and angrily began pouring and splashing, all the while shouting opinions about this *Américaine,* using some descriptors that weren't in my vocabulary but were still quite understandable.

Reeling, I finally discovered the problem: my dictionary was a bit too cheap or my mind a bit too slow or both. When looking up the French word for the noun "water," I instead had used a French verb meaning "to water, to pour." So each time he came by, this egocentric and lazy American was asking the waiter to pour his Coke for him. I laughed aloud and explained this to the waiter.

He didn't laugh. And I never got my glass of water.

What I was saying I wanted was quite different from what I really needed. You might say I was longing for one thing but unknowingly pursuing something quite different. My pursuit didn't fit with the longing I was trying to fulfill.

This fleshes itself out all over the place in our stories. For example, I think I'm longing for marriage when I'm really longing for something different—say, significance—while pursuing marriage. So the difference between pursuits and longings becomes something far more than semantics.

❧ ❧ ❧

Once I begin recognizing there's a difference between the two, I then begin to see the *mismatch* between some of my longings and the corresponding pursuits I attach to them. As actor and potential theologian Jim Carrey ruminates, "I think everybody should get rich and famous and do everything they ever dreamed of so they can see that it's not the answer."[3] Whatever the answer is he's referring to, it's a longing word, and the conventional pursuits most people go for don't address the deeper issue.

As God declares through the prophet Jeremiah, "My people have committed two sins: They have forsaken me, the spring of living water, and have dug their own cisterns, broken cisterns that cannot hold water" (Jeremiah 2:13). I am continually building my own cisterns (or water containers), adopting pursuits I mistakenly think will quench my soul's thirst, all the while avoiding the only One who can actually address it.

More often than not, it's impossible for a particular pursuit to fulfill a longing I've consciously or subconsciously attached to it—my expectation is simply beyond the capacity of the pursuit. The restaurant I've chosen doesn't even have what I'm longing for on its menu.

Take marriage as an example. Often a root of conflict in so many marriages is when a person expects from his or her spouse something the partner is incapable of providing. Often, those expectations are longings only God can address (deep significance, ultimate security, and so on). So when the no-contest mismatch between pursuit and longing is embraced, I can relieve my wife from my suffocating expectations.

> When I determine to go deeper with my longings, I'll ultimately and inevitably have to embrace something eternal.

Jesus was going deep with this Samaritan woman, calling her to evaluate whether her husbands had really addressed the thirst in her soul. The fact she'd had five husbands served as a sufficient answer to the question.

When I choose to start thinking along these lines, I begin to unmask the unrealistic expectations I've been attaching to many of my pursuits—whether it's trying to extract too much core significance from my job or too much fulfillment from fly-fishing. It doesn't mean I back off from my career or from fly-fishing, but I simply dial back my expectations of the type of longings that can be met by those pursuits.

Then, for deeper longings, I begin to reflect more carefully about what pursuits would begin to address those. (If you have the courage to do it, make a list of your frequent pursuits and try to match them up with your deepest longings. That's a scary but ultimately healthy way to really understand your longings.)

That's where Jesus heads with this woman, beckoning her to a deeper pursuit than marriage or men to address her ultimate longings.

❧ ❧ ❧

Jesus wanted this woman to understand that her ultimate longing was actually not for a man but for *living water*. She just didn't know it yet.

Living water. Life water. Something that addresses my soul's thirst. He's using the drinking of this living water as a metaphor of what it means to experience eternal life.[4] There's something eternal about what he's offering. Why is he bringing that up with a woman who's been pursuing her heart's longing through multiple failed marriages? Why not just offer a couple of marriage counseling tips and call it a day?

Hear the words of Ecclesiastes: "I have seen the burden God has laid on the human race. He has made everything beautiful in its time. He has also set eternity in the human heart; yet no one can fathom what God has done from beginning to end" (3:10–11, NIV 2011).

There's something embedded in every human heart: eternity. It doesn't matter who I am—young or old, male or female, a left-brained engineer or a right-brained musician, always or never in church—this eternity comes planted in my heart from birth. When I determine to go deeper with my longings, I'll ultimately and inevitably have to embrace something eternal.

Jesus is referring to water that addresses our thirst for eternity.

This woman is already thirsty for it, and she's been desperately seeking to quench it with any number of pursuits, the most obvious being men. Time and again she's come up wanting, disappointed, heartbroken. With her heart gasping for air as her soul is dying of thirst, the hopeless monotony of her story is now being interrupted by One who says he knows what kind of water she needs.

Blaise Pascal, a seventeenth-century French mathematician and philosopher, was also a passionate follower of Christ. In his classic *Pensées*, he conveys a resonance and understanding with this issue of longings, or as he put it, *avidité* ("ardent desire" or "craving"): "What is it, then, that this desire and this inability proclaim to us, but that there was once in man a true happiness of which there now remain to him only the mark and empty trace, which he in vain tries to fill from all his surroundings, seeking from things absent the help he does not obtain in things present? But these are all inadequate, because the infinite abyss can only be filled by an infinite and immutable object, that is to say, only by God Himself."[5]

As I begin to submit to Jesus's invitation to go deeper regarding my ardent desires, I increasingly realize that my ultimate longings—all of which are connected to my desire to be fully human—are bigger than any earthly pursuit can fulfill.

➤ ➤ ➤

In his children's classic *The Silver Chair,* C. S. Lewis brings his concept of *Sehnsucht* down to a level we can all understand.

A British schoolgirl named Jill has just arrived in the magical realm of Narnia. Dreadfully hot and thirsty, she sees a stream of fresh water and heads toward it for a drink. Then she sees the Lion. We know him as Aslan, the central character and Christ figure of the Chronicles of Narnia. She just sees him as large, intimidating, and potentially ferocious. She freezes.

"If you are thirsty, come and drink." From another child who had already been to Narnia, she remembered hearing of animals talking, which helped her identify that it was the Lion speaking to her.

She didn't move.

"Are you not thirsty?" said the Lion.

"I'm *dying* of thirst," Jill replied.

"Then drink," said the Lion.

Jill first asks him to go away. When he refuses, she asks for assurances that he won't do anything to her, and he again refuses. She concludes that she therefore won't go and drink, to which the Lion remarks, "Then you will die of thirst."

"I suppose I must go and look for another stream then."

Aslan's reply is both simple and sobering.

"There is no other stream."[6]

That sounds familiar. A bit like what a woman by a well in Samaria heard back in the first century.

A bit like what I'm hearing right now.

Accept this as an invitation for us to have a drink together.

Life, Our Ultimate Longing

He clothed Himself in our language, so that
He might clothe us in His mode of Life.
—EPHREM THE SYRIAN, fourth-century theologian

Jacob Brodsky knew what he desired, but his dad didn't agree. A central figure in Tennessee Williams's short story "Something by Tolstoi," Jacob was a shy Russian Jew whose father owned a bookshop. He longed for nothing more than to marry his childhood sweetheart, Lila, a beautiful, exuberant French girl.

Instead his father insisted he should go away to college.

A couple of months into his first year of university, his father died suddenly. So Jacob returned home, married Lila, and they blissfully moved into the apartment over the bookstore. The life of a bookshop proprietor suited him fine, but not his adventurous young bride. An agent for a vaudeville touring company heard Lila sing and talked her into touring Europe with their show.

In the process of explaining to Jacob that she had to seize this opportunity and leave, she also cleaved a chasm-sized hole in his heart. But before she left, he gave her a key to the bookshop. Handing over the heavy, old-fashioned key, he pressed, " 'You had better keep this,' he told her, still with complete quietness, 'because you will want it some day. Your love is not so much less than mine that you can get away from it. You will come back sometime, and I will be waiting.' "[1]

Lila went on the road, and Jacob went to the back of his bookshop. To deaden the pain, he turned to his books as someone else might turn to drugs or alcohol.

Weeks turned into years. When fifteen of them had passed, the bell above the bookshop's front door signaled the arrival of a customer.

It was Lila.

The bookshop's owner rose to greet her. But to her astonishment, her abandoned husband didn't recognize her and simply spoke like he would to any other customer.

"Do you want a book?"

Stunned and trying to maintain her composure, she raised a gloved hand to her throat and stammered, "No—that is—I wanted a book, but I've forgotten the name of it." Regaining some poise, she continued, "Let me tell you the story—perhaps you have read it and can give me the name of it."[2]

She then told him of a boy and a girl who had been constant companions since childhood. As teenagers, they fell in love, eventually married, and lived over a bookshop. She told him their whole story. The young wife's restlessness. The vaudeville company's offer and her acceptance. The husband's brokenhearted gift of the key before she departed. How, as years passed, the wife was never able to part with the key. How, after fifteen years, she finally came to her senses and returned home to him.

She culminated her summary with a desperate plea, "You remember it—you must remember it—the story of Lila and Jacob?"

With a vacant, faraway look, he merely said, "There is something familiar about the story. I think I have read it somewhere. It seems to me that it is something by Tolstoi."[3]

Only the heartbreaking, metallic echo of the key dropping to the hard floor interrupted her horrified silence. Lila, having let go of the key as well as her hope, fled the bookshop in tears.

And Jacob returned to his books.

❧ ❧ ❧

We find ourselves in the same heartbreaking story, each of us playing the part of both Jacob and Lila. I hear that story and put myself in Jacob's shoes: Do I remember what I'm actually longing for? Have I ever known? Have I buried myself in some pain-killing distractions? Jacob's incessant erosion of hope had buried his ability to identify his true desire.

He had forgotten what he had been longing for in the first place.

In the midst of our many pursuits—careers, relationships, aspirations to be a parent or a pro-golfer or a physician—we've lost touch with what we ultimately desire. We have been trying so many pursuits for so long and have been disappointed so often that we've forgotten what we're actually longing for.

But I also resonate with Lila. With every longing I have, it's as if I'm holding a key and wondering, "What door does this unlock?" My longings are the key I've been carrying my whole life that serve as a reminder of my heart's real desire.

In a poem entitled "Vowels and Sirens," C. S. Lewis talks about our longing as "vanished knowledge" and describes it as "Some earlier music / That men are born remembering." He then refers to a "backward journey to the steep river's hid source."[4] There is something about our longings that connects us with the saga our souls started long ago—a song we yearn to trace back to its source.

Every longing we have is ultimately part of the music that we're born remembering. That music is eternity.

That music is Life.

~ ~ ~

The disruption of our longings began in the Garden of Eden. Most of us have heard of the tree of life. It appears three places in the Bible: the beginning, in Genesis before humanity's Fall; the middle, in the wisdom book of Proverbs; and the end, in Revelation as a depiction of the New Creation is being unveiled.

In Proverbs, the tree of life is described as a metaphor of wisdom, righteousness, and healing. In Proverbs 13:12, we find a powerful defining statement: "a longing fulfilled is a tree of life."

I had seen that verse several times over the course of my journey. But just a few years ago I moved from seeing it to reading it to pondering it to being renovated by it. Whatever the tree of life is, access to it is closely related to the consummation of my longings, and being distant from it will result in longings that go unaddressed.

Before the Fall, Adam and Eve had unfettered access to the tree of life, keeping them as strangers to unfulfilled longings. My soul salivates when I read southern author and poet Wendell Berry's reflection about humanity's pre-Fall satisfaction and contented freedom. He envisions God's delight in Adam and Eve and their delight in him, proposing that their state of perfect contentment revolved around simply being who God made them to be. Since these complete humans lacked nothing and therefore had no desire for change or anything new, Berry contemplates that there was only one direction their yearning could take them:

> …Nor longed for change or novelty.
> The only new thing could be pain.[5]

Taking their almost unimaginable privilege for granted, Adam and Eve succumbed to the only new thing remaining: pain birthed by an individualistic rebellion against their Creator. Their intimate communion with God became polluted by a contrived self-sufficiency, one that presumed to have better knowledge than God himself of what would satisfy and fulfill. (That sounds familiar—it's what sin still looks like in me.)

With their—and our—embrace of this new thing called sin came the devastating reality of exile from the tree of life. We got what we wanted; yet it turned out to be anything but. Humanity, now banished from the undiluted fulfillment of the garden, became tragically familiar with unmet longings.

In the last chapter of the book of Revelation, a beautifully hopeful portrait of the new creation is being painted. Unencumbered proximity to the tree of life once again becomes a central part of the story of redeemed human beings. That is the hope of heaven!

> He had forgotten what he had been longing for in the first place.

It all sounds fantastic. But here I am now—dealing with car payments and computer problems, trying to carve out a few sane moments with friends, and battling periodic migraines. My journey is palpably suspended between a past, pre-fallen creation and the new creation that is yet to be. To say I'm daily aware that I don't have unfettered access to the tree of life would be a glaring and almost mocking understatement. My deep longings make themselves known through a variety of heartaches and inadequate pursuits that fall short of giving me what I most yearn for, so they continue their dejected complaint of being unaddressed and going unfulfilled.

Enter the gospel.

No, not the tame, sterilized version that accessorizes the religious Sunday compartment of our lives, but the outrageously good news that pulsates with hope and can invade our Monday morning realities. Could it be that what Jesus Christ offers us is restored access to the tree of life—even partially—while we await the completeness we'll enjoy in the new creation?

The symphony of the gospel trumpets a resounding and restorative "Yes!"

❧ ❧ ❧

Restoration to Life is at the core of what Jesus offers the woman by that well in Samaria—and us.[6]

In Jacob Brodsky–like fashion, we have forgotten what we've been ultimately longing for—we can't remember its name or identity—but we still long for it, deeply. Bottom line, the name and identity of that ultimate longing is eternal Life—but not in the trite or common way you and I may have come to understand it.

Flowing from an intimate relationship with God,[7] it's the Life Jesus promises and the Life that painter Nikolai Yaroshenko described as being possible everywhere. Life with a capital L. Deep, substantive water for my soul's thirst. An infinite ocean of his enoughness.

Since the day each of us was born, Christ's Life has hinted of its existence through the tributaries and rivers of our desires, dreams, and longings. So when I finally and truly grasp his offer of the gospel, his offer of living water, the most appropriate response should be, "This is what I've longed for my whole life!"

But, sadly, when we are taught that believing the gospel is merely a matter of filling out a conversion card, raising our hand at a religious meeting, or checking "Christian" in a census religious-preference box, our response is quite different from amazement. The underscoring yawn would be laughable if we weren't talking about something so potentially life changing and humanity altering.

Please hear this regarding Jesus's encounter with the woman by that well in Samaria we were talking about earlier: there was nothing yawn-worthy in the eternal Life he was offering her. Though a simple offer, it was not a simplistic appeal that merely targeted her religious habits. It was an invitation to address her ultimate thirst and deepest longings—to be catapulted into a journey of becoming fully human.

It was a summons to come Alive.

❧ ❧ ❧

A pivotal time for me in this journey was when I began to really unpack the term *eternal life*. Too many equate it as just another way to say *heaven*. I know I did—for years. In college, I became focused on my walk with God in a way I never had before.

And I was deeply grateful for the eternal life that was mine through Christ. Yet years passed before I began to realize that eternal life was more than a reference to heaven—that it also had a lot more to do with me and my humanity *right now.*

Oddly enough, my discovery was rooted in basic grammar.

I didn't pay much attention to grammar in school, but I did enough to figure out the difference between an adjective and a noun. I finally began to apply that to my understanding of the phrase *eternal life,* realizing both the noun as well as the adjective must be embraced if I was really going to grasp the gift Jesus promises. My problem, along with many, had been a tendency to emphasize the adjective at the expense of the noun, so I just focused on the word *eternal* and thought the phrase was only emphasizing the quantity of life Jesus offers us, as in forever life—a forever existence. Eternal life was just a synonym for heaven.

When Jesus promises eternal life, is he referring to heaven? Of course. But is he *only* referring to heaven? Of course not. *Eternal life* is a pregnant and massive phrase that refers to Life in both a *qualitative* as well as *quantitative* way, and it's a costly mistake to think otherwise. If I do, I'll miss the Life and restoration of my humanity that he promises right now.

Years ago, driving home from a backpacking trip in the Upper Peninsula of Michigan, I stopped at a little diner a few miles past the middle of nowhere. From its appearance it looked like it might have had a negative three-star rating from the *Michelin Guide to Restaurants,* but I didn't care. Dirty, exhausted, and starving, I slid into a booth and wasn't bothered by how sticky the menu was—or the seat. When the waitress came up, smacking on her gum, I conveyed my hunger and told her I was more interested in quantity than quality.

She responded way too quickly, never smiling or altering the rapid rhythm of her gum-fest, "Well, you've come to the right place." I had been joking—I wanted both quantity *and* quality.

But she wasn't joking.

I realized that when the food came.

To properly understand the meaning of eternal life, I've got to focus on quantity *and* quality. Yes, Jesus is promising a forever quantity of Life when he promises us eternal life. But when does it begin? When I die? That's where I once was in my journey—thinking that I wouldn't be able to experience eternal life until my heart stopped beating.

For too long I missed what Jesus emphasized: "I tell you the truth, whoever hears my word and believes him who sent me has eternal life and will not be condemned; he has crossed over from death to life" (John 5:24). He is teaching that once I enter into belief, I—present tense—*have life* from that moment on. He underscores the fact by saying once I have believed, I have moved out of a realm he calls death and into another called life.

I don't have to wait until I physically die for this to become a reality. It's true now. From the moment I believe.

So once I've put my trust in Christ, the question is not about whether I've received eternal life but whether I'm experiencing it.

Now.

❧ ❧ ❧

Eternal life—when I understand it in this way—becomes Life with a capital L. Realizing that it can begin now, I need to grapple with how all-encompassing it is. Eternal Life is not just about how long my life is but how full it is. It's an ability to live with a depth of engagement I've been longing for all my days.

Life with a capital L is a capacity Jesus gives me to fully embrace my humanity and experience the privilege of being human. Instead of living in the monotonous cadence of surviving to play and playing to survive, I really, *really* do life. Fully. Deeply. Widely.

"Livin' large" is a phrase you and I can resonate with. Certainly for some it might refer to a gluttonous engagement with life, dripping with excess, which is of course not what Jesus is talking about. But the expression nevertheless reveals a hunch we all have about the possibility that there is more to life than just having a heart that's beating, paying bills, taking out the garbage, and squeezing in a periodic vacation. That it's not only about how long I'm living, but how fully. The term divulges what kind of life we're longing for even if we can't quite put our finger on what it is. But, tragically, very few would turn in the direction of the gospel when trying to unpack what livin' large could look like in their journey.

Why? Because in cordoning off the gospel to the territory of Sunday and eternity, we've missed the centrality and daily relevance of the Life Jesus offers.

❧ ❧ ❧

Eternal Life—Life with a capital L—is at the core of the gospel. Instead of being some sidebar of Christ's message, eternal Life was absolutely central to what he announced to humanity.

It's why the disciples were so captivated with Jesus. They weren't passionate about his gospel because it was a cool religious ideology or new set of rules. That's not why they died for their belief. They gave up their lives because they were blown away that Jesus was the Truth and the Way to a new reality of Living, to a new humanity. They were gripped by the dance of Life he embodied and into which he invited them.

His new Life was at the core of the gospel they lived, proclaimed, and died for.

Listening to three of the dominant voices in the early church—Peter, Paul, and John—I hear this message of Life loud and clear. Peter told Jesus he would continue to follow him because he didn't know where else he could receive "the words of eternal life" (John 6:68). He later wrote that we are redeemed by Christ from "the empty way of life" (1 Peter 1:18) to which we're imprisoned without him, saying that because of Christ we are heirs of "the gracious gift of life" (1 Peter 3:7).

> We've missed the centrality and daily relevance of the Life Jesus offers.

Paul exclaimed that "because of his great love for us, God, who is rich in mercy, made us alive with Christ even when we were dead in transgressions" (Ephesians 2:4–5), and we can now "reign in life through the one man, Jesus Christ" (Romans 5:17).

John reveled in the reality of Life with a capital L, saying "we know that we have passed from death to life" (1 John 3:14) and that "he who has the Son has life; he who does not have the Son of God does not have life" (1 John 5:12), which is as about as blunt as he could say it. He even summarized the reason for writing his gospel in terms of proclaiming the Life that can only be found in Christ: "But these are written that you may believe that Jesus is the Christ, the Son of God, and that by believing you may have life in his name" (John 20:31).

They all grasped Christ's perspective: whether I'm ultimately Alive is not a matter of whether my heart is beating but whether my soul is alive, launching me on a journey of becoming a human being restored into the Life God originally intended.

If I miss Christ's teaching about eternal Life, I am missing the core of the gospel.

～ ～ ～

Something is dreadfully awry with the ways too many of us minimize and reduce the gospel: Receive forgiveness. Gain heaven. Behave morally in the meantime. Subscribe to a doctrinal statement. Go to church. Tell others about him.

Sure, those are all part of following Christ, but is that the extent of the reward[8] and blessing of following him? Is that the sum of the gospel?

The reward is eternal Life—to lovingly, submissively, vibrantly relate with God in such a way that it awakens my heart. Addresses my longings. Deepens my relationships. Permeates my work. Triggers my laughter. Authenticates my tears. Directs my journey. Fulfills my days. Restores my humanity.

And, yes, secures me for eternity.

I need to realize Life with a capital L is not secondary but primary to both my understanding *and* my experience of the gospel. A thoughtful business leader once excitedly blurted out to me, "I've been a Christian for a long time. How have I missed this? I've turned the purpose of Christ's arrival and my conversion into developing a moral list of dos and don'ts. I now realize that godly behavior comes from new Life, not just new rules. It's ultimately not about him making bad people good but making dead people alive. It really is about becoming fully human. This reframes the gospel for me."

It's a powerful moment when I let the gospel break out of the compartmentalized, pious playpen into which I've confined it, a realm where it's merely something that establishes my religious habits and church life. When I let the gospel invade every arena of my days and every aspect of my humanity, that's when Life with a capital L begins to transform me, regardless of the circumstances.

～ ～ ～

It was one week after sitting in the art gallery in Moscow in front of Nikolai Yaroshenko's painting of the prison railcar. I was beginning a monthlong sabbatical in Europe, something I'd dreamed of doing for many years. And I was standing in Milan's central train station.

When I bent over to tie a shoelace while waiting for a train, a thief who'd evidently been watching me saw his chance. During a three-second window, he glided by and, without stopping, sliced the strap of my overstuffed briefcase from its mooring on the pull handle of my roller suitcase, grabbed it, and ran up the stairs. With him went the essentials I'd packed for a month's stay in Europe: laptop, iPad, train tickets, headphones, glasses, books, files, sanity. Gone.

That night, after collapsing in my hotel from frustration as well as exhaustion, I thought about Yaroshenko's painting. *There Is Life Everywhere.* I had agreed with him in the calmness of the museum. But how about now? Is there Life to be embraced in the midst of *this* predicament?

I'll be honest about my struggle with the question: the soul tussle went deep (and so did my anger at being victimized). But I'll also be honest about my ultimate—and grateful—embrace of the answer: yes.

There Is Life Everywhere. Life with a capital L. Even behind the bars of a prison railcar and underneath the burden of being robbed.

A couple of weeks later, my family joined me from our home in Colorado for a dream vacation in Italy. During our first dinner together, my cell phone began to vibrate. And vibrate. Finally I picked it up, knowing something must be up.

It was a friend calling. "Matt, a wildfire has spread in the Waldo Canyon area near your home, and your neighborhood is being evacuated. A few of us are hurrying to your house now to gather anything you'd like us to salvage. What's the key code to your garage? What do you want us to grab?"

Welcome to vacation.

Things settled down over the next couple of days, and the fire was seemingly cordoned off in a wilderness area away from houses and neighborhoods. We were thinking the fire was under control. So did most people back in Colorado.

But on the third day we got word that the wind had picked up and was again moving the burgeoning blaze over tinderbox terrain primed by months of drought. The next morning, I woke early in the tranquility of a Piedmont village, picked up my cell phone, and was greeted by dozens of texts and voice mails. Serenity gave way to big-time stress. As I read and listened, my heartbeat relocated into my throat. Sixty-mile-per-hour winds had catapulted the flames over the defensive firebreaks, and an inferno had invaded our neighborhood.

While the voice mails and texts weren't able to definitely confirm whether our house was gone, they were assuming it. Instead of calling anyone while it was the middle of the night in Colorado, I went online. From the news photos and videos on the web, I saw why—there just didn't seem to be any way our home could have survived such a firestorm.

I woke my family and gave them the surreal and heartbreaking news. That day and into the next, we lived with the assumption that the structure we had called home for eleven years, along with everything but a computer and the few boxes of photos our friends had salvaged, was gone.

Then, incredibly, it was confirmed that our street had experienced only one destroyed home with another one damaged. In the smoke, ours was still standing. But our personal relief was short-lived. A tragic total of 346 homes around us had been destroyed. The most devastating wildfire in Colorado's history to date had left a painful scar, not only on the landscape of our beautiful city in the foothills of the Rocky Mountains, but also on people's lives and stories.

I flew back from vacation early and toured the smoldering and still evacuated neighborhoods. It was hard to get my head, much less my heart, around what I saw. Entire streets and neighborhoods were just…gone.

That afternoon, I had some reflection time. Again, I thought about Yaroshenko's canvas. *There Is Life Everywhere.* Seriously? In this? Is it really possible to experience Life with a capital L in the midst of such ashes and brokenness?

In days to follow, I had conversation after conversation with people impacted by the fire. Understandably, many were just lost. But with others, while juggling the stress of the evacuation and, for some, even the destruction of their home, there was something different. While still honestly and openly engaging with the reality of the pain, they were nevertheless experiencing something else: Life with a capital L.

They might not have had smiles on their faces, but there was a hopeful resolution in their hearts as they dealt with the drama of being human—and still alive—in a scorched and less-than-perfect world.

Do the difficult things in our days make it more of a challenge to experience Life? Yes, usually. But in the midst of those realities is Life still available? Absolutely.

In the maze of journeys that are more painful and circumstances that are much less perfect than we'd ever prefer, in the midst of Mondays that range from dull to dramatic, broken to beautiful, what we ultimately long for is Life with a capital L.

Not only behind the bars of a prison railcar or underneath the burden of being robbed, but even surrounded by the devastation of an out-of-control wildfire, *there is Life everywhere.*

5

Grace, the Doorway to Life

> "Babette can cook."
> —Isak Dinesen

The two sisters had lived in Berlevåg all their lives. Or at least they had lived as much as their religiosity had allowed. Their names are Martine and Philippa, and they are part of the central cast of characters in a short story by Isak Dinesen, the Danish writer who also penned the classic *Out of Africa*. In this beautiful tale titled "Babette's Feast," Dinesen not only writes about Life with a capital L but also how to begin to taste it.

The sisters are the leaders of a religious community in a little fishing village on an isolated part of the Norwegian coast. The church, founded by their father, is a religious sect that is not only small in number but also in its view of the world. Priding themselves in their denial of the world's pleasures, their focus is fixed on heaven (which is a fantastic reality to fix your eyes on, unless you deny your present-tense humanity in the process).

In their youth, the sisters were extraordinarily beautiful and desired, attracting would-be suitors such as—for Martine—a cavalry officer named Lorens Löwenhielm and—for Philippa—a Parisian opera singer named Achille Papin. Yet their father, who deemed such earthy pursuits as frivolous, discouraged their romances. So the suitors departed, and the daughters remained single.

It is decades later.

Their father, now deceased, has passed on the leadership of his religious vision to the two sisters, who now practice an austere faith while devoutly leading a diminished and elderly congregation.

On a rainy June night in 1871, their lives are interrupted by a knock at the door. A woman, "deadly pale," stands there for a moment and then faints. She carries a letter from Achille Papin, Philippa's suitor thirty-five years earlier. The letter explains that the woman is a refugee from the revolution in Paris. Her name is Babette. Would they take her in?

The letter concludes with a simple statement: "Babette can cook."

Despite some reservations, the sisters offer refuge to Babette, and she becomes their household servant. Suspicious of the extravagant French cuisine with which Babette is familiar, the sisters require that she confine her cooking to the compliant preparation of the fare they are accustomed to—underwhelming items such as split cod and ale-and-bread soup.

Over the years, Babette reorganizes the household, negotiates good terms with local merchants, and saves money on groceries and supplies. She doesn't speak much of her personal life, although she does mention she owns a ticket to the French lottery and that a friend in Paris was renewing it each year.

Mysterious as she is, Babette gradually becomes appreciated by the sisters and their small religious community.

Twelve years after she first appeared at the sisters' door, Babette receives the first letter ever delivered to her there. It's a lottery notice. Babette has won ten thousand francs.

She makes a request. The one hundredth birthday of their father is approaching, and the sisters had been planning to commemorate the anniversary. Babette asks if they would allow her to prepare, just once, a real French meal in celebration of their father's life. She offers to pay for the food herself.

Reluctantly, Martine and Philippa agree.

Babette proceeds to order an array of food supplies from Paris. When the exotic food shipments begin to arrive, suspicions and fear begin to germinate in the sisters.

Martine and Philippa soon develop great concerns over the lavish preparations being made. They alert the other church members who will be attending. They believe that "luxurious fare was sinful. Their own food must be as plain as possible." So they all agree to remain reserved at the dinner and not to speak of the food.

Encumbered by their view of God that excluded all notions of extravagance—including physical pleasures such as smell and taste—they agree to focus their minds on higher things.

After weeks of intricate preparations, including more mysterious shipments from France, the evening arrives.

The guests gather and are quickly overwhelmed as they see "the French dinner coming upon them, a thing of incalculable nature and range." Wines such as an 1860 *Veuve Cliquot* and an 1846 *Clos de Vougeot* fill their glasses. Dishes, including *Blinis Demidoff* and *Cailles en Sarcophage* are laid before them.

Their taste buds dance, but their hearts resist.

One of the guests is Lorens Löwenhielm, Martine's suitor decades earlier, who is in town to visit his elderly mother. Now a general, he has since married a member of Queen Sophia's court, traveled extensively, and become well acquainted with fine wine and cuisine. In fact, one of the dishes served this night reminds the general of a meal he enjoyed years before in Paris—a dish created by the culinary genius at the Café Anglais.

> The reason the religious crowd hasn't tasted Life is because they haven't tasted grace.

The only nonreligious person attending Babette's feast, General Löwenhielm is the one who ultimately awakens to the vision of grace—extravagant grace—embedded in the meal: its preparation, its cost, its beauty. Amazed, he stands to speak into the lives of people who, though religious for much of their lives, still don't know the taste of grace. He thoughtfully and thankfully proclaims, "In our human foolishness and short-sightedness we imagine divine grace to be finite.… But the moment comes when our eyes are opened, and we see and realize that grace is infinite. Grace, my friends, demands nothing from us but that we shall await it with confidence and acknowledge it in gratitude. Grace, brothers, makes no conditions and singles out none of us in particular; grace takes us all to its bosom and proclaims general amnesty."[1]

Slowly won over by the extraordinary foods and warmed by the fine wines, the guests begin to respond, not only to the feast itself, but to one another. Old quarrels are healed, past wrongs forgiven.

The dinner comes to a close, and the members of the church community depart.

Illuminated by moonlight reflecting off a blanket of new snow in the village square, they spontaneously join hands in a circle.

And they dance.

Inside, the sisters thank Babette for her extravagant feast. Assuming her plan will be to return to Paris, they are surprised to learn she will not be going and are shocked at why: Babette reveals she has no more money. She has spent all of her lottery winnings on the meal she cooked that night.

The sisters are speechless; they cannot fathom how a meal could cost that much money. Babette explains, "A dinner for twelve at the Café Anglais would cost 10,000 francs."

The sisters discover Babette's secret: Babette herself was the world-renowned chef of the Paris restaurant, Café Anglais.

Babette can cook.

Indeed.

～ ～ ～

No doubt I'm influenced strongly by my own heart hunger and religious history, but for me this story is saying something profoundly biblical. Something that's deeply rooted in the gospel message of Life with a capital L. And something we too often miss.

It's the echo of extravagant grace and fulfilled humanity that's embedded in the gospel.

At the core of "Babette's Feast" is a group of religious people who viewed spirituality as something that should repress their humanity instead of liberate it. Their refrains: isolate yourself from the world you live in, deny anything pleasurable, and hope that's enough to get you to heaven; to become more spiritual, you've got to deny your humanity. As a result, they were missing the Life of God and the privilege of being fulfilled human beings under his Life-giving leadership.

That sounds familiar. It's still what people often expect from church and religion: "Focus your eyes upon heaven, and avoid the things of the world." Many of those types of mantras might have their origins in Scripture, but we've wrestled them from their original context and twisted their meaning and thrown in our own legalism. The result for that church community in Berlevåg, and for many of ours today, is something that's gone terribly wrong.

❦ ❦ ❦

I let my mind wander a bit in the direction of Martine and Philippa's father, the founder of their religious community. I imagine him, a seeker early in his life, as someone yearning to fill some deep longings. He realized, at the core, those longings had a spiritual root. So far, so good.

Something similar happens with you and me. It starts with a hunch that, deep down, what we're longing for is God related. We then begin, in a variety of ways, to head down the road in his direction, which is fantastic. However, what often happens is that we take an exit off that highway. Instead of driving toward God, we detour toward religiosity.

Here's what that over-used exit looks like: instead of beginning to experience an actual relationship with God that's laced with grace and filled with Life, we start practicing religion in the presence of God. We start trying to do the right things—the list is long and riddled with both the appropriate (like being part of a church community) and the ridiculous (insert here your favorite fundamentalist rule not found in Scripture), with plenty more behavioral stipulations in between. The way we go about it is dangerously akin to trying to rub a bottle in just the right way to conjure a genie. *If I do all the right things at the right time in the right way, that might earn me a good seat at the blessings table, and hopefully it'll include more good things for me, along with a reduction of some bad stuff.*

That's not Life with a capital L but a legalistic religiosity that can lead us even further away from the fuller Life we long for.

Taking that route, we can join up with others—in churches ranging from mainline to fundamentalist—who've been raised in an environment of empty religion and are strangely settled in that realm. Church people who aren't Living but just existing, with nice religious résumés in hand. We begin to wish we could have it all together like them, and then we begin to suspect they are anything but together. It's a subculture that, at least by outward appearance, avoids the biggie sins. However, things like slander, superficiality, judgmental attitudes, neglect of the poor, hypocrisy, joylessness, and a lack of love make us suspicious. We probe. We don't like what we see in them.

Or what we're beginning to see in the mirror.

Fast-forward far enough, and we very possibly find ourselves among a group of religious refugees. Disappointed and repulsed by suffocating moralism and judgmental fundamentalism that's often passed off as Christianity, we leave the practice of religion altogether. Having never tasted Life, we throw out religion, but in the process we also discard God. We now find ourselves further away from God—and Life—than before.

Authentic seekers, after taking some sort of religiosity path, give up on it because it didn't fulfill us in the way we longed for—it didn't give us Life.

The tragedy is in the irony: what we thought would give Life actually led us further away. But the gospel wasn't tried and found wanting—religion was.

❧ ❧ ❧

So how do I avoid taking a religiosity exit and, instead, keep heading toward God... and Life? The distinguishing factor between Life with a capital L and the mere practice of religion can be summarized in one word.

Grace.

Life with a capital L can't be gained via the religious routine. It can't be earned— it can only be received. Once it's received, then I'm privileged to unpack it over the course of a lifetime. But first I must receive it. And that only comes through an authentic encounter with the God of grace—not just a one-time encounter when I become a follower of Christ, but a daily experience of his grace throughout my life.

Grace.

Sadly, I think many of the people who've heard the word the most experience it the least. So even if I think I understand grace, I better make sure. My Life depends on it.

I look at it again. And I listen to it.

Grace.

What happens when I hear that word? To many, that's all it is—a word. A woman's name. A characteristic of a particular athlete. Something someone says before a special meal. An act of kindness. We come within the walls of the church and add the word *amazing* to it when we sing a popular hymn, but is it really amazing? Are we really amazed? Am I?

Too many religious people I've met over the years, like the religious guests around Babette's table, aren't amazed by grace. There was a time when I wasn't. The gospel message of God's grace came into my life, but instead of letting it capture and transform me, I yawned. I kept grace at arm's length, turning it into a sort of spiritual souvenir while inserting it into my religious vocabulary collection. I then would pull it out from time to time when I needed a nice-sounding but nevertheless vague spiritual word.

Real grace doesn't play that religious game. The five letters of *grace* might settle onto the shelf of my religious alphabet collection, but the liberating truth behind those five letters doesn't follow. Instead, real grace heads where real humans are yearning to be really loved and fulfilled by a real God while doing real life.

Really.

When I finally realized my low-octane level of appreciation and engagement with grace in my life—that I wasn't really amazed—I started digging. I realized I had barely begun to understand grace. Consequently I had never really experienced it on a daily basis.

Grace was a word to me but not a way of life. I knew its spelling but not its meaning. I was familiar with its sound but not its taste.

> I finally had to discover that, bottom line, grace is
> God lovingly giving me what I need instead of what
> I deserve. It's God lavishly giving me what I long for
> but not necessarily all that I think I want.

"Lavish." It's not a descriptor you often hear when it comes to grace. Especially God's grace. But Scripture uses just that word. Paul's letter to the Ephesians tells us that God has chosen to adopt us back into his family and that results in us living for "the praise of his glorious grace, which he has freely given us in the One he loves. In him we have redemption through his blood, the forgiveness of sins, in accordance with the riches of God's grace that he *lavished* on us with all wisdom and understanding" (Ephesians 1:6–8).

Lavish is a unique and powerful verb used to describe what God does in grace toward us. The Greek word that's translated into "lavish" (*perisseúō*) is a word packed with stunning overtones. It appears several times in the New Testament in descriptions of God's grace. It invokes concepts such as abundance and even superabundance, more-than-enough excessiveness, and overflowing extravagance.[2]

A Babette feast. For us.

God doesn't grudgingly dole out the minimum amount of grace toward you and me. He *lavishes* us with it.

To many of us, *lavish* might imply an "extra" that's a nicety but not a necessity. Yet grace is simultaneously an overwhelming nicety and also an absolute necessity. It's necessary because my resistance and rebelliousness toward God's Life-giving leadership is pervasive, touching every aspect of my journey. I might rebel publicly or privately, legally or illegally, in socially acceptable or antisocial ways—but at the end of the day, it's all rebellion.

Because of my rejection of his rule, I fully deserve to experience the loss-of-Life consequences of being separated from God. However, he has opted for a different view of me than one of justly sentencing me to being distanced from him in a manner I deserve. Out of love for me, he comes toward me, wanting to restore me to the Life he made me for. So he offers to graciously give me what I need. And more. Much more.

Lavishly so.

~ ~ ~

Religious people struggle with this "lavished" business. Too often we have the opposite perception of God. Whether I take a path of practicing a minimal amount of religiosity or going all-in with my religious routines, both routes set me up to nervously and exhaustingly hope or expect that I can eke out some sort of approval and favor from a reluctant God, earning it by my good works and behavior.

This reveals a small, low view of God that I'm often tempted to embrace. Not only will my works and supposedly good behavior fail to bridge the infinite gap between him and me, but such a posture also diminishes his love by making it dependent on my performance.

We tragically think God is opposed to us until we impress him.

I don't know if you've noticed, but it's rare to meet a religious person who is living like they are loved by God. Instead, you get the feeling they suspect they aren't loved but are trying—whether feverishly or frivolously—to change things via their religious behavior. It's a scarcity mentality: there's only so much grace to go around, but "if I'm good enough, I'll get some. If I can impress God somehow, he won't be against me, and then he might pay out a little love my way." Taking the religious route, we're haunted by our inadequacy or deluded by our supposed competency, so we suffocate under the weight of our failure and pride.

I know this from personal experience. Early in my journey with God, I knew in theory about God's grace and that he loved me, but that knowledge was more theological than actual—for the most part it wasn't something I knew experientially. Deep down I didn't *really* believe God's love for me was unconditional. So I tried hard to be good.

That didn't go so well. Covetousness. Self-centeredness. Lust. Impatience. Familiar sins. New sins. They all hung around, impervious to my tactics of getting God to love me through self-improvement. So I tried harder. Then, when I still couldn't be good enough, I'd pretend and try to hide my failure. I knew God could see past my pretending, but it still felt better to think others didn't.

That had been my story. But a new chapter started. Not unlike General Löwenhielm, things changed when I began to "get" grace.

I began to realize Life with a capital L is received in the grace-filled context of a restored relationship with God. Yes, an actual relationship. Jesus couldn't have been more clear in his definition: "Now this is eternal life: that they may know you, the only true God, and Jesus Christ, whom you have sent" (John 17:3). Eternal life—Life with a capital L—is all about knowing God in the context of an intimate relationship in which his love and grace are lavished on me through Jesus.

It's a powerful thing when human beings begin to realize Jesus is inviting them into a relationship in which they can experience the unconditional and extravagant grace of God. That they have to do nothing to get God to love them. Only receive it.

Talk about Life-giving grace!

Sure, the battle with sin and self-centeredness continues—even though God loves me in the midst of my sin, he loves me too much to let me stay there.

But when the question of whether he loves me is taken off the table, the game changes. I move from trying to entice love from God to letting his unconditional love, through his Holy Spirit, transform me into a healthier human being. I press on with this crazy, up-and-down journey of transformation, knowing he is not mad *at* me but *for* me in the fight.

What I learned firsthand during my better-behavior-obsessed days was that the reason the religious crowd hasn't tasted Life is because they haven't tasted grace.

They haven't tasted the unconditional love and acceptance of God. They haven't embraced God's posture toward them through the person and work of Jesus Christ. They haven't really believed that he indeed loves them deeply, extravagantly lavishing them with his grace for his glory. That's what's behind author Nancy Spiegelberg's familiar words,

> Lord,
> I crawled across
>   the barrenness
> To You
>   with my empty cup,
> Uncertain in asking
>   any small drop
> Of refreshment.
>
> If only
>   I had known You
>   better,
> I'd have come
> Running
> With a bucket."[3]

What if God loved me more than I dare dream? How would it change me? Well he does. When I accept that realty, the transformation can begin.

～ ～ ～

But it's vital to understand that grace isn't just something that's lavished on us. Before we can enjoy his extravagant blessing, there's another reality we must embrace.

Grace is also a matter of Life and death.

We've talked about how the Fall stole our proximity to the tree of life. When separated from that Life, the only other option for me is death. That's what was behind Christ's cryptic statement in Luke 9:60: "Let the dead bury their own dead, but you go and proclaim the kingdom of God." He was describing spiritually dead people who were going about the task of burying those who were dead in both spirit *and* body. From birth, that spiritual deadness describes every one of us. I'm still created in the image of God, imprinted with the *imago Dei,* but things are muted. My lack of Life is hampering a fuller experience of my humanity.

Anne Lamott muses, "A friend said mournfully the other day that he'd lived his life like the Professor on 'Gilligan's Island.' While he found time to fashion generators out of palm fronds, vaccines out of algae, he never got down to fixing that huge hole in the boat so he could go home. How many people actually do?"[4]

No matter how impressively innovative I might be in various arenas of my life, until the main problem is addressed, I'm not going to get any closer to experiencing Life as it's meant to be. The fundamental issue I need to focus on is that, without Christ, I'm dead and need Life. Period.

This is the main reason the religiosity path is a dead-end (pun intended).

Religion isn't enough to address the immensity of my predicament. I don't just need some new religious habits; I need Life. The mere practice of religion might make death more acceptable in appearance, but it doesn't give Life. It simply but tragically just dresses up death, and we consequently become increasingly numb to both the seriousness of our spiritual deadness and the beauty of Life.

The result? Lifeless religious people can be a lot more miserable—in experience as well as appearance—than people who wouldn't consider even setting foot in church. Just ask General Löwenhielm. There's a reason Isak Dinesen chose a religious sect as the antagonists in her story. A huge enemy of Life with a capital L is empty religiosity. Religiosity that short-circuits grace and truth by focusing only on external practices—all at the expense of internal transformation.

That's why Jesus, when rebuking the hypocrisy of a group of religious leaders, used the metaphor of saying they were "like whitewashed tombs, which look beautiful on the outside but on the inside are full of dead men's bones and everything unclean" (Matthew 23:27). I read that and realize Jesus didn't come to dress up my deadness with religious decorations.

His aim is not to make me religious but to make me alive.

"As for you, you were dead in your transgressions and sins.... But because of his great love for us, God, who is rich in mercy, made us alive with Christ even when we were dead in transgressions—it is by grace you have been saved" (Ephesians 2:1, 4–5).

Grace is the only way to Live.

❥ ❥ ❥

To taste Life, I must taste grace. But to taste grace, I must first admit the reality of my sin as well as my longing for Life. I've got to own up to my need. Grace takes root in the soil of my spiritual deadness—when I admit I'm dead.

But admitting such a reality takes humility. Genuine humility doesn't fare too well in unbelieving circles, but the same is also true of the religious crowd. When I'm focused on my religiosity, I'm not too adept at owning up to my need.

After all, the whole point of my religiosity is to emphasize what I am able—not unable—to contribute to be okay with God. Through my pious habits and religious rule keeping, I begin to feel like I am subsidizing my standing before God. (*Surely God's impressed with me now.*) When jumping through man-made religious hoops, my ego gets a boost.

It's ironic how religiosity can cater to the same pride that keeps a person from coming to God in the first place. The pride of pseudo-belief is much like the pride of unbelief—religion just dresses it up more.

Embarking on the path of grace instead of pandering to my pride requires shoes of humility.

Humility embraces that, no matter how impressive I may or may not be in the eyes of other people, without Christ I have nothing but spiritual deadness at my core. That's scary for someone who is trying to bolster their religiosity. But for someone trying to recover their humanity, it's spot on. The reason? "God opposes the proud but gives grace to the humble" (James 4:6; 1 Peter 5:5).

Mary, in her *Magnificat* prayer of thanksgiving recorded in Luke's gospel, quoted from Psalm 107, "He has filled the hungry with good things but has sent the rich away empty" (Luke 1:53). That doesn't mean a person can actually be spiritually rich without God, but it does mean he can believe he is.

He thinks he's fine without God and that he's capable of fulfilling his own humanity. Sure, that includes unbelievers, but it can also include religious people who focus more on padding their religious résumés than on what God can do for them. Neither group will receive anything from him.

> God doesn't begrudgingly dole out the minimum amount of grace. He *lavishes* us with it.

It's only the people who know their need for grace and hungrily bring their longing to the feet of Christ who will begin to taste the good things of Life.

Remember our friend, the woman by the well? Jesus was probing to see if she was humble enough to admit her thirst and take a drink of Life.

She was. She did.

Am I? Will I?

It starts with a simple but honest—and humble—cry for help.

❧ ❧ ❧

To a lot of college students, a car is important. So is coolness. Ideally the two will be connected.

During my freshman year, that connection was absent for me—I drove a decade-old Chevrolet Impala. The summer before my sophomore year, I took my coolness and my car on the road to sell books door to door. It was quite a moment for people in Arkansas, when they opened their front door to see my smiling, selling face.

One evening after work, I pulled up to a Laundromat that was connected to a gas station. I put the car in Park and left it running, with the door open, while I helped my roommate unload some of our clothes to wash. While I was inside the building, my Impala—by its own free will—popped into Reverse. The persistent sound of a car horn got my attention.

I looked up to see my driverless car slowly moving backward at an angle, and to my uncool terror, scraping alongside another vehicle that was parked at a gas pump.

What stopped it was the inside of my open driver's door catching on the front right bumper of the other car. That vehicle was occupied by a freaked-out, horn-blowing woman helplessly sitting in the passenger seat. Suffice it to say, the impact caused the hinges of my car door to bend in a very uncool direction. I couldn't close it.

Since I was at a gas station, broke, in college, and in a hurry, my wise remedy was to borrow a sledgehammer from the mechanic on duty. I pulled my car to a corner of the property and proceeded to beat the living daylights out of the hinges to get the door to close. During this spectacle, a well-meaning Arkansas gentleman drove his pickup next to me and called out through his open window, "Need some help?"

I responded in the only way someone of my coolness caliber could respond. "No thanks. I'm good!"

Of course I was.

With my sledgehammer swings, I bent the hinges back enough to get the door to close. Mostly. But its partial close was a now permanent reality, causing me to have to crawl in the window the rest of the summer while, at stoplights, listening to well-meaning fellow travelers call out from their cars, "Hey, buddy, your car door's open!"

Not cool.

The next week I braked for a kid's ball bouncing in front of me, and in the process, my cool front-seat trash bin lurched forward, wedging under my brake pedal. I glided into the rear of a jacked-up pickup with a steel girder for a bumper.

His vehicle was fine. Mine was anything but.

Standing in the middle of the intersection with my front grill relocated, my radiator spewing steam, and the hood of my car buckled into an uncool shape that complimented my uncool door, a well-meaning Arkansas gentleman stopped his pickup next to me and rolled down his window. "Need some help?"

"No thanks. I'm okay."

Of course I was. I was still cool even if my car wasn't.

Two days later, with my buckled front hood bent back close to its original shape and secured by some uncool bailing wire, I was speeding down a highway. A big gust of wind came my way. The next thing I knew, the hood of my Impala had broken free of its wired mooring, peeled backward, and wrapped itself over my windshield. I blindly steered my way onto the road's shoulder.

While sitting on the side of the road, staring at the bird droppings on my hood, which was now draped over my windshield and inches away from my face, a well-meaning Arkansas gentleman with a slight smile in a pickup pulled up next to me and rolled down his window. "Need some help?"

Sitting there sweltering in the Arkansas humidity, my humility finally activated, and I put my coolness and pride aside. "Yes sir, I think I do."

What does it take for us to finally lay down our supposedly cool, yet contrived self-sufficiency and humble ourselves before God, admitting we need him?

In my dead condition, I need help. An infinite amount of it. The gospel is about God's infinitely gracious intervention in my story, but I will never experience that intervention without honestly owning up to my own desperation.

How desperate am I without Christ?

Well, I'm dead.

And to experience Life, I need to first embrace the reality of my death condition and my desperation for his love and Life. This admission means humbly engaging with the reality that my heart is beating, but my humanity is truncated because, spiritually, I'm dead.

Admission of my deadness and need for Life involves confession. Biblical confession, instead of being a mere religious ritual, is the heart cry of an honest human being. Confession of my sin. Of my mess. Confession of my dead-man-walking behaviors and attitudes. Confession that my deadness means distance from God. Confession of my need—for his Life-giving forgiveness, for his restoration. Yes, I need some help.

It was helpful when I learned the Greek word for *confess* is a word that literally means to "speak the same." In confession, I'm not informing God of anything (as if he didn't already know). Instead, I'm "speaking the same" as him, humbly agreeing with him regarding the reality of my need for him. For grace. For truth. For his love. For Life. And agreeing regarding his ability to lavishly provide it.

More than I'd like to admit, over the years I have found myself pretending instead of confessing. Pretending to be amazed over the grace of God, but not really amazed. I've now grown enough in my understanding, when that's going on, to realize the prideful roots of such a posture: I'm actually only *pretending* to believe in my need.

This reveals far more than I'm comfortable with regarding my low view of God (only pretending to believe in his holiness and love) and my inaccurate view of my need (only pretending to believe in my spiritually bankrupt condition). If I've been bitten by a poisonous snake, but for some strange reason, I'm not wanting to admit that I'm bitten, I'll only pretend to appreciate your gift of anti-venom—I won't really appreciate it and certainly won't use it. Such is the case with many of us while sitting in church and pretending.

Call me crazy, but instead of missing Life through prideful pretending, wouldn't humble confessing and eager receiving be better? Actually praying and receiving the amazing acceptance of an amazing God through amazing grace in order to experience amazing Life?

I vote yes.

Jesus has great expertise with requests like that.

❧ ❧ ❧

Babette can cook. It was a statement regarding her ability that the elderly religious sisters distrusted and minimized—a statement they listened to but did not really hear.

Jesus can redeem. Jesus can love. Jesus can give me Life.

These are statements of his ability that I too often minimize. When he says he came that I might have Life, instead of opting to just courteously listen, I want to humbly hear.

Babette lived with the sisters for a dozen years, and they still didn't know who she was. How long have I been hanging around the gospel? Do I still not know who Jesus really is? Am I still blind to what he wants to do for me?

The sisters had boxed Babette into their minimalist prescriptions of what they wanted her to do for them, having no idea what she was capable of. Do I really know what Jesus is capable of doing in my life? Am I boxing him in, prescribing that he help me only with my comfort-based agenda but otherwise not play too big of a role in my life until I die? Or can I join the apostle Paul and say, "Now to him who is able to do immeasurably more than all we ask or imagine" (Ephesians 3:20)?

Babette spent everything she had on the meal she lavished on them that night. Grace is free, but it's anything but cheap. It didn't cost me, but it did cost Christ. The extravagance of his love is matched only by the infinite nature of its price. Do I embrace his death out of Life-filled awe or merely nod toward the cross out of religious habit?

While General Lorens Löwenhielm was savoring one of the magnificent wines at Babette's feast, a proposal came from the religious guests around the table that it was nice lemonade. Incredulous, he clarified that it was an 1860 *Veuve Cliquot.* In response, "his neighbor looked at him kindly, smiled at him, and made a remark about the weather."[5]

At the table of God's amazing grace, may he rescue me from the appearance of politely nodding on the outside while yawning on the inside. From merely going through the motions of listening to the gospel of grace and pretending to appreciate it, without ever seeking to understand or submit to it. Or enjoy it.

~ ~ ~

General Löwenhielm, the one nonreligious person at the table, was the first to taste the grace. Sometimes it's easier to awaken from spiritual death when it's void of religious numbness. It's often the people who haven't been desensitized through mere religiosity who get grace first. And therefore get Life.

That happened during Jesus's ministry.

That happened in Isak Dinesen's phenomenal story of Babette.

It's still happening.

As the general finally realized, "But the moment comes when our eyes are opened, and we see and realize that grace is infinite."

Yes.

Whether I'm recovering from a junk-food binge of religiosity or not, it's time to realize my hunger for an extravagant meal of grace.

And a feast of Life.

ten
experiences
of life with a
capital L

Freedom

A Matter of Life and Death

> The world outside has not become less real
> because the prisoner cannot see it.
> —J. R. R. Tolkien

The presence or absence of prison bars is not the ultimate determination of whether a person is free. A friend who has taught me volumes about that reality is Dan, an exceptional prison chaplain who has enjoyed decades of credible impact behind bars.

It was he who introduced me to Chuck, Howie, and Carlos. They are all younger men, but between the three of them, they've spent more than sixty years in prison. Each of them came into a genuine relationship with Christ while in prison and, as a result, experienced a genuine taste of real freedom.

Long before they were released, I had the privilege of getting to know Chuck, a brilliant musician and worship leader, and Howie, a diligent Bible student and theologian. Dressed in the green prison garb of the Colorado Territorial Correctional Facility and their words echoing off the confining concrete of their cells, they each conveyed to me that they were free men, even though they were still behind bars. Delusions of an inmate? Not at all. Even though they were in prison on a literal level, their humanity had been liberated through authentic encounters with extravagant grace.

Howie, during four months of solitary confinement in the Denver County jail (before being sent to the state prison), found a tattered, coverless Bible stuffed behind a toilet. He read through it five times and finally found the freedom he had yearned for before being sent to prison. He chuckles at the irony, saying he had to go to prison to get free.

Chuck embraced Christ about four years into his then life sentence. "More than needing God to change my situation or change my circumstance," he said, "I needed God to change my life. God interrupted my dead routine in the joint and called me into something greater. I became a free man."

After spending decades behind bars, they were each finally released, and for several years I had the privilege of serving on a ministry team with them, along with Carlos, a man who's also contagiously amazed by grace on a daily basis. All three deeply treasure Christ and the authentic heart liberation he has lavished on them. During years of incarceration, they learned to depend on Christ alone for real freedom. In prison, you're not as distracted by seemingly endless recreation options, hectic schedules, and an abundance of possessions—all of which can mask how you're really doing at the core of your humanity—so you tend to perceive more quickly whether you're in a spiritual prison cell or not.

> "It's tough seeing somebody who's in church and in prison at the same time."

Also, discernment becomes a necessary life skill when doing time, so they also learned to spot inauthenticity. I'll never forget, after they'd been released a year or so and we were working together, when they conveyed to me a striking observation. They'd met a lot of people "on the outside"—many of them followers of Christ— who were not at all free, though they've never been behind the bars of a prison. Jail cells of guilt, fear, hypocrisy, judgmental attitudes, religiosity, perfectionism, and self-absorption enslave so many.

One of them remarked to me, "It's tough seeing somebody who's in church and in prison at the same time."

❧ ❧ ❧

"Freeeedom!"

Ask most movie lovers, and they can tell you the last word William Wallace cries out before his death, at the end of *Braveheart*. It is a word that resonates with us at our core. Political, social, and national freedom is powerful. Personal freedom even more so.

But we yearn for freedom so deeply that our judgment can become muddled, and we get sidetracked by a misunderstanding of what it really is. A ton of people have taken a supposed free fall into something they thought was freedom that turned out to be anything but. It's a painfully long list—people adopting an "I can do whatever I want when I want" definition of freedom who take a swan dive into a pool of no rules or restrictions. It's like diving into a concrete swimming pool without the water. The resulting devastation is immense to themselves, their relationships, their health, their hearts, and ultimately, their humanity and their culture.

As Frederick Buechner clarified, "To obey his strongest appetites for drink, sex, power, revenge, or whatever, leaves him the freedom of an animal to take what he wants when he wants it but not the freedom of a man to be human."[1]

The freedom of an animal is devastatingly different from the freedom to be fully human.

Paul wrote to some believers in first-century Corinth, a bustling, cosmopolitan city where flawed-freedom compasses were in abundant supply. You name the depraved, misdirected behavior, and the people of Corinth practiced it. To the men and women following Jesus in the midst of the fallen futility around them, Paul explained freedom: "Now the Lord is the Spirit, and where the Spirit of the Lord is, there is freedom. And we, who with unveiled faces all reflect the Lord's glory, are being transformed into his likeness with ever-increasing glory, which comes from the Lord, who is the Spirit" (2 Corinthians 3:17–18). Freedom is experienced when we're being transformed into his image by his Spirit. Freedom is experienced when we are becoming fully human.

William Wallace's passion for freedom cost him his life. Our passion for Life can lead us to freedom—the freedom of full humanity along the lines of what God originally intended.

~ ~ ~

Life with a capital L is liberation on steroids—the legal kind—and to enjoy that freedom I need to embrace my full humanity, which includes both the spiritual and physical realms of my journey. We often try to figure out freedom in the physical realm—the freedom to really live and enjoy our lives—without seeing its connection to spiritual freedom. But whether it's in my relationships or my emotions, from my vocation to my vacations, I'm never truly free until I'm experiencing Christ's liberating leadership.

Remember, our spiritual health and freedom are what unleash our full humanity. When Jesus, quoting from Isaiah's prophecy, said the Father "has sent me to proclaim freedom for the prisoners and recovery of sight for the blind, to release the oppressed, to proclaim the year of the Lord's favor" (Luke 4:18–19), he was addressing our core captivity issue. In bondage to our fallenness, we need the favor of God to set us free and enable us to see again and Live.

And Jesus emphasized that only if he sets me free will I be "free indeed." That our sinful rebelliousness is what holds us back from ultimate freedom. That the truth about the Life he brings is meant to make us free human beings, not refined religious people who are just as enslaved as unbelievers but simply confined to differently decorated prison cells.[2] A person can't truly be free in Christ and at the same time live a stifled human existence.

In coming chapters, I want to explore the Life that we've been liberated to enjoy. But first I need to let you in on something I overlooked in my journey for too long. I didn't understand that there's a difference between being set free and living free. Just because I'm free to enjoy his Life doesn't mean I will.

So let me tell you about the parable of the prison cell.

⌁ ⌁ ⌁

A metaphor that's helped me is to view the realm into which you and I and every other human being have been born as a prison cell. It's a prison cell called death.

The cell door is locked, so I live every day of my life in this place of spiritual death. I have not lost my *imago Dei* identity—I'm still created in the image of God—so I haven't lost my ability to laugh, cry, relate, create, dance, think, play, work, dream. But it's all muted, cloaked in this reality of spiritual death.

For the most part, I don't realize I'm imprisoned because everyone is in the same predicament. We each ingeniously decorate our cells—some more than others—with things like achievements, parties, job titles, families, bank account balances, degrees, vacations, friendships, volunteerism, hobbies, and, yes, religion. I know the envy when someone nearby decorates their cell a bit better than I've decorated mine. Some cells are pretty impressive in appearance, but bottom line, each is still a prison cell.

In the quiet moments when I'm willing to be honest about what it's like behind the facade of all my cell's decorations, I sense the hollowness that's still there. The longings that hint of Something Else. An awareness of the fallenness of the world around me, that things are not all fine.

To the surface come uncomfortable realities such as confusion, aimlessness, guilt, shame, frustration, emptiness, despair, superficiality, restlessness. Not knowing what else to do, I try to push them back down and submerge them like a stubborn beach ball in a backyard pool. Maybe some new cell decorations will prove to be enough of a distraction. That works for a while. But only a short while. And the cycle continues.

It's more like existing than living, pacing in my prison and trying to do some semblance of life. Days turn into decades. I can't escape.

During World War II, thirty-seven-year-old pastor and theologian Dietrich Bonhoeffer was in a Nazi concentration camp. At Christmastime, he wrote to a friend, "A prison cell like this is a good analogy for Advent. One waits, hopes, does this or that—ultimately negligible things—but the door is locked and can only be opened from the outside."[3]

No matter how well I decorate my cell or how good I try to be, I can't unlock the door and bring myself to Life.

～ ～ ～

Then I come in contact with the gospel. Not the religious replica but the real deal. I own up to my deadness. The confession gets sincere. Confession that I'm in a prison cell of death. That I'm in a fallen, broken world, and though I'm created in God's image, I admit I'm part of the problem due to my sinfulness.

I begin to understand that all my life, either actively or passively, I've been conveying to God that I can be a normal and fulfilled human being without him. That I don't need him for my security, significance, or self-worth—that those are longings I can address on my own. As a consequence of my sin, I'm in a prison cell of death. The under-the-surface realities of emptiness weighing on me are, fundamentally, the outcomes of my own rebelliousness.

"Death came to all men, because all sinned" (Romans 5:12).

～ ～ ～

I begin to see Jesus Christ for who he is—not the founder of a religion but the infinite God-man who came to lead me back into the Life and full humanity he originally intended for me. He came to show me Life but also to die. Fully human and personal, he came to experience the fallen reality of my prison cell. Fully God and infinite, he came to fulfill the death sentence that's the cause behind everyone's prison-cell existence, including mine. As the writer of Hebrews says, Jesus "suffered death, so that by the grace of God he might taste death for everyone" (Hebrews 2:9).

I then embrace the truth about Christ's death on the cross. As seventeenth-century theologian John Owen eloquently described it, the cross encapsulates "the death of death in the death of Christ."[4] Paul was referring to the same reality when he wrote to his friend Timothy of God's eternal grace revealed through Jesus, explaining that he "destroyed death and has brought life and immortality to light through the gospel" (2 Timothy 1:10). So I recognize that Christ's death was far more than a religious martyr's—his death was an in-place-of-me, substitutionary death motivated by love with an agenda of restoration. He was graciously paying my penalty, fulfilling my death sentence.

I learn that authentically and humbly receiving Christ goes much deeper than just being a rite of passage into a religious subculture. It means receiving his death on the cross as a payment of the penalty I owe—my eternal death sentence is fulfilled in Christ! Is that referring to hell? Certainly. But I'm also set free from my present-tense prison cell of death. That happens the moment I receive him. Jesus describes it this way: "I tell you the truth, whoever hears my word and believes him who sent me has eternal life and will not be condemned; he has crossed over from death to life" (John 5:24).

When I put my trust in Christ, I enter a new realm and receive a new status of eternal Life. One of restored, unencumbered relationship with God. I'm now alive!

Those prison-cell realities I mentioned earlier immediately become candidates for a Life-imbued antidote. The possibilities for Life-giving liberation abound.

Aimlessness giving way to purpose.

Guilt being relieved by forgiveness.

Shame being replaced by acceptance.

Restlessness being subdued by shalom.

Insight coming to replace the confusion.

Hope overcoming despair.

Completeness coming to occupy the emptiness.

Significance overtaking superficiality.

My shackled heart can experience freedom.

Does all this happen overnight? Yes and no.

My *status* as a dead man—a man locked in the prison cell of death—changes immediately when I receive Christ. I now have the unalterable status of being alive with a capital A, but that doesn't automatically mean I will have an immediate, perfect *experience* of Life with a capital L. That takes a lifetime of getting rid of the prison garb by growing, maturing, and learning to Live.

❧ ❧ ❧

Early in my journey, I was in a religious environment, but I wasn't an authentic follower of Jesus. Once I genuinely received him, I had an alive status but for too long didn't really enjoy the experience of being alive. I had my spiritual activities in one compartment and my physical pursuits in another. My spiritual side wasn't very active (an understatement), and my physical side, though it had plenty of distractions, wasn't very fulfilling at its core. But I didn't see the connection between those two realities.

Over the course of my life, I've met countless people in similar situations. Yes, many who are religious without being alive—I talked about them earlier. But I've also come across many who are alive but not living. Freed but not living free. I can recognize them because I've been there and still have to wrestle with it daily. I don't want to be in church and in prison at the same time.

The prison-cell door has been unlocked by the gracious hand of God. I've been gifted with Life. Yet I spend my days standing on the threshold of my prison cell with a new status but not much of a new experience. Will I, on a daily basis, become fully human and venture out of that place of death into this new realm of Life? Will I enjoy my relationship with God and the creation and the journey into which he's placed me?

For a long time, I thought my salvation only revolved around the death of Jesus. I didn't realize I was diminishing the gift of his Life with a capital L. "For if, when we were God's enemies, we were reconciled to him through the death of his Son, how much more, having been reconciled, shall we be saved through his life!" (Romans 5:10). Focusing only on his death left me in an in-between realm of having my past sins forgiven and waiting on heaven in the future. But what about now? That "wait until heaven" posture, which so many of us can have, divorces us from the new humanity into which he is calling us—now. "We were therefore buried with him through baptism into death in order that, just as Christ was raised from the dead through the glory of the Father, we too may live a new life" (Romans 6:4).

When I receive Christ, I'm receiving his death but also his Life. As my death sentence is vicariously fulfilled through Christ, something else arrives: his new Life. Life with a capital L.

Instead of just continuing to exist in my prison cell, it's time to learn to Live. And the choices I make—primarily about my willingness to obey and follow Jesus in the midst of every spiritual and physical realm of my journey—will determine the amount of Life I experience.

➤ ➤ ➤

Like the *Star Trek* crew of the USS *Enterprise* who would determine, with each planet they encountered while hurtling through the galaxy, whether its environment was compatible with human life, I must learn to look at potential paths of behavior and ask the same thing regarding Life with a capital L: is this behavior compatible with my new Life?

But I don't always get it right.

I venture out, seeking to become fully human by following Jesus and experiencing his Life. But sin and selfishness don't just exit the scene once I become a follower of his (just ask my family and friends). I still don't always choose behavior that's compatible with Life. So when I opt for rebellion against God's leadership, taking a sinful path, it's as if I'm going back into my prison cell and sitting down in the stagnation.

Even as an authentic follower of Christ, I can fall for the lie that my old prison cell offers what will fulfill me at that moment (my cell often looks better from the outside looking in). Of course, it didn't fulfill me before, but like wannabe kicker Charlie Brown repeatedly falling for Lucy's lie that she won't move the football and, kicking only air, he again ends up flat on his back—I try it again. So I sin. It could be a thought. Or an action. Or an omission of something I should do. You know the routine. In doing so, experientially, I head back into my prison cell. I'm still loved by God. Still his kid and headed for heaven. But for the moment, I've returned to a place of death. The freedom of becoming fully human is once again stifled.

But I'm not trapped there. I can get up and leave because, when I first trusted Christ, the cell door was unlocked and will never be locked again. The difference between a follower of Jesus who's walking in behavior that isn't compatible with Life and an unbeliever who is doing the same is that the prison-cell door always remains unlocked for the Christ follower. I have the option to leave at anytime. I am free even though I'm not looking like it at the moment.

~ ~ ~

So why do we head back into that prison cell? Why, once we've become a follower of Jesus, do we still sin and let that rebellion suffocate our enjoyment of Life?

In our years before becoming a follower of Jesus, we developed a comfort with the attitudes and behaviors of our prison cell. Even after we trust Christ, the more time we spend in our now-unlocked cell, the familiarity can continue to deepen. Even a dependence. It's a dependence that takes a long time—a lifetime—to unlearn and overcome. As Morgan Freeman's character, Red, ruminates about decades behind prison walls in *The Shawshank Redemption:* "These walls are funny. First you hate 'em, then you get used to 'em. Enough time passes, you get so you depend on them."[5]

> I've come across many who are alive but not living.

My friend Chuck and I were talking about the high number of guys who, after being released from prison, miss the familiarity and, strangely enough, the security of being behind bars. He has seen this firsthand in some inmates. The notion of returning to a prison cell that's familiar and secure is, at times, strangely more attractive than having to figure out freedom.

Our conversation then shifted into the parallel arena of spiritual freedom. So often we sin and go back into our prison cell because it's familiar. But we also head back there because that's where we feel like we have control over what will satisfy us. Bottom line, we don't like the vulnerability of having to trust God, which is what we must do when we're living free.

When we sin, yes, we're disobeying God, but it's deeper than rule breaking. We're not trusting God with our longings.

Instead, we pair up ordinarily appropriate longings with pursuits that are sinful by definition or pursuits that are healthy but inadequate. In either case, longings we should be entrusting to God are given over to inappropriate or inadequate pursuits. We long for self-esteem, so we might sin by slandering someone else—it temporarily distracts us, but it doesn't ultimately help our self-esteem (which is a God-sized longing). Or to bolster that same longing for self-esteem, we might hijack an ordinarily great pursuit like parenting and sinfully smother our child with our own unfulfilled ambitions while withholding our love. (That's how some otherwise beautiful and enjoyable pursuits can become so joyless.)

Instead of being free human beings, we're chaining ourselves to pursuits that can't address our God-sized longings. Our dogged but deceived determination to squeeze that kind of fulfillment from an unworthy pursuit imprisons us with unmet expectations. We end up being escorted back into our prison cell that reeks of death. Our prison cell is not only a place of rebellious postures and actions. More deeply, it's the place where the celebration of our humanity is hampered by our refusal to trust God and bring our ultimate longings to him. Not only is he grieved, but our Life is diminished.

~ ~ ~

I can often find myself tempted to blame Jesus for the ways I'm not experiencing Life with a capital L, thinking he's not delivering. But it's actually a matter of me, instead of pursuing Life, disobediently spending too much time in my prison cell and not choosing behavior that's compatible with Life. As a friend of mine said, "It's like I'm blaming God for the conditions of a prison cell that I built for myself."

Several years ago Congress passed a measure that was nicknamed the Cheeseburger Bill, which would prohibit class-action obesity lawsuits against fast-food companies. Several overweight Americans had been filing lawsuits against fast-food chains as the culprits behind their obesity—their food was too fattening. One of the bill's sponsors, Wisconsin Representative Jim Sensenbrenner, explained, "This bill says, 'Don't run off and file a lawsuit if you are fat.' It says, 'Look in the mirror because you're the one to blame.' "[6]

This is what's behind Paul's famous instruction in Romans 6:23: "For the wages of sin is death, but the gift of God is eternal life in Christ Jesus our Lord." Is that a statement about trusting Christ and going to heaven? Of course, but that's not its only meaning.

The original context of that verse is Paul addressing the question many Christ followers have: if I'm going to receive God's grace and forgiveness regardless, then why shouldn't I just go ahead and sin?

Fair question.

He responds with the warning that, when I rebel as a follower of Jesus, I won't lose my salvation, but I will head back into that prison cell and experience the stench of death. I've been set free from the "law of sin and death" (Romans 8:2), but I'm not exempt from it. So when I sin, Life-laced blessings are replaced with death-tainted wages, such as insight being replaced with confusion and shalom being chased out by restlessness. Instead, Paul urges you and me to behave "as those who have been brought from death to life" (Romans 6:13).

I'm alive and free, so I can go ahead and live like it instead of blaming Jesus when I'm experiencing the "wages of sin."

❧ ❧ ❧

Before talking about what it means to head out of our prison cell and pursue Life, I need to address a toxic reality that has devastating consequences, even for followers of Jesus. It's one of the most paralyzing ways that sin pays us. And it's one of the tentacles that keeps us, even though we are free, from thinking we can leave.

Shame.

Once I've sinned and returned to my prison cell, I might stay there for a few minutes or a few weeks. It all depends on how long it takes me to get up and leave. The biblical words for that process of leaving my cell are *confession* (my agreement with God about my sin, but also about his grace) and *repentance* (turning around and, with the Holy Spirit's strength, walking back out into freedom). I took that route when I first trusted Christ, but I must still daily practice it, not for salvation—that's a done deal—but for the experience of Life.

But I need to warn you about something I've fallen for too often. When I find myself back in my prison cell with some new rebellion on my résumé, among my response options is a debilitating counterfeit of confession called shame. Beware. Confession restores Life. Shame does anything but that.

Here's how it works. Once back in my prison cell, the Holy Spirit convicts me, and I sheepishly realize the lie I've fallen for yet again. I see my sin, but instead of agreeing with my Life-giving Father about my error, tasting a new dose of his grace and walking back out toward freedom, I opt to sit in shame. Instead of humble confession that leads me to Life, wallowing in shame keeps me in prison, showing up in defensiveness, inauthenticity, pride, denial, religious obsessiveness, isolation, deflection, and a judgmental posture toward others—not unlike Adam and Eve in the garden after they lost their access to the tree of life.

Shame offers little hope and lots of condemnation. It doesn't let me just honestly confess, "I have failed." Shame instead forces me down the poisonous path of saying, "I am a failure." Over the cliff I go, losing sight of my identity as an *imago Dei* and forgetting that I am loved by a God who is graciously beckoning me to restoration and Life.

Even though the door is unlocked, I spend another night in prison. Or longer.

In that moment, Paul encourages me from his own experience. It's a vital truth I must grasp to experience Life: "Therefore, there is now no condemnation for those who are in Christ Jesus, because through Christ Jesus the law of the Spirit of life set me free from the law of sin and death" (Romans 8:1–2). I'm always free to get up, leave my cell, and head back toward Life. But will I believe that? Will I act in faith that it is so, and Live?

∽ ∽ ∽

I just finished reading a riveting account of freedom. Hampton Sides, in his book *Ghost Soldiers,* tells the story of "a jailbreak on an epic scale, the largest and most triumphant mission of its kind ever undertaken by the U.S. Army."[7] On January 28, 1945, as World War II was groaning to a close, 121 elite Army Rangers liberated over 500 POWs, mostly Americans, from a Japanese prisoner of war camp near Cabanatuan in the Philippines.

The prisoners, many of whom were survivors of the infamous Bataan death march, were in awful condition, physically and emotionally. Before the rangers arrived, the primary Japanese guard unit had left the camp because of Japan's massive retreat from the Philippines. The new situation was precarious. Japanese troops were still around and in the camp, but they kept their distance from the prisoners. "The men of Cabanatuan didn't quite know what to make of their new freedom—if freedom was in fact what it was."[8] And then, without warning, the American Rangers swept upon the camp in furious force.

What struck me was the reaction of many of the prisoners. They were so defeated, diseased, and familiar with deceit that many needed to be convinced they were actually free. Was it a trick? A trap? Was this real?

One prisoner, Captain Bert Bank, struggling with blindness caused by a vitamin deficiency, couldn't clearly make out his would-be rescuers. He refused to budge. Finally, a soldier walked up to him, tugged his arm, and said, "What's wrong with you? Don't you want to be free?"[9] Bank, from Alabama, recognized the familiar southern accent of his questioner. A smile formed on his lips, and he willingly and thankfully began his journey to freedom.

Finally, well away from what had been, for years, the site of an ongoing, horrific assault on their humanity, the newly freed prisoners began their march home. In the description of one prisoner, contrasting it with the Bataan nightmare years earlier, "It was a long, slow, steady march…but this was a life march, a march of freedom."[10]

But, at first, there was an incapacitating and devastating voice deep within those men that told them they weren't really free.

We know a similar voice. We get caught up in our own prison resulting from a new binge of rebelliousness. At that point, our own sin—bolstered by shame and bitterness—can blind us to the truth that grace is available and Life is not lost. We can easily begin to question whether we were ever really free in the first place (*Maybe I never was a true believer after all*), or we let the voice convince us that the cell door has finally been relocked (*I've blown it one too many times—I'm stuck here now*).

Of course, the more mature I become, the less I'll revisit my prison cell. But another big maturity indicator is the length of time I'll spend wallowing in the stench of my cell once I do blow it—again. The more mature I become, when I do sin, the less time I'll spend paralyzed by shame and self-pity and the quicker I'll humbly grasp grace and forgiveness—and actually believe the gospel.

I'll also realize forgiveness is not just an end in itself but a provision God gives me in order to, once again, experience Life. So I repent and walk out to again set my feet on the path of Life with a capital L.

❧ ❧ ❧

So how do I pursue the Life that awaits me on the freedom side of my prison-cell threshold? What will my Life march, my march of freedom look like?

A key passage that has rocked my world and liberated me to Live fully is in the fifth chapter of Romans. In talking about the benefits of grace-laced freedom, the apostle Paul refers to what he calls *reigning in life*.

I love that phrase.

Here's the context: "For if, by the trespass of the one man, death reigned through that one man, how much more will those who receive God's abundant provision of grace and of the gift of righteousness reign in life through the one man, Jesus

Christ.… So that, just as sin reigned in death, so also grace might reign through righteousness to bring eternal life through Jesus Christ our Lord" (Romans 5:17, 21).

Part of our problem is we've lost so much of the emancipating *substance* of the gospel. That sad reality has not only watered down our understanding, but it's diluted our Living.

One of the casualties revolves around a powerful word we see a lot of in Scripture, including the passage that, just now, you were careful to read slowly.

Righteousness.

Yes, it's a word we don't hear much these days. In fact, it seems like only surfers and skateboarders use it but not with its original meaning.

Biblically speaking, righteousness is intimately related to the experience of grace and reigning in Life.

But what does it mean? It's important not to get too complicated with it and also to avoid attaching a straitjacket of suffocating religious connotations to it. Instead, I've found that a great place to start is to simply think "rightness."

Righteousness is being rightly aligned with the person, character, and truth of God. With him. With his path. With what he originally intended for me as a human being.

You might say, "We're talking about righteousness? That seems like a long way from our discussion awhile back about longings."

Not so fast.

Jesus, in a sermon summarizing what will bring us the greatest joy, said, "Blessed are those who hunger and thirst for righteousness, for they will be filled" (Matthew 5:6). Actually, the Greek language is emphatic—he was saying "they alone" will be filled. Hear him. He's saying the only human beings on this planet who are having their longings addressed are those who are bringing their thirst to the water fountain of righteousness. So in the presence of whatever longings I'm going deep with, I need to also deeply evaluate my rightness with God's original intentions for me, realizing the connection between the two.

There's one more vital clarification I've learned to grasp regarding this powerful truth: when I see the word *righteousness* in the New Testament, it could be referring to one or both of two aspects of righteousness. It's helpful to understand that first there's the gift of righteousness, which is *positional*. Then there's the behavior of righteousness, which is *practical*.

Positional righteousness is the gift fully given to me when I first come to faith in Christ—when the prison-cell door is unlocked. When I trust Christ's work on my behalf, before God, I immediately become clothed with Christ's righteousness (theologians will use the phrase *imputed righteousness*). From then on, when God looks at me, he does not look at my sin and screwups but instead sees Christ's righteousness. You might say, "That sounds too good to be true."

Well, that's why it's called grace, and that's why it's called the gospel.

But even though I'm now eternally dressed with Christ's righteousness, I've got a lifetime to live while still in a fallen body and still in a fallen world. That's where practical righteousness enters the picture. *There is Life everywhere,* but will I seize and experience it? It's one thing to be gifted with Life and righteousness. It's another thing to pursue Life and live righteously.

You might say, "Distinguishing between positional and practical righteousness sounds similar to the whole deal about the difference between being free and living free."

Exactly.

Also a bit like the difference between being alive and actually living Life.

Yes.

~ ~ ~

So as someone who has been set free, if I'm going to actually experience freedom, I've got to learn to pursue Life by *practicing* righteousness—learning to walk righteously. That will involve—drum roll here—*obedience.* For many of us, when I say that word, the air goes out of the room because most of us don't initially think of obedience as a freedom word and certainly not something that gives Life.

But I have to understand a key reality: there is an enormous difference between legalistic obedience and Life-giving obedience.

Legalistic obedience is a debilitating attempt to get God to love me, earn his favor, impress others, and bolster my religious pride. Ironically, it's actually a prison-cell activity that avoids important, weighty commands like caring for the poor and instead invents its own superficial rules that are easier to keep though anything but Life giving.

I once met some seriously religious people who had a swimming pool. On Sundays they wouldn't let their kids swim in the deep end. Deep-end swimming was considered work, and Sundays were a day of rest. Instead, the not-so-delighted kids could stay in the shallow end so their feet were touching the bottom and thereby avoid the strenuous effort of treading water.

It's that kind of legalism that drove Jesus nuts. And keeps kids from learning to swim.

Life-giving obedience is a response to the favor of God that I've already received through Christ (any type of practical righteousness we're called to is always *after*, not before, we've received his gift of positional righteousness). Instead of living like an orphan, it's me living like the accepted child of God that I am, responding to his love, and following his path. Instead of imprisoning myself and those around me with suffocating, legalistic expectations, it's enjoying my walk with God in the context of a Life-giving community. That road, instead of stifling me, will be liberating.

> Obedience—to God's instruction, not human rules— enables me to experience Life.

Paul speaks of the freedom of being transformed by the Holy Spirit in an ever-increasing way into a healthy human who is glorifying God more and more.[11] Obedience is what is best for me as a human being—it's behaving and becoming like the healthy human God intends for me to be. True freedom is being anything but free of the loving leadership of God. The God who created me, who knows what I need to really Live and what will protect me in the process.

That's why Jesus taught that being "free indeed" involves following his instruction, "Then you will know the truth, and the truth will set you free" (John 8:32). It's what's behind his saying things like "If you want to enter life, obey the commandments" (Matthew 19:17) and "I know that his command leads to eternal life" (John 12:50).

Obedience doesn't make me alive, but obedience—to God's instruction, not human rules—does enable me to *experience* Life.

❧ ❧ ❧

That obedience-enabled experience of Life is something that happens in every arena of my journey, not just my spiritual life. My obedience to Christ infuses my experience and enjoyment in all the physical realms of my life as well.

Again, the freedom I experience when living Life with a capital L is not just related to spiritual pursuits. Jesus has a holistic agenda to free me in every arena of my life. My spiritual freedom, instead of being cordoned off from the rest of my life, is to be the springboard of Life that impacts my entire journey.

The freedom I have in Christ is the liberation to experience my humanity to the full, integrating both my spiritual as well as my physical realm—from relationships to vocation to emotions to finances to cultural impact to creativity to recreation. When I'm set free, I'm free to enjoy Christ's Life in all of life, whether talking with him, designing software, volunteering at a homeless shelter, or riding a horse in the mountains. They are all part of being a redeemed human and embracing the significance of my existence in God's creation.

When I exercise discernment in appropriately pairing my pursuits and longings, I'll be free to experience renewed enjoyment of some everyday physical pursuits that, while fundamentally healthy, have at worst become sinful and at best grown stale under the pressure caused by attaching mismatched longings to them.

I'll be free to enjoy relationships instead of getting imprisoned by codependency because I'm expecting the other person to be God for me. Free to enjoy my vocation as a calling instead of succumbing to workaholism as a means of self-identity. Free to enjoy material possessions without becoming a greedy materialist who defines my significance by accumulation. When I free my spouse from needing to do for me what only God can, marriage is liberated to become the gift that it is.

And cheering for the Denver Broncos becomes much more enjoyable when I'm not staking my life's fulfillment on their winning the Super Bowl (as a former Chicagoan myself, that's especially important for Cubs fans to hear).

~ ~ ~

Someone told me about his cousin who was an army infantryman in Vietnam. One night, his patrol was bombarded with mortar fire. An explosion hit so close to Jeff that the force of the blast rendered him unconscious. When he woke up, he was still paralyzed from the concussion.

That problem was horrifically amplified when he realized he was now zipped up in a body bag.

The medics, thinking he was dead, had bagged and lined him up with other casualties they were loading onto a transport vehicle. Though conscious, Jeff couldn't move, he couldn't speak. He could only look through the pin-sized holes along the zipper to see the light of day and listen to the crew go about their jobs. Panic began to set in.

Concentrating every fiber of strength toward his mouth and tongue, he finally channeled enough energy to shout out a deafening declaration: "No! I'M ALIVE!"

Jeff survived his concussion.

The medics survived their heart failure.

❧ ❧ ❧

Because of Jesus, I'm alive.

And I'm free.

May I overcome my prison-cell paralysis of sin or shame or legalism, and,
instead of being in church and prison at the same time,
May I experience the freedom of my freedom.

Heart

The Wellspring of Life

Money lost little lost,
honour lost much lost,
heart lost all lost.

—Inscription on the Watson Mazer,
sixteenth-century Scottish silver bowl

attoo. I had never realized how the volume of that word magically increases when contained in a sentence from one of your own kids. Especially when that sentence is in the form of a question.

My oldest son was the one doing the asking, and I listened intently. It wasn't just because of the content of the question, but more notably, its backstory. It had started years before as a sort of motto I had come up with to encourage my three sons, starting in their early teens.

"Fight for Your Heart, Fight with Your Heart."

At key moments along the way, I'd lock eyes with them, sometimes with a smile and sometimes much more seriously, but always with a spirit of support. I'd then say the now-familiar phrase, hoping it would go past their ears into a deeper place. Maybe it related to a big game they were playing in. Or feeling overwhelmed with schoolwork. Or going out with friends. Or facing a big decision. Or just navigating potential teenage pitfalls and opportunities.

FFYH-FWYH.

On Post-it notes and text messages, the shorthand of eight initials still carried the full message. When my oldest, Andrew, entered the Air Force Academy, I used some stationery cards on which I wrote him short, strengthening notes to get him through the first sixty days of basic training (aptly nicknamed "Beast"). Engraved on the letterhead were those eight letters, the meaning of which would be known only to him.

Now, here we were, sitting around a fire as we had countless times, in one of those moments dads want branded on their memories. Andrew was the initial spokesman of this band of three brothers, accompanied by Joel, also in college, and Stephen, almost there. He started with a proposal. They wanted to create a sharp-looking family coat of arms centered on FFYH-FWYH.

I was enthusiastic. "Cool. Think it's an awesome idea. Look forward to seeing it."

Conversation moved to other things. But later the subject came back around. "Dad, if we all really like the look of the coat of arms—you know, that it's cool with zero cheesiness—what would you think about us getting it tattooed on our chests, right over our hearts?"

I just stared through the flames and smiled. *My boys.*

But there was a follow-up question.

"And, Dad, if we do it, we'd really like you to do it with us."

It wasn't the request, but the meaning behind the request that got to me. Obviously they'd been talking about this before bringing the idea to me. They had all weighed in; they were willing to have a permanent reminder emblazoned on their chests, signifying their mutual commitment to being men who lived with heart.

My opinions about my sons getting a tattoo faded in the presence of my heart's fullness. My boys had gotten it—not just as a slogan, but as a way of life.

And a way *to* Life.

~ ~ ~

If I'm yearning to become fully human, Proverbs has a nonnegotiable exhortation for me. It's the basis for the motto I used with my sons: "Above all else, guard your heart, for it is the wellspring of life" (Proverbs 4:23). The heart is both the battleground and dance floor of Life with a capital L.

My heart is where I fight for my humanity, and it's where I relish and experience Life. Paul talked to the Ephesians about people who are "separated from the life of God because of the ignorance that is in them due to the hardening of their hearts"

(4:18). He couldn't be more clear: the health of my heart will determine whether I'm experiencing Life or not. But it's a reality I missed for way too long in my journey.

The problem is that we tend to be illiterate when it comes to matters of the heart. Sure, we'll talk about someone being cold-hearted, fainthearted, brokenhearted, halfhearted, wholehearted, lighthearted, or hardhearted. But what are we referring to? When we're exhorted to "above all else, guard your heart," do we know what that means?

We tend to equate "heart" with emotion, as in a movie tugging on our heart-strings or someone speaking from her heart. It *is* that, but it's more than that. When we use "heart" to refer only to our emotions, I'd offer that we are referring to heart with a lowercase *h*. But when Scripture refers to the heart (in Hebrew the word is *lebab* and in Greek it's *kardia*), it's referring to much more than just our emotions. Heart with a capital *H*, the type of heart described in Scripture, refers to the core of a person. Having a healthy *kardia* is how I experience Life with a capital L.

My heart is what activates and enhances my humanity. My heart is the center of who I am, encompassing three very human activities: thinking, feeling, and acting.

It's helpful for me to visualize a wheel with three sections, or spokes, and a hub in the center. I picture those three spokes as my mind, my emotions, and my will. Then I look at the hub. That core is my heart. An engaged heart brings balance to the interplay of the three spokes. As a human being, I am involved every day with thinking, feeling, and decisively acting, and it's the business of the heart to synchro-nize all three. Without engaging my heart, I'll be imbalanced in the direction of being overly cerebral, excessively emotional, or exceedingly impulsive. When that imbalance is taken to an extreme, I will shut down in all three arenas.

Imagine someone at the end of his rope—perhaps a drug addict on the street begging for a fix. You glimpse a dramatic loss of humanity, namely, a person who is hollow, aimless, and desperate. You might say that person has lost heart. He has deeply, profoundly lost the core of himself. Like the prodigal son who ended up in a pigsty, the drug addict has lost touch with his humanity.

He has lost touch with his mind, his emotions, and his will. He is no longer thinking clearly. He's become emotionally numb. And he has no will to do anything but survive—barely. Bottom line, his heart is totally unengaged.

It's an extreme example, but it gives us a glimpse of a complete loss of heart and consequent loss of humanity. Maybe we aren't so hollowed out as that addict, but our hearts are just as vulnerable to neglect as his. When our hearts aren't engaged, we lose touch with our humanity.

When we get in the rut of routines that numb our minds, squelch our feelings, and cause us to walk aimlessly through life without taking any steps toward Life, our hearts are hard from a lack of use. In an interview, actor and comedian Tim Allen provided a great image of heart engagement without using the phrase: "I look at it this way: How much of the day are you awake? You think, 'I've gotta get that dry cleaning, I gotta get this going, and this, and this, and this.' And all of a sudden it's dinnertime. And then there's a moment of connection with your spouse or your friends. Then you read and go to bed. Wake up and then it's the same all over. You're not awake, you're not living, you're not experiencing."[1]

We've all been there, seasons in our lives when "it's the same all over." It feels like we're not awake, not experiencing, and certainly not living. We're not realizing life while we live it.

Why? It's because our hearts—as organs of awareness, of longing, of passion— aren't engaged. Fighting for our hearts is choosing to think clearly, feel deeply, and then act intentionally during our days. Engaging our hearts moves us from being spectators to participants in our journeys.

To engage my heart is to reclaim my humanity and actually experience Life.

～ ～ ～

An attorney friend of mine, tussling with this issue of living from the heart and going deep with his longings, was walking along Pearl Street in Boulder, Colorado, an avenue known for its creative artisans and street vendors. Catching his eye was a typewriter—those things are not far from being archeological artifacts these days. Sitting behind it was a poet who, at a customer's request, would craft a poem on the spot, pecking it out on his typewriter.

My friend Jeffrey walked up and made his request. "How about a poem on 'The Longings of the Heart'?"

"You got it." Keys started tapping out a rhythm of sidewalk brilliance.

Later that day I received a text from Jeffrey with a photo of the poem written by the sidewalk Shakespeare. Twenty thoughtful lines, starting with these:

The brain is second.
It's the heart that gives the orders.

Gives the craving to the bones,
The blood.

Right on.

But I realize some will object to any notion of the brain being second. They think the *mind* should give the orders.

Years ago, I know I would have. I'm a logical guy, and for too long I emphasized my mind over feeling in my life. Not wanting my life to be run by emotion, I downplayed feelings and focused just on matters of the mind.

I didn't realize by doing this that I was muting my Life with a capital L.

Like it or not, you and I are products of history and culture. Whether the culprit is the scientific age or Western civilization or the Enlightenment, we are products of philosophies and historical trends that incline us to worship rational thinking and logic and to look down on feeling and experience.

One result of that has to do with the word *emotion*. We connect that with the word *emotional*, which suggests someone who's out of control or psychologically fragile. Emotion is often considered a weakness in one's character. And emotion is sometimes thought of as an unreliable response to situations and circumstances.

The church contributes to this too. Often we preach the knowledge of God over the experience of God, the study of Scripture over the living out of the gospel, the facts of the Bible over the supernatural power of God's Word in our lives. A powerful picture of this problem is the church community depicted in "Babette's Feast"—that group of devout Christian people sitting down to a dinner of pure grace, but intentionally hardening themselves against the imagined dangers of joy and feeling, vowing instead to focus on higher thoughts. Imagine how much Life they were missing out on by rejecting the things of the heart.

The same is true of us. As a result of culture and history and sometimes the church, we are trained from an early age to develop the intellect of our heads and the skills of our hands, but regarding the importance of emotion and passion, not so much. So we miss out on Life with a capital L. But let's go back to that street poem:

The brain is second.
It's the heart that gives the orders.
Gives the craving to the bones,
The blood.

On the other end of the spectrum, there are those, because they equate the heart with emotions, who might respond to the poem by saying, "Amen!" They think *emotions* should give the orders. This also mutes Life with a capital L.

I don't know whether the sidewalk Shakespeare intended it with a capital H or not, but the heart that "gives the orders" in our lives, with Life-giving results, is more than an organ of emotion. At this point it might be helpful to paraphrase the street poem:

> The brain is not number one.
> But neither are our emotions.
> The heart gives the orders.

While some people live entirely in the realm of the mind and miss out on the *experiences* of life that God's grace lavishly provides, others live entirely in the realm of emotions, bounce from thrill to thrill, and miss out on the *meaning* of life that God's grace lavishly provides.

When I'm engaging my heart, I'm engaging both my mind and my emotion. My heart is the conductor of the great symphony of thoughts *and* feelings.

~ ~ ~

So how does my heart "give the orders" to both my mind and my emotions?

The heart, remember, is the core, the hub of our humanity, able to balance our thinking, feeling, and acting. When we engage the heart, we're giving ourselves to that balance—literally, to that check and balance between the mind and emotions and the actions that follow.

Without that balance, if I'm just an emotions person—engaging my emotions without my heart—I'll respond to events solely in an emotional way and, without the rational wisdom the mind brings to the table, miss the actual *truth* of a situation.

But when I'm engaging my heart, my emotions are balanced by my mind. A newspaper editorial might elicit powerful feelings in me and lead to a drastic reaction, but my mind tells me that the emotions of the story are contrived and haven't been written honestly. With my emotions, I'll fall in love with a new car in a dealer's showcase, but my mind tells me I can't afford it. With deep feeling, I'll want to come to the rescue of my child who's gotten into a mess at school, but my mind tells me it's important instead to let him learn a life lesson.

Similarly, if I'm just a mind person—engaging my mind without my heart—I'll respond to events solely in terms of facts and, without the wisdom that feeling and intuition bring to the table, miss the deeper *significance* of a situation.

But when my heart's engaged with my mind, I understand an event, but I also let my emotion give me a fuller experience of that moment. With my mind I evaluate a job applicant in an interview, but it's my intuition that gives me a gut feeling that something's not right. With my mind I'll evaluate my future, but my passion highlights my priorities within those possibilities. As Victor Hugo wrote in *Les Misérables,* "That which enlightened this man was his heart. His wisdom was made of the light which comes from there."[2]

My heart can enable me to contemplate the implications of the facts of the world and of the events taking place in my life. My heart can see and appreciate things about my life that my mind doesn't perceive on its own. It's what Blaise Pascal was referring to when he famously mused in his *Pensées:* "The heart has its reasons, which reason does not know."[3] Without my heart being engaged, I'll notice events in my life, but I won't experience the moments—whether they be celebrations or disappointments—within those events.

～ ～ ～

Emphasizing reason at the expense of the heart will also leave me ill prepared for the shocks doled out daily by a fallen world, shocks that often come in the form of disappointments and unanswered questions. This side of eternity, I enjoy some certainties—from $2 + 2 = 4$ to the scientific laws of the universe to the powerful credibility of Christianity's essential historical claims.

But the last time I checked, there is also uncertainty in the world. We don't know it all and everything's not black or white. There are a ton of unanswered questions and gray areas in the universe, which brings a lot of mystery to our Mondays. So even with some certainty in hand, we're still waiting for a lot of answers.

My mind by itself is not equipped to deal with the resulting mystery. My mind wants resolution and, if lacking the maturity that the heart can bring, will be tempted to allow no room for mystery, forcing resolution and inventing answers that aren't there. Those kinds of answers can be shallow and superficial, leading me to become disappointed when they're easily dismantled, and then cynical, insecure, or dogmatic, or all of the above. Which is why a reminder was written in the margins of a preacher's sermon notes: "Argument weak here—yell louder."

My heart can handle unanswered questions more easily because it goes deeper than mere facts for a sense of security. For the follower of Christ, my ultimate security comes through not only his truth but also his love. So in the face of mystery, I deliberately and intimately relate with him instead of only trying to get, or invent, all the answers. Engaging both my mind *and* heart in relationship with my Creator and Sustainer who promises to be enough for me, I am able to bend instead of break in the face of fallenness.

I just talked with a friend regarding a young acquaintance of hers: an eight-year-old boy who is in an intensive care unit due to heart failure. I hung up the phone, reeling. Eight-year-olds aren't supposed to have heart failure. If I try with just my mind to think of answers capable of bringing comfort, I'll come up empty.

> My heart is where I fight for my humanity, and it's where I relish and experience Life.

Reactions such as anger, denial, despair, or cynicism will quickly arrive on my doorstep. Instead, what if I engage with that news and use my heart, both mind *and* emotion? That's what I choose to do, with tears welling up even as I type.

With my mind, I review that the world is fallen, why it's fallen, and that we're not exempt from fallenness—yet. I focus on the truth that Christ came. I lean into the validity of his resurrection, which assures me of the trustworthiness of all that he taught about his ultimate rescue and repair of creation.

Against that backdrop, my feelings engage with the reality of the pain, and I authentically grieve without moving into despair. In the context of my relationship with Christ, with my will I *choose* to pray for this little boy and cry out with honest *emotion*, lamenting that this is not the way it should be, but I also worship, *knowing* it will not always be so. I then begin to consider what I can *do* to come alongside this family.

Hope is a gift embraced only when mind and emotion and will are all engaged together—united and fueled by the heart.

～ ～ ～

At this point, a recap might be helpful. Full humanity means an engaged heart. An engaged heart means I am actively balancing my mind and my emotions, which will activate my will in a healthy way. If I use only my mind and neglect my heart, I might end up being smart in some areas but also superficial and a bit too fragile to thrive in a fallen world. If I view my heart as only my emotions and neglect my mind, I might end up being sensitive but also overly sentimental and a bit too fragile to thrive in a fallen world.

God intends for me to engage life with my mind—fully.

God intends for me to engage life with my feelings and emotions—fully.

God gave me a mind. He gave me emotions. And he gave me a heart to balance the two—and, with my will, to experience Life with a capital L.

❧ ❧ ❧

Movies—at least many of them—are a great opportunity to practice some heart engagement and learn that balance of thought and feeling. Great films can impact us on not just an emotional level but on a heart level through our thinking as well as our feeling.

My sons—the FFYH-FWYH gang—have learned not to hop up and head out when a movie is done. If we're watching at home, we take a minute to process. They now know the question is coming: How'd that impact you—on a heart level? Early on, when I first started doing this with them, it was slow going. They would offer unreflective, grunt responses that we chuckle about today: "Good." "Cool." "It was okay." However, these days, the whole family enters into the question with more re-flection. Including me.

But that's not typical in our culture these days. Unfortunately, instead of engag-ing with great movies on a heart level, we tend to just watch them for amusement. The word *amusement* derives from two root stems: *muse,* which means "to think carefully," and the prefix *a,* which means "not." So *amuse* literally means to "not think."

Unfortunately, our culture worships this kind of amusement. It seems that the more amusement—mindlessness—we can experience, the better. We approach movies and many other things in life as a means of escaping reality by not thinking.

I'm not saying that we shouldn't have some fun or find an escape once in a while. That's fine. But we've gone overboard. We've made entertainment the purpose of our lives and amusement the object of our worship.

Engaging our hearts means choosing to engage with something using both our minds and our emotions. It means experiencing the significance of something by appreciating both its physical and spiritual dimensions. It means going deeper and not settling for the superficiality of amusement.

Take the final scene of the Academy Award–winning Best Picture *Gladiator*. Rome is headed for a catastrophic implosion under the selfish agenda of Commodus, the warped and wicked emperor. He is holding hostage his sister, Lucilla, by threatening to kill her young son, Lucius, if she doesn't support his schemes. A couple of senators know of the impending doom if Commodus isn't stopped, but the people of Rome are still unaware of the danger seeping into the very bedrock of their society.

At this point in the film, the only one who can stop Commodus is Maximus, the former general who had been condemned by the emperor, narrowly escaped execution, was sold into slavery to become a gladiator, and has now returned to Rome as part of traveling troupe of fighters. As a result of his resounding victories in the majestic Colosseum, Maximus has become the loved and lauded gladiator.

Commodus, jealous as well as fearful of the former general's popularity and influence, knows Maximus's death will end the final hope of opposition to his evil reign. He arranges to fight Maximus in the great arena, but first he ensures it won't be a fair fight. Before their contest, in the bowels of the Colosseum, he stabs Maximus secretly, has his mortal wound concealed, and then brings him before the people for their duel to the death.

In the climactic conclusion, Maximus, struggling to breathe, is barely able to raise his sword. Yet he manages to kill Commodus, thereby freeing not only Lucilla and Lucius but Rome itself. He then succumbs to his wound, heads into eternity to join his murdered wife and son, and his body is carried out of the arena in honor. Commodus's body remains behind, disgraced in the dust of the Colosseum floor.

Now, if I don't care to engage my heart with this scene, I can, with my emotions, just be sentimental about a good guy dying. Or, with my mind, stick with just the facts. When asked for a summary, I can simply say that the hero died, but he killed the bad guy, and everyone was relieved. That's all accurate. But it doesn't engage the heart. Or win an Academy Award.

Remember, my heart enables me to go beyond the facts and events to the implications and realities behind the events. So let's do that with this scene. What does the movie make me think? What does it make me feel?

Through Maximus, I engage with true leadership, authentic courage, and the conquering of evil. I'm inspired by his perseverance. I connect with my longing for resolution and my desire for justice to be done. I want freedom for those who are oppressed. I feel the power of protecting others. Deep down, through Lucilla's character, I sense what it means to be rescued. I also engage with an abundance of other realities: love of family, enduring through pain, sacrifice for others, the joy of triumph, living a life that matters, leaving a legacy. The thrill wells up in me to see what true strength and honor look like, prompting a desire to live accordingly. And because of what Maximus did, as a follower of Jesus I'll freshly reflect on Christ's sacrificial death on my behalf.

All that in one scene? Absolutely. That's the power of listening to your heart.

So, right now, hear this, with your heart: *Your life is immensely more significant than any movie.*

On any given day, a succession of events unfold in your story, their significance concealed only by a thin curtain. A curtain easily moved aside by a heart that is willing to engage and muse instead of amuse.

❧ ❧ ❧

Last night our family gathered around a table to commemorate my middle son's twenty-first birthday. It took about ten minutes. Each of us congratulated him for twenty-one years, gave him a cake and a card, and then we all moved on with a normal evening.

Of course that's not what happened. That would have been a mind-only response to a momentous event.

Instead, our hearts got involved. Instead of just commemorating, we celebrated. Yes, we acknowledged the *fact* that he'd been on the planet for twenty-one years. But with our hearts we experienced the *significance* of that reality. We thanked God for preserving his life when he was just a couple months old and almost died. We acknowledged the gift of life and the fascinating progression of growth that occurs in the first two decades of a person's life. With his requested New York strip steak, we opened a twenty-one-year-old bottle of Bordeaux, birthed the same year as he, and savored those years of majestic maturing. We joked about his funny escapades, affirmed his unique traits, and talked about God's purpose for him on this planet. We dreamed about the next two decades.

At the end of the evening, our stomachs were full from the birthday dinner, but so were our hearts.

You've done similar things with your family and friends. But how often do you and I—on a daily basis—miss out because we simply don't do this enough? How often do we miss out because we don't engage our hearts and allow ourselves to *think* about and *feel* the deeper dimensions of life? As T.S. Eliot mused, "We had the experience but missed the meaning."

Once, as I sat down to a memorable meal with some Italian friends in Piedmont, they urged me to slow down as I ate, to savor the food and wine. In doing so, I experienced the significance of the meal—the care and expertise of preparation that went into it, the pairings of different wines with various courses, the special delight of the never-to-be-repeated moment we were enjoying.

I was engaging my heart with the dinner. But I learned an even bigger lesson: engaging my heart will mean savoring not only a meal but my journey as well. That will mean noticing the significant realities that otherwise I would miss. Yes, the bad things become more painful, but the good things become more beautiful.

My heart is not an avenue for me to milk sentimentality from my days, but instead to more deeply notice the significance of them. Being fully human involves letting my heart speak—and savor. That's what I have it for.

❧ ❧ ❧

As I'm learning to engage my heart, what difference does a relationship with Christ make?

Among the hundreds of prophecies in the Old Testament about Christ's coming, one of the most powerful is a word picture of a valley of dry bones into which God breathes his Spirit. In Ezekiel, the impact of the Messiah's coming is prophesied in terms of his impact on men and women who are spiritually dead, even though they're breathing and walking. God promises, "I will give you a new heart and put a new spirit in you; I will remove from you your heart of stone and give you a heart of flesh.... Then he said to me, 'Prophesy to these bones and say to them, "Dry bones, hear the word of the LORD! This is what the Sovereign LORD says to these bones: I will make breath enter you, and you will come to life"'" (Ezekiel 36:26; 37:4–5).

He is saying that, when Christ comes to give Life to me, he gives me a new heart. In Isaiah's prophecy, the voice of the Messiah announces his mission: "The Spirit of the Sovereign Lord is on me, because the Lord has anointed me to preach good news to the poor. He has sent me to bind up the *brokenhearted*" (Isaiah 61:1). Before I come to Christ, I have a heart, but it's shattered and therefore unable to adequately fulfill its purpose. I have a heart and can use it, but things are blurred.

The writer of Ecclesiastes points out that God "has made everything beautiful in its time. He has also set eternity in the hearts of men; yet they cannot fathom what God has done from beginning to end" (Ecclesiastes 3:11). Without Christ, my heart can indeed, for example, perceive beauty (which we'll look at in the next chapter), but I'm unable to really fathom the ultimate eternal significance of it all.

> Living from the heart isn't what most of us have naturally learned.

Turntables are making a comeback. But for some, they're in the same archeological category as typewriters, so I'll review. Basically, a turntable will spin a vinyl album and produce sound with a needle following the grooves in the album. What's been recorded on the album is revealed only when the needle comes into contact with the vinyl. That needle provides a word picture for the purpose of my heart. If I engage my heart, if I allow the needle of my heart to come into contact with the album of my life's journey, my heart vibrates with the rattle and hum of my journey. Just as I can choose when and where on the album to place the needle, I can choose when and where in my journey to engage my heart.

When I was a kid, we played around with an old record player, trying to devise needles out of tiny nails with which we could get some distinguishable noise from a record. But it was nothing like what a real needle could produce. The nails were too hard, which limited their sensitivity. Ezekiel's prophecy tells us that Christ comes to transform the broken needle of my heart, removing my hard "heart of stone" and giving me a soft "heart of flesh." When I trust Christ, I "believe in [my] heart" (Romans 10:9), and a heart transformation occurs. He gives me a new heart with which to experience my journey and begin to fathom fully what God is up to. *There is Life everywhere,* and now I'm able to participate in it.

So is it possible for a person who is not a follower of Christ to engage their hearts? Of course. In fact, many not-yet believers who are engaging their hearts are experiencing much more of their journey than some followers of Jesus who aren't engaging theirs. A broken needle that's engaged with the album will produce more music than a repaired needle that isn't even touching the vinyl. That's why some heart-engaged Christians are more comfortable doing life with unbelievers who are engaging their hearts than they are with fellow believers who aren't—more humanity is experienced from engaging a broken heart than from leaving a redeemed heart unused.

This is also why a lot of heart-engaged unbelievers look at some unengaged Christians and wonder why they need Jesus. They see religiosity but not redeemed, heart-throbbing humanity. This takes us back to the distinction between being alive and actually living. Just because I have a new heart doesn't guarantee I'll enjoy it. I must engage it to enjoy it.

In order to engage my heart, I must protect and nourish it, submit it to God, and soften it before him in humility. I must be wholehearted in my walk with him, paying attention to what fuels it, shrivels it, numbs it, or enlarges it. I must hang around with others who care for my heart.

In short, to be fully human, I have to guard my heart and fight for it.

C. S. Lewis referred to the music "men are born remembering."[4] It's with my heart that I hear it. It's also with my heart that I release that music into the story of my life. It was Oliver Wendell Holmes who sadly reflected,

> Alas for those that never sing,
> But die with all their music in them![5]

The gospel enables me to engage my heart so I can get the song of my humanity off the album of mere existence and into my daily experience. Once I have received Christ, thereby receiving a new heart, I must learn to engage it. I don't want to go to my grave with the song still in me, unheard and unsung.

❧ ❧ ❧

Because of my embrace of the gospel, I have a new heart. But am I experiencing the gospel on a heart level? Am I letting the gospel liberate the song that's in me as a human being?

As he was encouraging some believers, Paul prayed something unique for them: "I pray also that the eyes of your heart may be enlightened" (Ephesians 1:18). I love that phrase. Right after that, he proceeds to tell them how, through God's lavish love and extravagant grace, they had been made alive. To really understand what it means to be alive in Christ, and then to experience his Life, will involve embracing that reality not just with my head but on the level of my heart as well. If I don't, it will result in a loss of Life, which will lead to fake spirituality and less-than-authentic humanity. Does that sound like some religious people you know of?

In many churches over the years, head knowledge has been emphasized over heart engagement. But these days, intellectual engagement is now waning as well. The result? We're lacking substance *and* we're lacking passion.

No wonder the watching world yawns.

Deep thinking and robust theology are absent, but a contributing factor to that predicament is the lack of heart engagement. Once I engage my heart, I will want more context and truth, and therefore I will be motivated to use my mind. Then, with the truth I'm absorbing, my heart will seek to apply it as sort of a drumbeat to enrich the cadence of my lifestyle. I'll celebrate more fully and grieve more honestly. And live more fully. When we encounter someone who intellectually knows a lot of truth but isn't living it out, it's a sure sign that their heart isn't engaged with the truth.

Jesus exhorts us to "love the Lord your God with all your heart and with all your soul and with all your mind and with all your strength" (Mark 12:30). When I interact with the gospel on merely a head level, the result is not just a lack of balance but barren religiosity and a lack of Life. That was the flaw Jesus exposed in some religious leaders when he quoted from the prophet Isaiah: "These people honor me with their lips, but their hearts are far from me. They worship me in vain; their teachings are but rules taught by men" (Matthew 15:8–9). If my heart's not engaged with the Life-giving gospel, I might be going through religious or legalistic motions, but I won't be living. And I'll go to the grave with the song still in me.

❧ ❧ ❧

The renowned architect Frank Lloyd Wright used to enjoy telling about a day during the winter when he was nine years old. He was walking across a snow-covered field with his reserved, no-nonsense uncle. As the two of them reached the far end of the field, his uncle John stopped him. He pointed at his own straight, unwavering tracks in the snow, and then he pointed to Frank's boyish tracks meandering all over the field. His uncle reprimanded him, "Notice how your tracks wander aimlessly from the fence to the cattle to the woods and back again. And then see how my tracks aim directly to where I was headed. There is an important lesson in that, Frank."

When telling this story, Wright would then say, with a twinkle in his eye, "There certainly was—I determined, right then, not to miss most things in life, as my uncle had."[6]

Even as a boy, Wright understood that there's a lot of life to be experienced by following one's heart. The straight, rational path might get you to a destination more quickly, but at the cost of missing out on a lot of life.

Our hearts help us not to miss things. A redeemed heart, if we engage it, even more so.

Christ came to restore our humanity. He wants us to open ourselves to the experiences of our hearts. He created us mind *and* emotion; he wants us to live and follow him with both/and, not with either/or.

That will take effort. As we've seen, living from the heart isn't what most of us have naturally learned. But it's essential to living Life with a capital L.

So fight for your heart and fight with your heart. Live your days thinking clearly, feeling deeply, and acting intentionally.

Fighting for your redeemed heart could not be more important, and fighting to live with your redeemed heart could not be more fulfilling.

Or more fully human.

❧ ❧ ❧

You might be wondering about the tattoo. Did it happen? You can ask my boys. They might tell you. But be warned, they'll probably say something like, "More important than what's happening on the outside of my chest is what's going on the inside of yours."

Beauty

Relishing Life

> I did not have to ask my heart what it wanted
> because of all the desires I have ever known,
> just one did I cling to
> for it was the essence of all desire:
> to know beauty.
> —St. John of the Cross

It wasn't a museum, but a golf course, and it wasn't a tour guide, but my son. It was a Life-giving moment—a Life-giving moment that was bursting with beauty.

And I had forgotten my camera.

But that was a good thing.

Two weeks before, my life had been permanently altered when my dad died suddenly of a massive coronary. My wife, Arlene, and the boys had been with me at my mom's home for the funeral, followed by ten days of helping the family take care of the myriad details accompanying the aftershock of an unexpected death. We had just returned to our home in west Michigan, and I had brought my heartache back with me.

It was a couple of days later when my grief and the weather coaxed me into taking Andrew, my then four-year-old son, to play golf. Adjusting to my new fatherless status, it was a way for me to begin to heal—enjoying an activity with my son that my dad had loved sharing with me, and I with him, countless times over the years. It was midafternoon on a gorgeous Indian summer day in the third week of October.

In Michigan, you seize those kinds of days in late autumn because, when the snow arrives, you say good-bye to the grass until Easter (or the Fourth of July, depending on the year).

We stood on the tee box of the fourth hole at Railside Golf Club. A par-five, slight dogleg to the left. I had connected for a decent drive that, to my young son who was still of the opinion that I was the most talented and interesting man in the world, seemed like a cannon shot. Now it was his turn.

He teed up his ball, and as he was taking his five or so practice swings that only a toddler can pull off without maxing out the patience meter of whoever's watching, everything seemed to shift into slow motion. The way I would put it now: my heart engaged, and it escorted me through the event into the significance and beauty of the moment. Since this was in the dark ages before smartphones, I winced when I realized I'd forgotten my camera. So the only thing I knew to do was to dial up my attention gauge, which is why, twenty years later, I can still remember the details.

The two of us had that section of earth to ourselves, together drinking in a big gulp of grace. The sun danced through shimmering leaves onto my back and made the little blond-haired boy in front of me glisten. He stood against the backdrop of a small pond, its sleep disturbed by some paddling ducks underneath a cloudless azure blue sky. He was wearing a red-striped Charlie Brown golf shirt with a yellow sweater vest, khaki pants, and Velcro tennis shoes. He delivered a mighty swing, his tongue strategically positioned out of the corner of his mouth, and watched his ball bounce and skip across the manicured grass. He then stood frozen, holding his miniature club over his shoulder and against his back, mimicking a classic golfer's finishing pose.

It was as if he were not just looking down a long fairway, but ahead into a long life that would be filled with moments like this. I wanted to be a part of as many of those future highlights as I could, before yet another coronary, or something else, brought the privilege to an end. I relished not only the beauty of the landscape and the little man in front of me but the privilege of being human—and alive.

One resounding word is all I could utter.

"Beautiful."

My son beamed, not realizing I was referring to a heck of a lot more than just his golf shot.

~ ~ ~

Fast-forward a few years. This time it was indeed a museum, and one of the most beautiful. The State Hermitage Museum in Saint Petersburg, Russia, is within the enormous complex of the Winter Palace of the old Russian royalty and is home to the most paintings of any museum in the world. For many years I had wanted to visit this collection, and in particular, I especially wanted to see *The Return of the Prodigal Son,* a seventeenth-century oil painting by Rembrandt.

It's one of the Dutch master's final works, based on Christ's parable recorded in the gospel of Luke. I had appreciated the painting for years, and then, after reading Henri Nouwen's book by the same name, it was catapulted to an even higher place of meaning for me.

> Our ultimate longing is not actually for beauty, but for the Author of beauty.

Now, here I was, finally standing in front of the masterpiece. Fittingly, it's the only piece of artwork in the small room it calls home. Massive in size at over eight feet tall and six feet wide, it dominates the space that's constantly bulging with admirers. I remained in its presence for well over an hour, viewing it from different angles, observing the changes in light from the enormous windows to the right of the painting, eavesdropping on tour guide monologues, and letting Rembrandt's image of God's gracious embrace seep into my hungry heart. The word *beautiful* quietly crossed my lips more than once as I tried to take in as much of the experience as I could.

Midway through my time there, I saw him as his quick pace brought him into the room. He was a tall American man with a bright NFL hat, so when he entered, I noticed him immediately. When traveling abroad, you never know if a fellow American will make you proud or prompt you to fake an accent.

This one made me nervous right away. What really caught my attention was the fact that as he sprang through the large doorway opposite the painting, he was holding his camera phone up high to clear the heads of those in front of him. I watched as he rapidly moved on across the room and exited the doorway left of the painting, his video camera aimed at the masterpiece the entire time. What struck me was that he never broke stride and barely looked at the painting. His stressed expression was primarily focused on the sea of people in front of him in order to facilitate the most efficient navigational route through them.

I was so intrigued that I left my post and followed him for a few minutes. I had to move quickly because he did the same thing through the next couple of rooms, never slowing. I broke off my pursuit and headed back to my time with Rembrandt, grinning at what I had witnessed and imagining an earlier conversation he might have had with his wife: "Honey, we only have an hour to enjoy some of the most famous works of art in the world. I'll take a video and that'll help us cover more ground. We can watch the paintings later... Oh, was that a picture of Rembrandt's I just passed?"

I chuckled out loud.

Back with *The Return of the Prodigal Son* and reflecting further on the drive-by approach to art appreciation I had just observed, my smile subsided and I actually returned to that moment years earlier on the golf course with my son when I had forgotten my camera. If I had brought my camera to the golf course that day, I would've done just what I'd seen this guy do with Rembrandt's painting. But I recalled how instead I had been extra careful to soak it all in precisely because I didn't have a camera and how, as a result, I had actually engaged more with the moment—and its beauty. Yet, cringing, I had to admit that so often in life I'm more typically like the guy with the funny hat I'd just watched, snapping shots while missing moments—and rarely slowing down to actually pay attention.

The result is tragic: a life filled with detours around beauty and procrastinations of the heart.

"Beautiful moment! I'll look at it later."

❧ ❧ ❧

Rollo May, in his book *My Quest for Beauty*, excavates this more clearly for me: "Beauty is eternity born into human existence." That resonates with the words from Ecclesiastes that we looked at earlier: "He has made everything beautiful in its time. He has also set eternity in the hearts of men" (3:11). There's a connection between beauty and that larger sense of eternity that each of us has ingrained in our heart.

May continues, "A chord of music, such as the one that opens Beethoven's 'Hammerklavier Sonata,' sets loose within us a quality of eternity, a sense that this moment is ultimate. One thinks, 'I could live or die tomorrow but *now I have this moment*.'"[1]

Hmm. Sounds a lot like *realizing life while I live it*.

Wherever I am and whatever I might be doing, an encounter with beauty can escort me more deeply into whatever particular moment I'm in and, through that moment, enable me to engage with something far bigger.

Beauty can uniquely enable me to experience the significance of being human and, ultimately, be a portal through which I enter into the Life that's everywhere.

❧ ❧ ❧

When I speak of beauty, I'm not referring to something that's just pretty, sentimental, or superficial. I'm not equating beauty, as many in our culture do, with glamour, image, or even excitement. If I choose to pursue that definition of beauty, I'm settling for counterfeits and easy amusement, indulging in an almost narcotic form of entertainment to serve as a diversion from my boredom or difficulty. Whenever I confine myself to such imposters of beauty, my heart and mind become numbed rather than nourished and my humanness will remain confined to merely getting through my days (with little doses of anesthesia sprinkled here and there) instead of experiencing them.

Instead of being something to just passively observe, beauty requires me to actively engage with it. The Greek word for "beauty" and "goodness" (*kalon*) is related to the Greek word for "call" (*kalein*). There is a calling I experience when I encounter beauty.

That call can come through any of my senses—sight, sound, smell, taste, or touch. It can come in a variety of locations, from national parks to ballparks, from galleries to theaters, from churches to restaurants, from living rooms to conference rooms. It's a call that I encounter in both the physical and spiritual realms of my journey, awakening me to the significance of my humanity.

Harvard professor Elaine Scarry, while expounding the thoughts of great minds such as Augustine and Dante, refers to beauty as an invitation, a greeting.[2] Beauty speaks to me, sings to me, welcomes me, and summons me into the presence of something that is life saving, life affirming, and life giving. Irish poet and priest John O'Donohue observes, "When we experience beauty, we feel called. The Beautiful stirs passion and urgency in us and calls us forth from aloneness into the warmth and wonder of an eternal embrace. It unites us again with the neglected and forgotten grandeur of life."[3]

True beauty calls me to live and not just exist, to celebrate the privilege of being human and not just deaden the pain of being fallen. Sure, beauty can and should provide for me a momentary shelter from the storm of ugly fallenness that assaults us all. But instead of being just a tranquilizing escape from fallen realities, the refuge of beauty comes in the form of a vibrant portal into that which is good and true and fully human in the midst of Monday morning realities that are often way less than perfect.

In the midst of chaos, tragedy, and evil, beauty can be a portal through which I see and taste shalom. An encounter with beauty can stop the drowning sensation caused by the undertow of a fallen world—and breathe Life into me. When Nikolai Yaroshenko asks if I am noticing that *there is Life everywhere,* his query undoubtedly includes beauty. To him there was something beautiful in the simple act of a child feeding some birds. The beauty of the child's—and adults'—hope is all the more poignant against the horrific backdrop of a prison railcar headed to Siberia. "That's beautiful."

> Beauty, ultimately, can be a portal through which I enter into the Life that's everywhere.

Beauty can also be a portal for celebrating the best of our humanity in the best of times. The third baseman in a World Series game launches his body lengthwise to snare a screaming ground ball that is barely in bounds, and then, amazingly, he rights himself to one knee and fires a bullet across the diamond to throw the batter out by a half step. "That's beautiful."

An architect creates the remarkable design for a public building, then craftsmen arrange brick and mortar and glass into an extraordinary array of space and form, a breathtaking display of the creativity God has entrusted to human beings. "That's beautiful."

Bank employees brainstorm about ways, in their words, they could "re-humanize" their bank and care for their clients and community. The employees, using their own money, start a fund for people in need. The next day the car of a struggling single mother of two breaks down at a teller window. The employees take care of the repairs. "That's beautiful."

Beauty can also be a portal through which we gain a glimpse of God. A father tells his daughter, while they gaze at a rainbow, of God's promise to finish what he started when he created humanity. That even in the blackness of a storm, we can find the beauty of grace. That, whether we're in times of desperation or celebration, God is always present. While the child smiles, the dad is reminded, in the midst of his overwhelming stress at work, that hope is real. "That's beautiful."

All occasions of beauty—true beauty—are marks of significance. They tell us that something is important, worthy, substantial. They point us to the Creator of creation, the Creator of human artists, craftsmen, musicians, chefs, writers, farmers, caregivers, athletes, homemakers, actors, and businesspeople, and the Creator of all human endeavors. As we behold their beauty, our stimulated hearts soar.

Beauty is a call to more than merely observe. It's a call to engage with the significance of the beauty, to acknowledge its meaning, and to embrace its origin.

It's a call, in that moment, to become more fully human.

❧ ❧ ❧

So why do we neglect beauty in our life journey? It's related to the neglect of the heart we've already talked about. The two go hand in hand. If I'm not focused on heart health, then beauty will be low on my priority list.

Take my American friend in the art museum—the guy with the video camera and a schedule to keep. Of course I have no idea about the rest of his life, but when he was rushing through that room, there was a lack of engagement with both his heart and the beauty before him. I'm capable of doing the same thing when I'm in the presence of beauty. When I do, is my heart unengaged because I'm missing the beauty or am I missing the beauty because my heart is unengaged?

Yes.

If I disregard my heart, I will be deaf to the value of beauty, which is a primary language and source of nourishment for my heart. And dismissing beauty will have a dehumanizing effect on me. If I neglect beauty, my heart will eventually and instinctively turn to lesser things to awaken it, ranging from mere amusement to deadly addictions. The result might be titillation, but not nourishment, and my heart will starve, usually without my knowing it, because the superficial stimulation masks my malnourishment until it's too late.

Learning to care for my heart leads me to embrace and experience beauty, making me more fully human in the process.

Plato and plenty of others over the course of history have talked about the three necessary and universal ideals of the good, the true, and the beautiful. You can even see them in this exhortation of the apostle Paul in his letter to the Philippians:

"Finally, brothers, whatever is true, whatever is noble, whatever is right, whatever is pure, whatever is lovely, whatever is admirable—if anything is excellent or praiseworthy—think about such things" (4:8). Paul is urging us to use both our hearts and minds to ponder goodness (noble and pure), truth (true and right), and beauty (lovely and admirable).

Goodness, truth, and beauty aren't synonymous with each other, but they are interdependent. You can't have one without the other two. If someone says, "I want beauty, but I want nothing to do with goodness or truth in the process," whatever they end up with won't be beauty. If I propose, "I want goodness in my life," then it must also involve truth and beauty or else it will be a version of goodness that is more akin to image management. And if I want truth, an application of its goodness and engagement with its beauty will have to be in the mix as well.

An imbalance of these three categories is a major reason why so many church people end up neglecting beauty in their journey and unknowingly opt for hollow religiosity instead. It's the natural outcome of focusing on goodness and truth while ignoring beauty. Again, the religious community in "Babette's Feast" is a great example: they intentionally ignored the beauty of the lovingly crafted meal placed before them, and in doing so missed the grace and the Life.

It's a pitfall we succumb to as well. We view Jesus as the Way and the Truth, but overlook our present-tense engagement with his Life.[4] If we do that, it will result in applying our will toward his way and our mind to his truth, but neglecting our heart's engagement with his Life. The consequence is anything but beautiful: a legalistic demonstration of supposed goodness and a prideful and judgmental use of truth while the heart is going elsewhere for fulfillment (which is where a lot of Christians' secret, "out of the blue" sin stories originate). It's the peril of taking the necessary seeds of morals and doctrinal statements out of the rich soil of beauty and placing them in a potted plant of religiosity.

It took a long time for me to learn, but once I did, it was Life-saving. If I'm keeping beauty at arm's length, the goodness in my life will be something less than good, and truth will be something less than true.

Christ's way and truth must include his Life.

❧ ❧ ❧

When I begin to grasp the importance of getting more beauty into my daily diet, a temptation is to shelve my new esteem for beauty instead of celebrating it. I procrastinate engaging with it, justifying, "My life's just too hectic or troubled to try to focus on beauty right now."

But that's actually when I need beauty the most.

In one of my favorite movies, *The Shawshank Redemption,* Andy Dufresne is a young banker wrongly convicted of murdering his wife and her lover and sentenced to consecutive life terms at the Shawshank State Penitentiary in Maine.

At one point, Andy locks himself in the warden's office and plays a recording of Mozart's *Marriage of Figaro* over the prison's loudspeakers. His friend Red, commenting on why the beauty of that moment caused everyone all over the prison to stop and listen, reflects aloud about the music that soared over them: "It was like some beautiful bird flapped into our drab little cage and made those walls dissolve away. And for the briefest of moments, every last man at Shawshank felt free."

For his stunt, Andy is confined to a brutal two weeks in "the hole." When he gets out of solitary confinement, he joins his buddies at dinner. They ask him if it was really worth two weeks, and he tells them it was the easiest time he'd ever done because "I had Mr. Mozart to keep me company."

"So they let you tote that record player down there?"

Shaking his head, Andy clarifies. Pointing to his head, "It was in here," and then to his heart, "in here. That's the beauty of music. They can't get that from you. Haven't you ever felt that way about music?"

Red responds, "I played a mean harmonica as a younger man. Lost my interest in it though. Didn't make much sense in here."

Andy counters, "Here's where it makes the most sense. You need it so you don't forget.... Forget that there are places in the world that aren't made out of stone."

In the midst of whatever cyclone of a circumstance I'm in, my mind and heart can provide a sort of landing strip in the midst of the storm on which beauty can descend. But in the midst of difficulty, I have to open myself up to allow the beauty to land into my life.

A reality that has encouraged me is in that passage from Philippians I mentioned earlier. It's not only what Paul encourages me to do (choose to dwell on that which is good and true and beautiful), but the context from which he encourages me. He's not on a beach playing a game on his phone under the rays of a Caribbean sun; he's in prison, on death row, and under the watch of a Roman guard. And his exhortation is intentionally sandwiched between two references to God's peace.[5]

He is encouraging me, in the midst of whatever fallenness I'm grappling with right now, to invite shalom into my difficulty by pursuing goodness, truth, and beauty.

That sounds similar to some people in a prison railcar choosing the Life that's everywhere. And if I'm choosing to ignore that Life (remember the silhouetted individual in the background of Yaroshenko's painting, looking out the window on the opposite side of the railcar), hopelessness, despair, and cynicism will result.

Boston College philosopher Peter Kreeft talks about the roots of that cynicism: "The closer we are to God, to divine attributes—such as absolute truth, goodness, and beauty—the more we wonder. When we separate ourselves from truth, goodness, and beauty, we lose wonder and become cynical."[6]

I think it's interesting that so many who are confronted with extremely difficult circumstances—cancer, loss of a spouse or child, a natural disaster, imprisonment in a railcar—seem to find wonder in the simplest things. And those of us in seasons of comfort and ease seem to have such a hard time seeing the beauty around us.

❧ ❧ ❧

That brings up the most powerful—and beautiful—aspect of beauty. The core reason behind the nourishment beauty can bring to my days is rooted in a simple reality: all true beauty bears the fingerprint of God. And, again, that may be the reason those in tough circumstances find wonder and beauty against all odds. They desperately need to see God in something, and in those simple things, he is there.

Beauty reunites me with the Author of beauty. When I start viewing this world as a gallery of beauty and acknowledge these as God's own fingerprints, I begin to understand that beauty is a way of connecting personally and intimately with God himself.

Jonathan Edwards, the brilliant eighteenth-century philosopher and theologian, wrote that God is the "foundation and fountain" of all beauty.[7] That's why, whether we realize it or not, beauty is "what we are more concerned with than anything else whatsoever."[8] To be enthralled with beauty is, essentially, to be enthralled with our longing for God, because all beauty begins with him, "perfect in beauty" (Psalm 50:2).

Beauty can, if I let it, escort me into an intimate encounter with God.

David, one of the poets of the Psalms, wrote that his ultimate desire was, daily, to "gaze upon the beauty of the LORD" (27:4), acknowledging that "the heavens declare the glory of God; the skies proclaim the work of his hands. Day after day they pour forth speech; night after night they display knowledge" (19:1–2). He intimately relates with the beauty of God's person through encountering God's personal works of beauty.

Unfortunately, we live in a secular culture that actively disconnects beauty from God. That's not to say that a work created by someone who denies God is not beautiful and does not have merit. God still shines through. But something is lost when we intentionally ignore the ultimate Creator of beauty.

When I divorce beauty from God, I not only limit my appreciation of that beauty, but I also dilute the nourishment it provides my heart and humanness. Because, when in the presence of an object or experience of beauty, if I separate this beautiful fragment from the whole, I'm not letting it connect me to God as the ultimate Author.[9]

Take something like a football, a jar of paint, a four-pound sack of sugar, or a box of fly-fishing flies. All of those, by themselves, are meaningful and even beautiful to various people, but the real reason for the value of their enjoyment is due to their larger context. When I put that football on a field with twenty-two players, take that paint and put it on a canvas, put some of that sugar in a cheesecake recipe, or take that box of flies with a rod to a trout stream, my appreciation deepens. Why? Because I'm engaging with the fragments in the context of their greater whole.

Living in a secular culture where the hand of God in exhibitions of beauty, truth, or goodness is at least downplayed and often denied completely, I can, on a personal level, be tempted to disconnect it from him. I daily have to choose to resist aligning with the beauty-shriveling tendencies of my culture that deny the whole while nevertheless attempting to fully enjoy the fragments. As Dostoyevsky's character Father Païssy observes about atheists, "But they have only analyzed the parts and overlooked the whole, and indeed their blindness is marvelous."[10]

> Learning to care for my heart leads me to embrace and experience beauty.

When we disconnect beauty from God, we become overly focused on the mere parts and miss the significance and greater meaning of the whole.

C. S. Lewis pointed out the dangerous result of separating the fragments of beauty from the whole when he wrote, "The books or the music in which we thought the beauty was located will betray us if we trust to them; it was not *in* them, it only came *through* them, and what came through them was longing. These things—the beauty, the memory of our own past—are good images of what we really desire; but if they are mistaken for the thing itself, they turn into dumb idols, breaking the hearts of their worshippers. For they are not the thing itself; they are only the scent of a flower we have not found, the echo of a tune we have not heard, news from a country we have never yet visited."[11]

Our ultimate longing is not actually for beauty, but for the Author of beauty.

Embracing this, I can experience the epic in the every day when I see the beautiful things and experiences of my journey—whether a sunset over the mountains, the belly laugh of a child, a fantastic strategic plan, or the beautiful gospel itself—as a bridge to the One who is truly, originally, and perfectly Beautiful. No wonder Lewis wrote, "The sweetest thing in all my life has been the longing...to find the place where all the beauty came from."[12]

\~ \~ \~

In 1912, Lawrence, Massachusetts, was the largest textile-producing city in the nation, employing about thirty-two thousand workers. But the working conditions facing those laborers, people from dozens of nationalities, were deplorable, resulting in astounding mortality rates. On the first of January that year, a law went into effect that reduced the workweek from fifty-six to fifty-four hours—but only for women and children. The owners retaliated by cutting the workers' wages while increasing the workload by speeding up the assembly line. The workers responded with an enormous—and successful—two-month strike that began on January 12.

It became known as the Bread and Roses Strike because of a slogan the workers adopted: "We want bread and roses too." It was based on a poem by James Oppenheim, published in the *Atlantic Monthly* the previous month, which included these lines. Read them carefully—your humanity depends on it:

Our lives shall not be sweated from birth until life closes—
Hearts starve as well as bodies: Give us Bread, but give us Roses....
Small art and love and beauty their drudging spirits knew—
Yes, it is Bread we fight for—but we fight for Roses, too.[13]

Am I fighting for beauty in my life—and my culture—or just going through the motions of survival? My answers to those questions will play a large role in determining whether I'm thriving as a human being or just enduring.

It's a powerful moment in my journey when I wholeheartedly embrace my desire and need for beauty. When I submit to the reality that my heart will not live without it and I cannot know God apart from it. When I realize that Life with a capital L necessitates, on a daily basis, that I fight to nourish my mind and heart with beauty.

Yes, it's a fight, because the world is fallen. But it's still a world that has its Creator's fingerprints all over it, so I open the eyes of my heart and behold his beauty. And the greatest reward of the journey is growing closer to this Author of all the beauty. Growing closer to the Christ who slowed down to acknowledge the beauty of wildflowers[14] and who celebrated the extravagant beauty of an expensive perfume a woman poured on his head.[15] Growing closer to the Holy Spirit who breathes into us the ability to create beauty.[16] And to relate with the heavenly Father who, in the beginning, beautifully created it all and called it "good."

My intense hope for you—and me—is that we'll start uttering, "That's beautiful," more often and more deeply than we ever have before. And that we, as men and women created in the image of the Creator himself, will experience the freedom of using our unique and creative abilities, whether we call ourselves artists or not, to generate more beauty on the canvas of our relationships, our careers, our stories, and our culture.

May we embrace the daily reminders that, truly, *la vita e bella*—life is beautiful.

And that Christ's Life is beautiful.

And, above all, that *he* is beautiful.

~ ~ ~

I now know what was going on that afternoon on the golf course years ago. As my son swung a golf club, I chose to engage with the layers of beauty contained in that moment, and it brought shalom into my grief over the loss of my dad.

Yes, I live in a fallen world where fathers die of massive coronaries long before the rest of us think they're supposed to. But beauty still abounds. And that beauty is not meant to serve as a mere distraction or even a painkiller but instead as a Lifeline...

enabling me to embrace the residue of what once was,
    to get a taste of what will one day come again,
        and to relate with the beautiful and gracious Author of it all,
            who can bring beauty even from ashes.
That day, beauty breathed into me a resolve and ability to keep moving forward.
And Live.

9

Illumination

The Light of Life

In the middle of the road of my life, I awoke in a
dark wood where the true way was wholly lost.
—DANTE ALIGHIERI

It's quite complicated, but I'll try to explain it. There are two key factors to understand about a night dive: One, it's a scuba dive. Two, it's at night.

For most people, the notion of being underwater in the dark is sufficient to nix such a ludicrous idea from their bucket list, and they move on to other, more sensible endeavors—things that happen with unobstructed vision or at least above the surface, where breathing is free.

For other people with less sense, like me, it's all the more reason to give it a try.

Cozumel, Mexico, is home to one of the largest coral reefs in the world, thus a magnet for scuba divers. I was there with a friend to get an advanced scuba certification, and as an additional activity one evening, we signed up for a spur-of-the-moment night dive. It was to be the first for both of us.

Flashlights are sort of important for a night dive, and I had not brought one with me. (If this were a movie, you'd be hearing some faint, melodramatic music starting up about now.) In the dive shop, they said I didn't need to buy one because I could rent a good one from them. (More music, a bit louder.)

I agreed to their offer and rented a large dive light. While still in the shop, just to be sure of things, I switched on my future ticket to observing a world I'd never seen before. Looking at the bright beam, I wanted to be sure of a slight detail with the dive shop attendant. "This has new batteries in it, correct?"

"*Sí, señor!*"

"You're sure?"

"*Por supuesto, señor!* And, *señor,* even if something were to happen, your dive-master will have an extra one!" (Big-time music here.)

At dusk, my friend Rick and I showed up at the dive boat with all our gear, dive lights, and excitement in tow and cruised toward a dive site named Punta Dalila. The word *site* is a bit misleading since reef diving off the Yucatan Peninsula is always a drift dive because of the strong current; you drift with it instead of staying in the same place. (Also, the current does not stop at night. Just thought I'd clarify.)

With scuba diving, the buddy system is one of the fundamentals. You always stick with your dive buddy and watch out for one another. Rick and I buddied up, along with two other pairs of divers and our divemaster. As our forty-two-foot dive boat skipped along the shadowy surface on the southwest side of the island, we reviewed the dive plan, agreed on the hand signals we'd use to communicate with each other, and began putting on our gear.

"Okay, *señors,* masks and fins on!" That was our cue to finish gearing up so we would all be ready to drop in the water at the right moment in order to hit our desired entry point along the reef. Just a few minutes later, I was excitedly descending through wet

> We all know what it's like trying to do life in the dark.

darkness. The black water mirrored the moonless night, and I was instantly ushered into a dependence on artificial light in a way I've never before known. Simultaneously needing to keep a watchful eye on my dive buddy and our divemaster while avoiding the outcroppings of the reef and paying attention to the underwater animals, I instantly fell in love with my dive light.

I'll pause to acknowledge the non-wetsuit crowd's incredulity, "And why exactly are you doing this *at night*?" Simply put, the reef is an active thoroughfare of marine life during the day, but at night it erupts into a rush-hour-like display of even more creatures, their shyness diminished by the darkness. Within moments, our presence in the black water was rewarded with up-close sightings of a slipper lobster, large octopus, spotted eagle ray, huge grouper, banded sea snake, and a large moray. Hands down, it was the most fascinating dive I'd ever taken.

That is, for twenty-two minutes. (That earlier music—it crescendos here.)

With my depth gauge showing fifty-three feet below the surface, my dive light suddenly went dim and within a minute it was totally out. In the blink of an eye, my blink became permanent. Total darkness enveloped my vision and quickly began engulfing my nerves as well.

I'm not sure if you've noticed, but most wetsuits are black. Not sure what people were thinking when they made that design decision, but one significant result is that it camouflages you completely from your dive buddy in the dark. To this day Rick talks of never forgetting the moment when Matt totally disappeared into thin water. How would he explain that to my wife and sons?

I felt my way through the swift current and dark water, swimming up to my stunned friend to confirm my continued existence. I think he was relieved, but his eyes didn't show it. I conveyed to him what had happened and then propelled my invisible self with my invisible fins over to our divemaster for his extra light. My surprise for him was the shock of a sudden arm tap out of the dark. His surprise for me, after I pantomimed my problem, was a shrug of his shoulders, which turned out to be sign language for "I have no extra light, and you're on your own. Have a nice dive." Don't ask me why I thought the dive shop guy, having also assured me that the batteries were fresh, would have been trustworthy about the divemaster's possession of an extra light. I guess an underwater panic in the dark muddles one's judgment.

I returned to my dive buddy, once again emerging from the darkness, and signaled to Rick's saucer-sized eyes that it was just him and me with one light between us and that we were about to be closer friends than ever. It was then a matter of drifting with the current and just sticking together. I stayed as close as the current allowed and was totally dependent on the direction of my friend's beam of light. I kept an eye out for his light, the coral, his light, more creatures, and, yes, his light. It is a relative term in those conditions, but considering the dilemma we were in, I guess "fine" was as good a word as any to describe things.

At least for a few minutes.

(Is there any soundtrack music left?)

I drifted a few feet ahead and below Rick, still following his light beam coming from behind me and over my shoulder. As I was turning with the movement of his light, abruptly illuminated in front of me, about seven feet away, were the black eyes and large snout of a nine-foot shark. It was staring right at me. (Forget music—it's time for a cymbal crash.)

I think I inhaled half of my remaining tank of air, which thankfully gave me the buoyancy to rise above the shark. It turned out to be a nurse shark—a species relatively harmless to humans—but when it's bigger than you and in your face in the dark, adjectives aren't that comforting. As I hovered a few feet above the shark, the other divers all gathered around it while I again disappeared into the blackness.

Hoping to avoid unseen coral and any more sharks in the dark, I focused on remaining calm and was only partially successful. Without a light, I used my patented "swim-up" approach—actually an ill-advised method by which I'd swim up to each flashlight-bearing member of my dive group to search for my dive buddy. Of course, for each them, the experience of being accosted by a big, dark approaching hulk was fairly unnerving. But I finally figured out which of them was my friend and reunited with him yet once more. He and I then voted, and it was a unanimous decision: it was time to surface and deal with the dark—and a flashlight refund—from *above* the surface.

I now understand the unsettling disorientation of darkness in a way I never had before. Light is something I've taken for granted. I now appreciate it differently and more deeply.

The first thing I did when I returned home was buy a killer dive light of my very own. Experienced divers have already been screaming that solution at these pages.

Why head into unsettling darkness without a credible source of illumination?!
Great question.

❧ ❧ ❧

You may not have tried doing a dive in disorienting darkness (which shows your astuteness), but we all know what it's like trying to do life in the dark.

Desperately needing wisdom, perspective, and light to be able to walk the privileged path of being human, you and I are also navigating our way through unforeseen obstacles that seem to crop up on a daily basis. Robert Frost's words ring true for us all: "I have been one acquainted with the night."[1]

The Italian poet Dante Alighieri penned his classic, *Comedia,* in the fourteenth century. Two hundred years later, the adjective "divine" was added to it, and his *Divine Comedy* has become known as a preeminent piece of Italian literature. In his poem, Dante places himself as the central figure, a thirty-five-year-old man in the year 1300. He's reflecting on his life and the afterlife, engaging with the nuances of what it means to be human and who God is in our lives and stories. He begins his massive work of literature with these words: "In the middle of the road of my life, I awoke in a dark wood where the true way was wholly lost."[2]

The honest among us know what that is like, whether it be for a moment's decision or a dilemma we're facing over a season. It's as if we are doing our lives in the dark. Missing the big picture. Not fully understanding what it means to be human. Missing the path of Life and the taste of hope. There are plenty of times we find ourselves groping in the darkness. Wanting to have our path illuminated, we shout into the shadows, "Would someone please show me the way?!"

Enter Jesus.

Along with an enlightening promise. "When Jesus spoke again to the people, he said, 'I am the light of the world. Whoever follows me will never walk in darkness, but will have the light of life'" (John 8:12). He is referring to the "great light" promised in Isaiah's prophecy seven centuries before, the great light that would be the source of Life illumination for people who were living in "the land of the shadow of death" and stumbling around in the darkness of their days (Isaiah 9:2; Matthew 4:16).

～ ～ ～

The Spanish phrase meaning "to give birth" is *dar a luz*. Literally, that phrase means "to give to the light." To come alive is to come into the light. Redeemed human beings don't have to walk around in the dark. To come into Christ's Life is to come into his light.

When I am freed from my spiritual prison cell, I am ushered from death into Life but also from darkness into light. Illumination for Life is now available to me. That's why David exclaimed, "For you have delivered me from death and my feet from stumbling, that I may walk before God in the light of life" (Psalm 56:13). God's light serves as both my summons and my enablement to come into the Life he alone can provide. Enjoying his light on a daily basis is a significant part of being fully human. It also enables me to realize life while I'm living it.

But what does God's light look like?

Ultimately, it looks like Jesus. We've already heard his credible claim to be the light of the world. That's why John begins his gospel with this statement about Jesus: "In him was life, and that life was the light of men" (John 1:4). In that same paragraph, John also describes Jesus as "the Word" (1:1, 14). In Greek, the term John uses is *logos*. It was an ancient concept, already in use for centuries, referring to that mysterious influence that creates as well as describes all that exists. In an astounding revelation, John is saying Jesus Christ is the Logos, the living Word of God. To relate with him is to relate with the One who created me and, as my author, can shed light on me—the me that I currently am as well as the best version of me that's possible as I walk with him.

But in addition to relating with Jesus, how else do I get God's illumination? Jesus not only referred to himself as the truth about the way that leads to Life (John 14:6), but he also referred to the Word as truth (17:17). And he taught that "whoever lives by the truth comes into the light" (3:21). That insight is echoed in the psalmist's words when he explains how he finds illumination for his path: "Your word is a lamp to my feet and a light for my path" (Psalm 119:105). I receive the light of God through the living Word—Jesus—but also through the God-breathed written Word—the Scriptures.

For many of us who might think the Bible is just an ancient religious manual, a doctrinal handbook, a devotional prop, or just a platform for judging others, viewing it as our source of illumination for really living can be a game changer. Light for our Life is the truth of God's Word—reading it, studying it, listening to it, meditating on it, memorizing it, applying it, living by it.

Bottom line, relating with Jesus through the Scriptures is my dive light in the dark.

❧ ❧ ❧

So if it's such a great source of light, what makes us hesitate to turn off the dark by getting into God's Word? Why, instead of switching on the light, do we just focus our efforts on adjusting our eyesight to the dark? In the words of Emily Dickinson,

We grow accustomed to the Dark—
When Light is put away....

A Moment—We uncertain step
For newness of the night—
Then—fit our Vision to the Dark—
And meet the Road—erect—[3]

That is my tendency more often than I would like to admit: to stiffen with determination and simply try to keep stumbling and bumbling ahead in the dark, existing but not living. Missing too much of the Life that is everywhere.

Referring to my diving debacle in the dark, an appropriate question would certainly be why in the world would I do a night dive without a credible dive light? But when we find ourselves in the disconcerting dark on Dante's "road of my life," a much bigger and potentially life-altering question confronts us. Why don't we take—and use—the light God offers us?

~ ~ ~

One reason we avoid the light of God's Word is that we live in a culture suspicious of an ancient religious book that offers what it claims to be absolute truth. For many of us, this can embolden or at least reinforce a dismissal of the Bible entirely.

At best, our culture has a tendency to be skeptical and, at worst, to disdain the notion of absolute truth and meaning. A dominant tenor of our age proposes that, instead of needing to perceive God's objective reality about our life, we must create our own reality.

As a result, the light of the Bible and God's authority is passed over in favor of human reason. Specific, absolute truth is replaced by relativism and tolerance.

Yet Jesus himself flies in the face of that philosophy. He clearly teaches there is a specific (narrow) path to Life and that he can illuminate it: "Enter through the narrow gate. For wide is the gate and broad is the road that leads to destruction, and many enter through it. But small is the gate and narrow the road that leads to life, and only a few find it" (Matthew 7:13–14). If I'm going to throw out the notion of objective truth because it seems so narrow and noninclusive (a popular posture these days), then I must also discard the credibility of Jesus (a not-so-popular position).

But the absolute nature of God's light-giving truth doesn't mean it's a restrictive, suffocating blanket over my human journey. Jesus says the exact opposite, telling me that his teaching and truth, when I embrace it, sets me free.[4] By illuminating the way to humanity as it's meant to be experienced and life as it's meant to be lived, the light of his truth can lead me to a liberated life, not a stifled existence.

Richard John Neuhaus, in a lecture at the Veritas Forum at Yale University, addressed our culture's "loss of truth" in a speech titled "Is There Life After Truth?" He proposed we do not understand the deadly nature of this trend in our culture and that it "dances and makes jokes at the edge of the abyss." His answer to the question of his speech's title? "Yes, there is life after truth, but it's not a life that's really worthy of human beings."[5]

~ ~ ~

We also avoid the light of truth because of the misuse of God's Word that you and I may have been exposed to in our religious upbringing. In some religious traditions, the Bible is used for a lot of purposes, but Life is not one of them.

We might have learned to think of the Bible as a doctrinal position paper but not as the way to Life. It's an approach to Scripture that engages the mind but not the heart. That tactic isn't wrong, just incomplete, causing us to merely rely on the Bible for what to believe instead of also how to live.

Certainly what we believe is foundational, and we must intellectually grapple with truth from that standpoint, making great efforts to be theologically sound and substantive. But if we stop there, truth ceases to be a Life-giving light and becomes a mere collection of propositions and dogma (which is a word that doesn't even sound appealing). We end up looking to Scripture merely as a source of indoctrination regarding our belief instead of an illumination about our humanity.

The truth I embrace is not meant to just establish my doctrinal position but to illuminate and guide the way I go through my Mondays—whether they be filled with difficulty or delight. His Word is meant to shed light on a way of Life, not just a system of belief.

Others just use Scripture as a legalistic rulebook and religious lifestyle manual. Yesterday I received a familiar-sounding letter from someone who is learning for the first time to feast on God's Life-giving grace and truth. That's the good news. But for that to happen, she had to, in her words, "heal and break free from a shame-based, controlling, works-based religion." It was a religiosity that used Scripture as a source of life-stifling regulations instead of Life-giving illumination. In those environments, the Bible tragically becomes a weapon of shame and human judgment that some are weirdly drawn to and others are tragically wounded by. (In an emergency, it might be okay for a police officer to use a flashlight as a weapon, but not church people.)

That's the background of an admonishment Jesus delivered to a group of religious leaders who had taken Scripture study, which is a beautiful and necessary ingredient to Life, and turned it into a barren, religious routine: "You diligently study the Scriptures because you think that by them you possess eternal life. These are the Scriptures that testify about me, yet you refuse to come to me to have life" (John 5:39–40). They might have started on the right path, but their use of Scripture stopped short of God's intent. His truth is meant to provide illumination, yes, but in the context of a relationship with him. It's not a matter of just reading the Bible, getting some doctrinal insights or fortune-cookie clichés, and moving on, but instead I'm to actually relate with him through my time in the Word—letting him, the living Word, speak wisdom into my darkness through the written Word. It's a matter of learning to "walk in the light of your presence" (Psalm 89:15), not just have some Bible data to pull out in a pinch.

❧ ❧ ❧

It was Christmas Eve, and my brother and I were assembling his three-year-old daughter's tricycle. It had those dangerous words printed on the box: "Some Assembly Required." When we emptied the contents onto the floor, they were accompanied by an instruction manual that looked like it belonged to a Ford truck, not a toddler's trike. We looked at each other, rolled our eyes, and as many red-blooded American males would do, we tossed it in the trash. Surely enlightened guys like us didn't need instructions for a toy. We'd figure it out.

> What if I were to view the Bible that way, as a book that's not only about *Christianity* but about restored, redeemed, and thriving *humanity*?

We did indeed get it assembled on our own, except for the slight detail that one of the wheels wouldn't turn. So we took it apart and started over. This time, the wheels all worked, but it wouldn't steer to the left. After more of the same, we finally humbled ourselves, went to the trash, and brushed the coffee grounds off the instruction manual. It was remarkable how illuminating the manufacturer's instructions were. Maybe we weren't as enlightened as we thought.

At the root of my refusal to benefit from the light of his Word is sheer pride. Letting God illuminate my path requires humility, an admission that he knows—better than I—what will fulfill me and lead to Life. It will involve a submission to his way over my way.

It's one thing to be prideful in the presence of a toymaker's instructions and stubbornly say I don't need the manufacturer's insight and can figure it out on my own. The consequences become infinitely more significant when I become prideful in the face of the illuminating instructions of my wise and loving Creator—the One who knows what's best for me and what's necessary for me to really Live. Without humbling myself before his leadership, the prognosis isn't good. "There is a way that seems right to a man, but in the end it leads to death" (Proverbs 16:25).

Humility is birthed by being honest about my need. When I was in the darkness of the ocean without a dive light, it never occurred to me to refuse the guidance of my friend's light—I was all too aware of my desperation. I'm learning that when I'm honest about my inability to pierce the darkness, it paves the way for humble receptivity to light. But if I think I can figure out a way on my own, it merely sets me up for further stumbling or worse.

I once heard someone pointedly observe, "It's easy to forgive a child who is afraid of the dark, but the real tragedy of life is when grown-ups are afraid of the light." In the face of truth's light, it's either prideful fear or submissive humility—those are my options. The pride pushes me further into the dark, but a response of humility is the key that unlocks the light.

A lack of humility is also present when I just politely or religiously read the Bible with no intention of obeying and following his insight. That's why Danish philosopher Søren Kierkegaard made the distinction between merely admiring the truth and following it, saying Christ "never asks for admirers" but that he "calls disciples" and "consistently used the expression 'follower.'"[6] To just be a polite admirer only thickens the crust of religiosity over my heart while I remain as befuddled as ever by the dark.

~ ~ ~

My friend Joy is an emergency room physician and also a budding private pilot. One afternoon, a few weeks after she got her pilot's license, she decided to take a small plane for a late afternoon solo flight from Kansas City to a small town in western Missouri. She took off, flew east, and arrived at the rural airport just fine. With sunset approaching, she headed back for an ER shift at the hospital that was starting later that evening.

Nearing the end of her return flight, her GPS indicated she was approaching the airport in Kansas City, so she looked down to get a visual. The sky's horizon had bid the sun good-bye, and in the darkness of the ground below, she couldn't make out the runway or even the airport. She thought her GPS was malfunctioning and began trying to make out any landmarks, but everything was shrouded by dusk. She remembered the highest structures in the area were below a thousand feet, so she made sure she stayed above that altitude while she figured things out.

Confusion quickly turned into panic. She could have called air traffic control or the downtown tower for help, but she did neither. Instead, this ER physician who was accustomed to pressure surprised herself by beginning to cry.

When she reached up to wipe the tears, she discovered the solution to her crisis. She was still wearing the sunglasses she'd donned as she had flown into the setting sun. She sighed and took them off, and everything came back into sight: airport, runway, and home.

Removing our sunglasses of pride, religiosity, or skepticism—all of which dim the Christ light that's already there—is a frightening prospect for many of us. But considering the alternative of trying to find the fulfillment of my humanity in the dark and attempting to land my heart's pursuit on a runway that isn't there, it's a step I need to take.

～ ～ ～

So if I'm to embrace the light of Scripture, what does his light illuminate? It gives me instruction on how to be human. A compartmentalized view in which I confine the Bible to just a religious manual will make it unappealing and, for most of us, unread. Scripture is not primarily about how to live a *Christian* life but how to experience a *human* life as it's meant to be lived in the presence of the God who made me and redeems me. It's not about how to be religious but how God enables me to be restored to Life as a rescued human being. It's how David found such great joy. God had made known to him the "path of life" (Psalm 16:11).

When the Bible moves from being a book on the shelf or the nightstand and becomes something I actually read and apply, I begin to realize it includes illumination for how a human being who has come alive can work, love, rest, recreate, and relate with God. It brings light into arenas as diverse as finances, physical health, fear, sex, courage, beauty, time, temptations, joy, contentment, justice, trials, relationships, calling, and priorities. And the list keeps going.

In the process, Scripture sheds light on the path of obedience I need to follow in order to taste Life. While certainly involving a pursuit of right and an avoidance of wrong, that path of Life is still very different from a constrictive route of religiosity that involves meaningless rules. Instead, obedience becomes the way to live as a fulfilled human being who is glorifying and enjoying God. I learn to embrace his instruction and parameters not as ways to demonstrate my religiosity, but as the path to fulfilling my heart's longings as a human being. I realize his guidance of me is rooted in the same types of reasons I would tell my sons to do fun stuff as well as eat their broccoli and not play football in the street. It was all to ultimately protect as well as enhance their enjoyment of being a kid, not stifle it.

> To have a light that understands me is one of the great privileges of Life with a capital L.

What if I were to view the Bible that way, as a book that's not only about *Christianity* but about restored, redeemed, and thriving *humanity*? Guaranteed, I'll read it differently. And in the process, I'll gain much-needed perspective about being human, not just about being religious.

❧ ❧ ❧

The Bible also gives me insight into the big picture of my journey as a human being, involving matters of meaning, purpose, and destiny. Darkness is frustrating because it shrinks our vision and we all like—and need—to be aware of the bigger landscape.

Climbing a fourteen-thousand-foot peak in Colorado requires that you start in the dark so you can summit before dangerous lightning and bad weather rolls in. If I'm hiking in unfamiliar terrain in the dark, to have a context—an understanding of where I am in the big picture—I'll need either a good flashlight or an accurate topographical map. Preferably both. If I don't, I'll slow down to a crawl that's anything but enjoyable.

To be able to walk and live with freedom, I need the light of God's context for me. I won't do well if I don't have some type of understanding of where I am and my purpose (more on that in the next chapter). Bewilderment regarding the big picture and the right path to take is debilitating to Life with a capital L.

Legendary American frontiersman Daniel Boone, when asked if he had ever been lost, is said to have replied, "Nope, but a few times I've been a bit bewildered."

I was once on a day hike in a dense rainforest, and my companions and I got a bit bewildered. We even had a local guide with us (when your guide gets disoriented, you know you're in trouble). After a couple of hours of increasing confusion and finally admitting we were lost in the hilly terrain, I climbed to the top of the tallest tree I could find. I didn't do it to get a great view of the scenery but to gain perspective, to gain a sense of context for where we were and the direction we needed to head to get out of there.

A regular intake of Scripture gives me a boost to the top of the trees where I can gain a renewed perspective of life's landscape. As Fyodor Dostoyevsky observed, "We have never truly breathed air nor seen light until we have breathed in the God-inspired Bible and see the world in the Bible's light."

This doesn't mean I'll gain all the answers. To understand the topography of an area doesn't mean I can explain every boulder in my path. The Bible indeed gives credible, specific answers to the great questions of our existence. But there are plenty of smaller questions, albeit important in our individual journeys, which are left unanswered and with which we learn to trust God (yes, easier said than done much of the time).

For example, does the Bible explain why sickness exists? Yes (the Fall, for starters). Does it explain why I get sick with a particular disease at a particular time? No. But it does credibly assure me of his companionship and sufficient strength in the midst of the sickness. It also takes me back to the larger story of his promise to ultimately repair a creation that's groaning under the weight of its rebellion.

Illumination does not eliminate mystery in my story. The power of the Bible is that it leads me not to all the answers but into relationship with the resurrected Christ who promises to walk with me in whatever difficult and dark terrain I might encounter.

❧ ❧ ❧

One of the most powerful aspects of illumination that truth brings into my life is intimacy. Truth shines its light on me and into me, illuminating the brokenness that's present, as well as the beauty of what can be.

And that can be intimidating. As Anne Lamott observes, "Light reveals us to ourselves, which is not always so great if you find yourself in a big disgusting mess, possibly of your own creation."[7]

But thankfully, along with God's truth comes his grace, and it's important to embrace both. If I take the truth about me while shunning grace, I'll plummet because of the hopeless lack of resolution of what's exposed, which is why many of us avoid the light in the first place. If I take grace without truth, I'll end up with a superficial, feel-good imposter of grace while living in a whitewashed house of self-delusion. But when I humble myself in the presence of both God's grace and truth, his merciful posture toward me through Christ is illuminated, as well as my mess, and I receive his conviction and correction as well as his compassion. Then some of the biggest arenas of darkness in my life—my failures, sins, and regrets—are illumined not with shame but with the light of his forgiveness and instruction, and the once-dark path ahead becomes ablaze with hope.

In his book titled *Journey into Light,* twentieth-century Princeton philosopher Emile Cailliet tells a story of illumination. Growing up as an atheist in France, he had never even seen a Bible until he was twenty-three years old, when his wife brought one home. He took it and began to read. Deep into the night he delved into the Gospels. He explains the impact it had: "And suddenly the realization dawned upon me: this was the Book that would understand me."[8]

To have a light that understands me, illuminates the bigger picture of my journey, and guides me regarding how to be a fulfilled human being is one of the great privileges of Life with a capital L.

～ ～ ～

My first major research paper assignment came during my sophomore year in high school and the assigned topic was photosynthesis. The only thing that exceeded the stress of the first major deadline of my education (I still remember the December 17 due date) was the impression the research made on me. It's something that people have known through both science and gut instinct for millenniums: light is necessary for life.

It's also necessary for Life.

Therefore I need to dig into the Scriptures not only more often but differently. Every time I open a Bible, it's an opportunity to shine a flashlight on my story. It's an opportunity to receive understanding to address my confusion, and courage to face the fear that comes from being disoriented as a human being. It's an opportunity to turn off the dark by using it as a light for my life instead of just a religious reference book.

We've already taken a dive in the dark, so the most Life-giving decision we can now make is to go ahead and grab a light.

~ ~ ~

This summer I returned to Cozumel and did another night dive—this time with my three sons. It was in the same area of water as my previous night dive and, yes, just as dark. But this time we had a blast because the stress factor was greatly reduced. Perhaps a reason for that was, in addition to the colored strobe lights I attached to their tanks, each of them had his own light with brand-new batteries. And a backup light. And a small backup for the backup. And I had an extra.

Their eyes rolled and mouths grinned, but my heart rested.

And we all could see in the dark.

Story

Your Life Is Bigger Than You

"Seem like we're just set down here," a woman said
to me recently, "and don't nobody know why."
—ANNIE DILLARD

The ale was the same one they had always ordered before, but now it somehow
tasted different. But not because *it* was different. *They* were. What had changed
them was what they had learned—and experienced—since the last time they had
raised their foaming mugs in this place.

The tavern, the Green Dragon, was in Bywater, near Hobbiton. It was a fondly
familiar place to Frodo, Sam, Merry, and Pippin—four unassuming hobbits, main
characters in J. R. R. Tolkien's classic Lord of the Rings trilogy, and brilliantly depicted by filmmaker Peter Jackson in his epic three films.

Unbeknown to the other pub patrons around them, the four of them had been
centrally involved in the battle for the future of Middle-earth. And now here they
sat, having just returned from their yearlong adventure, sharing a pint.

As they gathered together around the table, the four companions looked the
same to all of their old friends. But they themselves knew they were far from being
the same hobbits as before. Yes, they were sitting in the same seats they had occupied
on many an evening before they left. Their friends were the same as before. The
jokes and stories being tossed about the room were familiar, as was the music and
food.

But they were drastically different because their perspective of life had been enlarged. Their eyes had been opened, their hearts had been impacted, and their lives had been transformed by what they now knew as the greater reality regarding the world they lived in. And their role within that reality.

A year before, they had departed Hobbiton as self-absorbed young hobbits looking for adventure—as long as it was fun and beneficial for them and not too demanding.

But in the months since, they had been entrusted with responsibilities they had never before considered, much less dreamed they would be capable of handling. They had witnessed unimaginable beauty and unspeakable pain. Each of them had demonstrated courage and strength they hadn't known they possessed. They had developed an ability to discern the powers—seen and unseen—around them, learned to relish that which was good and not back away from evil. They had pressed on through fear, tragedy, conflict, overwhelming opposition, and seemingly certain defeat. They had learned to go without comforts they previously had thought essential. They had willingly risked their lives and learned to savor every breath of each day for what it offered. Fortitude and perseverance had become habit to them, and they had prevailed victorious.

Ultimately, these four hobbits had been lauded as heroes by the world's great leaders—men, dwarfs, and elves alike.

What brought about their transformation?

In a nutshell, it was the larger story. More specifically, they were now aware of it.

A bigger story that was more beautiful and more dangerous than anything they had considered before leaving their familiar surroundings a year ago.

It was a story they now not only understood, but a story in which they now knew they had a part to play. A role that also was more significant than anything they could have imagined a year earlier.

So here they found themselves, aware they weren't just sitting in the midst of a tavern full of friends and acquaintances but also sitting in the midst of the great story.

Embracing that story had changed the way they viewed each other. It had changed the way they approached difficulty—lessening their frustration about some struggles and heightening their resolve with others. It had layered their lives with purpose and heightened their sense of significance. It had even deepened their laughter.

This time around, they were savoring and enjoying the familiar ale more than they had before, and, yes, more than the hobbits around them who were still unaware.

❧ ❧ ❧

Let's move from Middle-earth to the real earth—your world and mine. How *aware* are we? When we sit in our taverns or our offices or our kitchens or our churches, when we walk through our day's routines, is there a bigger story gripping and guiding us? Without a bigger context, the monotonous heart-numbing pace of just getting through our day, our month, our lifetime is killing us before we even make it to the grave.

"Getting tired of living till I die" is the way an indie-rock band from Cleveland called Cloud Nothings describes it. In their strikingly honest "Wasted Days," they articulate a drudgery-induced despair that's deep within many of us, resulting in the haunting realization: "I thought I would be more than this."[1]

Three years before his tragic suicide, novelist David Foster Wallace delivered a candid commencement address at Kenyon College in Gambier, Ohio. "The plain fact is that you graduating seniors do not yet have any clue what 'day in, day out' really means. There happen to be whole large parts of adult American life that nobody talks about in commencement speeches. One such part involves boredom, routine, and petty frustration."[2] To combat that, he explained, will require intentionality about the choices we make.

> It's when I lose my life in his bigger story that I find my life.

After Wallace's suicide, in an online forum regarding that commencement address, one commenter reflected, "I really like this speech and I've honestly tried to put its moral into practice, but for me life is still boring, still banal, still repetitive. I'm not even a very negative person, and I probably lead what many would consider a fairly exciting life, but the fact is I'm not happy and I'm not sure that I ever will be.… I'm probably not going to kill myself or anything, but I wouldn't mind peacefully passing away in my sleep tonight."[3]

His words are as disturbingly insightful as they are brutally honest.

Where does our boredom and unhappiness come from? It's certainly not from a lack of things to do. It's ironic, whether in work or play, we've never been so busy—or so empty. No matter how fast we pedal, we never get anywhere. No matter how frantically we pursue pleasure and purpose, we still aren't fulfilled. Meaninglessness has become an epidemic in our culture and a soul sickness in ourselves.

Why?

In the movie *Hugo,* director Martin Scorsese tells the story of a twelve-year-old orphan who lives in the walls of a Paris train station in the 1930s. Gifted at fixing things, he's fascinated by the way machines work and the purpose behind them. In a powerful scene, he reflects aloud with his friend Isabelle, "Everything has a purpose, even machines. Clocks tell the time, trains take you places. They do what they're meant to do.... Maybe that's why broken machines make me so sad, they can't do what they're meant to do. Maybe it's the same with people. If you lose your purpose, it's like you're broken."[4]

When we are disconnected from what we're meant to do, it's like we're broken—we run and run without getting anywhere. When we have no idea about the role we are called to play in life, we miss out on our greater significance in the world and the experience of being fully human.

Without that overarching sense of purpose, we're unable to fully realize life while we're living it.

~ ~ ~

The purpose of anything comes from its maker. What is a person's reason for being? The answer to that question isn't determined by what's been created but by its Creator.

Over the course of my life, there have been precarious moments when I've veered down the futile path of trying to deal with my purpose as if I were self-created. I start to devise my own direction for my life. I begin to forge my own selfish goals.

Thankfully, the illumination of God's Word draws me back.

When my alarm clock buzzes on a Monday morning, the first five words of the Bible carry an enormous amount of significance: "In the beginning God created..." If God created me, then he has a purpose for me.

Now, if God didn't create us, if we just accidentally happened in a cosmic petri dish, then we have no overarching purpose, just our own individual goals that we set for ourselves. It was atheist philosopher Albert Camus who proposed that, since we are in a meaningless universe, people must repeatedly attempt to devise purposes for themselves. But, he observed, such purposes are found to be superficial and disappointing, so people start over and try again with something else. In his view, life was an endless cycle of trying to create purpose and being disappointed by its emptiness. But since the only other option was suicide, Camus was okay with the futility, asserting that at least the struggle itself would occupy us.

That sense of futility is dismantled if I accept that I'm not a cosmic accident, understanding I am created by God.

As an intentionally created human being, I don't have to come up with a purpose for myself. I instead need to discover the purpose God has for me. As God's creation, I don't have to contrive my own self-worth; I just need to see that the gifts, personality, experiences, abilities, and journey I've been given are all part of a story unique to me. And as a child of the Creator, I don't have to fabricate a purpose for my life in the universe; I just need to discover the role God has intended for me since the day I was born.

To experience my full humanity is to embrace that I'm fully purposed. And so, for the sake of my own humanity, it becomes imperative that I become a student of my own story.

Nineteenth-century poet Walt Whitman proposed that the key to life's meaning is discovering your identity in that larger drama. "The powerful play goes on, and you may contribute a verse."[5] We are drawn to that. Something within us resonates with the notion of contributing a verse to a larger story.

Why?

Because finding the place where our pages fit into a bigger narrative is crucial if we are to grasp our meaning, pursue some sort of purpose, and in the process, make sense out of our Mondays.

So the question "What will my verse be?" is absolutely vital.

However, that's actually the second question.

First, a deeper question must be addressed.

"What is the play?"

〜 〜 〜

We each have something deep within that seems to indicate there's a play—a larger story—in the works, but we can't quite put our finger on what it is. We get the sense that our lives are part of a progression of events, but toward what?

Singer and songwriter Sting, in his song "The Book of My Life," proposes that his life is indeed a story. But, he muses, there is still a lingering question: "Though the pages are numbered, I can't see where they lead."[6]

That play, that progression of events, that tale we've fallen into is at the heart of the gospel. It is the plot of the Bible. It is the larger story.

For me to be able to make sense of *my* story, I've got to understand how it fits into *the* story. Understanding what the larger story is all about is anything but a matter of mere curiosity.

So what is it?

I'm about to make a statement that may intrigue you, drawing you in, or it could well tempt you to dismiss what you suspect is just another rendition of a religious cliché. Please don't take that second option. The stakes are too high. Hanging in the balance is your fulfillment as a human being and your experience of Life with a capital L.

So here we go.

The larger story is the glory of God.

The risk for many is that the phrase *the glory of God* can make our eyes glaze over. Many of us have heard it countless times before, and it's always seemed too general, too immense, too ambiguous to really make much practical sense to us. Many of us just file it away in our church jargon file folder.

But let's give it another chance. Read it again. *The larger story is the glory of God.*

It's a simple statement, but not at all simplistic. The size and drama of the statement isn't something I've contrived—God's glory is referred to almost three hundred times in the Bible. It's core to Scripture's message for us, and it is anything but ancillary or insignificant to the story of our lives. Bottom line, I can't dismiss it and still hope to understand my role in God's story and unpack and pursue the purpose of my life. Nevertheless, a lot of us—indeed, much of civilization throughout time—have tragically ignored, neglected, and omitted the glory of God from consideration. And from life.

When the movie *The Sound of Music* was released in South Korea back in the 1960s, it was enormously popular, so much so that some theaters were showing it four or five times a day. One ambitious theater owner wanted to squeeze in even more showings. The only way to do that in the one-screen cinemas of the day was to shorten the film, which he did. The problem was he chose to edit out many of the *songs*. I guess the irony—cutting the music from a movie that was actually about the sound of music—was lost on him. But the response from the rest of us is obvious: why would you edit out something so central to the movie's identity and purpose?[7]

I do something eerily similar when it comes to the larger story on this planet as well as my individual story: I edit out the glory of God. In the process, I leave myself defenseless in the substantive battle with boredom, meaninglessness, and insignificance. And miss out on Life with a capital L.

～ ～ ～

At dinner a while back, I asked my friends Matt and Jess about a movie they'd seen. They get into movies, and I always enjoy hearing their take. Matt said the movie explored the "current complexity of relationships" in our culture. He added that it addressed the aimlessness of his generation and that it made some pointed observations about the wisdom of age and experience.

I turned to Jess, and she focused on the maze-like journey the characters went through and the events they experienced, basically summarizing the plot.

I was intrigued by how two people could talk about the same movie so differently. Yet both of them were accurate in their descriptions. Basically, Matt described the movie's ideas, its *propositions,* and Jess conveyed to me the movie's relationships and *plot.* Actually, the dual review was pretty effective—I received a fuller sense of the movie by hearing both of them from their different perspectives.

When it comes to the larger story of the glory of God, I started realizing it's critical to understand it in terms of *proposition* and *plot* as well. It's not either/or, but both/and. For example, how about that first phrase of the Bible: "In the beginning God created..."

Is that a statement about proposition or plot?

Yes. (The proposition of God creating the world is also the beginning of an incredible, plot-filled story.)

The gospel is anchored in propositional truth, but that truth comes clothed in a plot that exhibits the value and relevance of those propositions. If we don't get the gospel as plot as well as proposition, we're not getting the gospel. We don't gain purpose from propositions only; we need to know the plot as well. And nowhere do the plot and story of the gospel come through as beautifully as when grappling with the glory of God.

I first must wrestle with the propositional part. As I begin to reflect on the story of God's glory of which we, as human beings, are a part, I need to have some grasp of what "glory," in general, and "God's glory," in particular, mean.

When you and I speak of a person's glory, we're referring to what's notable about them in terms of their uniqueness, appearance, or capability. It's something that can be admired by others.

Likewise, when Scripture speaks of God's glory, it's referring to what's notable about him.

But different from a human being's glory, I need to understand that God's glory is not just a few laudable characteristics. *Everything* about who he is and what he does is praiseworthy. God's glory is his *essence*. His glory pertains to all of him in his infinite worth. The Hebrew word translated as "glory" literally means "weight" or "heaviness." God's glory is his weightiness. His glory is referring to the heavy substance of his ultimate *significance*—he is other and above all else. It also refers to his *self-existence*—he is dependent on nothing else. And it refers to his *sufficiency*—he is enough for everything creation needs to exist and thrive, including us.

So the glory of God is referring to his weighty importance and, if I can make up a word, his "enoughness" for all of creation.

I also must realize God is all about his own glory. That's not a matter of a needy ego, because he doesn't have one. Because he is God, his motivation is always the highest and purest possible. So to be motivated by anything less than his own glory would be a flawed motivation, and he has no flaws.

So if I do the *propositional* movie review, I would say something like this: God created you and me. Why? I can be sure it is for his glory, to be a part of the story of his glory. He made us so that our individual stories would revolve around the fulfillment of relishing and reflecting the weightiness of his supreme importance and enoughness in all that we do. Life with a capital L is about embracing and enjoying God's glory, acknowledging his importance, and experiencing his enoughness.

The proposition of God's glory is vital, certainly, but the fuller picture becomes more clear and understandable when I place those propositions within the plot.

So, for the *plot* of God's glory, like Jess's review of the movie for me, I'll tell you a story. Correction, I'll share *the* story. While hearing it—especially if you're familiar with the story—it's important to pay attention to his glory and how central it is to the story. If I don't see the glory in it, I don't really know the story.

❧ ❧ ❧

Once upon a time—actually, at the start of time—God created a world. The birth and rhythm of his creation was to be a story of his glory.

Supreme in this tapestry of a tale that God was writing in creation was his formation of human beings, whom he made in his image as male and female. He breathed life into their lungs and Life into their hearts. He loved them deeply and freed them to flourish on the earth in flawless relationship with him and one another.

Fully enjoying God, his creation, and the gift of existence, man and woman were blessed with the whole taste of the Creator's glory. Their enjoyment of God's significance was constant, and their experience of his loving enoughness was undiluted. They were given total access to the tree of life and every longing was fulfilled. With hearts that were fully awake, they loved him back and glorified him in all they did. Walking a path that was fully illumined by God, work was a pleasure, play was a delight, and relating with him was authentic and Life giving.

In this new world, nothing—no behavior, attitude, or object—failed to reflect God's glory. His glory perfectly overlaid all that existed on the planet. Everything glorified him. It was indeed Beautiful with a capital B.

Then paradise was lost.

The cause was a combination of both volition and villain.

Volition—choice, decision making—is always part of a great story. It's also an essential ingredient of an intimate, fulfilling relationship. Intimacy, by necessity, involves a choice, and nowhere is that more true than in a human being's relationship with God. He loves them zealously, but always standing in the balance is their response, their decision of whether they'll reciprocate his love. The experience of intimacy with him requires a human's continual decision to love God back.

Villains are also a part of all great stories, because they reflect this, the ultimate story. It is here that the original and ultimate villain enters the drama. Call him Lucifer, Satan, or the devil, he is the enemy of God and, above all, despises the glory of God. In creation's infancy, he saw the vulnerability in the volition of these naive human beings. With slithering stealth, he attacked with precision. At the core of his lie was "you do not need God's glory to Live."

Temptation was born, a deadly choice was made, rebellion was birthed, and sin entered the story.

The seamless canopy of God's glory over all his creation now had a tragic, gaping hole in it. The Creator's enoughness had been defied by his creatures, and for the first time, something now existed on this planet that did not glorify him.

Humans had been warned that death would come if they rebelled.[8] The reason was not as a vindictive punishment because they hadn't done as he instructed them, but essentially because they could not thrive in a mode contrary to the way they were designed. They could not Live without God. But they chose to believe a lie:

That they could indeed find better fulfillment on their own.

That they didn't need God to be fully human.

That their individual stories could flourish without God's glory.

So they stepped off the path. It was the path God had lovingly prescribed for the health of their humanity and the significance of their stories. As they strayed, their hearts continued to beat and their lungs continued to breathe, but they died inside. Discarding his glory, they had left the path of Life. "Although they claimed to be wise, they became fools and exchanged the glory of the immortal God for images made to look like mortal man and birds and animals and reptiles" (Romans 1:22–23)— things they deemed to be more significant and capable for their fulfillment than God. They thought they could turn to other pursuits to satisfy, assuming they could have the same satisfaction they had previously enjoyed from God's glory, but now with autonomy from his authority.

> The larger story is the glory of God.

Yet God is clear about his unique ability of displaying and conveying his Life-giving glory: "I will not give my glory to another or my praise to idols" (Isaiah 42:8).

Nothing can fulfill a human being like the glory of God.

Because of their rebellion, they could no longer have perfect access to the taste of God's glory. In fact, the epitome of sin's impact on them was falling into an existence that was "short of the glory of God" (Romans 3:23). They were still *imago Dei*, in the image of God, but they were now blemished and his image was marred. Remnants of the paradise they had lost were still with them—gifts like laughter and love and beauty—but now, as part of their existence, there was also a hollowness that their rebellion had escorted into their lives. The story of God's glory was still being written, but they were now blind to the plot. Using pens filled with the futile ink of self-absorption, they began to write themselves out of the great story.

Creation also was impacted. It, too, had now fallen from perfection and would groan because of the humans' fall from glory.[9] The perfect overlay of God's glory with all that existed on the planet was gone. His glory still permeated the atmosphere of his creation, but it was no longer undiluted. Beauty remained, but pollution had come. There were now portions of creation as well as people that did not glorify God. From devastating diseases to debilitating shame, from random accidents to calculated selfishness, from disappointing physical decay to destructive emotional anger, from deadly tsunamis in the oceans to hurricanes in the hearts of people—the fall from glory would show itself.

However, instead of destroying his now less-than-perfect creation and starting over, God purposed to glorify himself even through this tragedy. He promised then and there that his love would prevail and he would complete his story. He would re-create. He would redeem humans and restore creation. He would triumph, showing himself to be supremely and gloriously enough even in the face of this rebellious rupture of his handiwork.

In days to come, God prophesied the return of his undiluted glory to his creation, saying, "Though it linger, wait for it; it will certainly come" (Habakkuk 2:3). What would come? "For the earth will be filled with the knowledge of the glory of the LORD, as the waters cover the sea" (verse 14). It's a fantastically descriptive and hopeful metaphor: "waters cover the sea" with absolute totality. Before the Fall, the earth had been totally filled with God's glory. He was promising that, one day, it would again be so.

With the renovation underway, promises from God about his plan continued to come. Resolute assurances that he would restore humanity's access to his glory. "I will say to the north, 'Give them up!' and to the south, 'Do not hold them back.' Bring my sons from afar and my daughters from the ends of the earth—everyone who is called by my name, whom I created for my glory, whom I formed and made" (Isaiah 43:6–7). Unwavering in his intent to graciously reclaim and restore human beings to the purpose for which he had created them, he prophesied the return of his glory. "Arise, shine, for your light has come, and the glory of the LORD has risen upon you. For behold, darkness shall cover the earth, and thick darkness the peoples; but the LORD will arise upon you, and his glory will be seen upon you" (60:1–2, ESV). The glory of the Lord would be revealed, and all the people would see it together.[10]

How would the restoration of glory come?

In addition to writing the story's pages, the Writer would now inhabit them. To accomplish his restoration, the Author personally entered the story. God the Son—"the radiance of God's glory and the exact representation of his being" (Hebrews 1:3)—clothed himself in our humanity. For the first time since before the Fall, a human fully reflected the glory of God in all he said and did. "The Word became flesh and made his dwelling among us. We have seen his glory, the glory of the One and Only, who came from the Father, full of grace and truth" (John 1:14). It was a sight to behold and a hope to embrace.

Christ's agenda? Ultimately, it was described as one of "bringing many sons to glory" (Hebrews 2:10). He came to restore human beings to the opportunity of having their stories enveloped by the great story of God's glory. So great was his love, to accomplish this he would give himself up to be crucified as their infinite substitute. The promise of renovation made in the garden would be fulfilled, and the lingering penalty of that offense would be paid.

The night before the cross was raised as an exclamation point in the story of God's glory, the Son conversed with the Father and reflected on the completion of his mission. How would he summarize it? In addition to giving eternal life and God's Word, he confirmed the restoration of glory to human beings who become his people. "I have given them the glory that you gave me" (John 17:22).

In three days, that mission's success would be publicly and historically validated by an empty tomb.

But the end of the story, while assured, hasn't yet arrived.

Yes, the glory of the Lord has already come, but it is not yet fully covering the earth as the waters cover the sea. But the tide is rising and the story is progressing. God is reclaiming his creation for his glory and, in that process, populating a new kingdom with men and women who are responding to the call of his glory.[11]

Men and women who realize that the greatest avenue of fulfillment for them is to realize they live, above all else, "for the praise of his glory" (Ephesians 1:12). Men and women who realize their "chief end is to glorify God, and to enjoy him forever."[12] Men and women who, with the turn of every page of their stories, discover new paragraphs of purpose as they echo God's significance and experience his enoughness in the drama of their day-to-day lives.

Men and women who are learning Life with a capital L and demonstrating through their stories why Irenaeus, in the second century, proclaimed, "The glory of God is man fully alive."[13]

❧ ❧ ❧

Fast-forward a couple of millennium. Today. In theme parks and expansive public areas, when I see one of those large Plexiglas maps of the area, I can't help but walk over and check it out. I'm a big-picture guy, and I love getting an overview. But a key to the effectiveness of those drawings is whether they have that little star with a *You Are Here* label beside it. Without that star, the map might be interesting but only mildly beneficial. But when it has that star, and I can get an idea of where I am, it becomes extremely helpful. Which is why, on many of them, the star has been rubbed off by so many people putting their finger on it—a grungy testimony of gratitude from a multitude of people who've been able to figure out where they are in the big picture.

I just shared that story of God's glory not because it's a neat religious tale but because of how helpful it's become to me as I'm figuring out my humanity. And it's only helpful to the degree that I enter into each day with the courage to proclaim, "I am *here*. By the grace of God, I am in the midst of his story. My destiny—with my job, my hobbies, my relationships, my fears, my foibles, and my flaws all in tow—is to enter into this great story being authored by God and bring a smile to his face."

> Life with a capital L is a matter of asking great questions of myself regarding why I am here and what my role is.

But, to be honest, even though that's my destiny, it's not my tendency. The reason? The seismic vibrations of the Fall are still messing with my internal compass regarding my heart's true north.

Our natural tendency is to presume that we're the star of our own story. We mistakenly think, in order to be significant, we must be the star. Yes, I have a role—a vital role—to play, and my story is immensely significant, but I'm not the star. The story is not being written for me or even about me but *with* me. Not as a disposable pawn but as a loved and purposefully created instrument.

It's when I lose my life in his bigger story that I find my life.[14]

As the captivating southern writer Flannery O'Connor resolved, "Don't let me ever think, dear God, that I was anything but the instrument for Your story—just like the typewriter was mine."[15]

My natural tendency includes just looking at the individual events in my days with blinders on, like unrelated snapshots. I don't effortlessly see the big picture—it's a learned posture.

Cultural commentator David Brooks, in his book *The Social Animal,* refers to a study that explored why chess experts are so accomplished. The reason? It's because they can see the entire game board at once. How? A higher IQ? Not necessarily. It's because they have learned over time to see the game board in a different way. "When average players saw the boards, they saw a group of individual pieces. When the masters saw the boards, they saw formations. Instead of seeing a bunch of letters on a page, they saw words, paragraphs, and stories."[16] When I go through my day, instead of just seeing the individual events of a supposedly ordinary twenty-four-hour span of time, I'm learning to see the bigger story that's unfolding within and around those events.

This isn't something I can do on my own. Without God's illumination, it's impossible for me as a human being to fathom what he is up to "from beginning to end" (Ecclesiastes 3:11). But when he illumines my path and I respond to his loving offer of restoration in salvation, the result is a story saturated with renewed vision. When I became a follower of Christ, this is how the Bible summarizes what happened to me: "For God, who said, 'Let light shine out of darkness,' made his light shine in our hearts to give us the light of the knowledge of the glory of God in the face of Christ" (2 Corinthians 4:6). In Christ, I am now able to perceive the story of the glory of God, which is what humans were intended for in the first place.

No wonder atheist-turned-believer C. S. Lewis, in an address to the Oxford Socratic Club on November 6, 1944, testified, "I believe in Christianity as I believe that the Sun has risen, not only because I see it, but because by it I see everything else." He included a transcript of that speech in a collection of addresses that quite appropriately was titled "The Weight of Glory."[17]

～ ～ ～

Ralph Winter is a Christ follower as well as film producer of such Hollywood blockbusters as the X-Men, Fantastic Four, and Star Trek series. At a gathering in New York, he made a comment that struck me: "Great movies ask great questions. In my movies, the hero learns something about himself—such as, 'why am I here?' and 'what is my role?'"

Learning to live Life with a capital L is a matter of asking great questions of myself, of realizing the big picture regarding why I am here and what my role is. Like Frodo and Sam sitting in the Green Dragon after they had grasped the larger story, I will, on a daily basis, begin to see things differently.

It will mean paying attention and being aware of the ultimate story that's always there and is being written on a daily basis. As Neo was finally able to see the "code" of *The Matrix* and perceive the world as it really was, I now—as a redeemed human being—have the ability to see the story of God's glory. But will I choose to? Daily? In all types of activities—not just the spiritual ones but the physical ones as well. "So whether you eat or drink or whatever you do, do it all for the glory of God" (1 Corinthians 10:31).

Embracing that I am part of the larger story of God's glory will change the way I live out my humanity. It will change the way I eat, drink, do the dishes, and mow the lawn. It will change the way I pursue my vocation and enjoy my vacations. It will change the way I love, laugh, and cry.

It will mean realizing that the main story line of God is deeper than avoiding sin or becoming an instrument of hope in my community or even being good at my job. It's also a matter of realizing the *why* behind those behaviors: to glorify him and enjoy him.

Embracing the story of God's glory will enable me, like nothing else, to realize life while I live it.

～ ～ ～

A couple of years ago, I was in Malpensa Airport in Milan, Italy, walking through the tunnel from Terminal 1 to the main terminal area. I just happened to glance down and see a small slab of stone with some engraving on it, unpretentiously fitted into the floor of the walkway. Placed in the middle of the traffic area, you could step on it and walk right over it. There was no border or light denoting its presence. You either saw it or you didn't.

The writing on the stone stopped me in my tracks (almost causing a crash of luggage carts behind me). The words were in Italian, with the English translation underneath:

Tutti i passi che ho fatto nella mia vita mi hanno portato qui, ora.
Every step I have taken in my life has led me here, now.

At first blush, this appears to be written by someone with a similar ability to the one I have—to clarify the obvious with great gusto.

But I continued to stare at the sentence, letting my fledgling tongue that was attempting to learn a little Italian mouth the words. And then I let my fledgling human heart that is learning Life embrace the truth. It's a statement about journey. About story.

I stepped off to the side and watched to see how many people actually saw the plaque. Out of the next fifty people, maybe four noticed it. I wondered if that ratio is similar to the number of people who pay attention to the story. It might even be similar to the ratio of hobbits in the Green Dragon, between those four who were aware of the great story and the rest who weren't.

During a lull in the traffic pattern, I went back over and read it again.

I thought about those lines as someone who is learning the gift of being human. I read them as someone who is realizing that the experience of Life with a capital L is intricately linked to his ability to embrace his story within God's larger story.

And I smiled.

That plaque was like one of those *You Are Here* signs. But instead of being on a mall map, it was on my life path. Literally.

I took inventory.

Every step I have taken has been anything but the random behavior of what some have referred to as "lucky evolutionary mud" in a petri dish called humanity. I have a story that matters because, by grace, it fits into a larger story that's more beautiful and more dangerous than, much of the time, I dare dream.

God is the Author of it, and he's also the Finisher. Instead of worriedly clutching the pen of my story, hoping I don't screw up the script, I revel in the reality that the pen is actually in his hand. I respond not with passivity but determination to take the next step with submissive and joyous confidence that the Author has and will continue to write my story into his. And I can trust his sovereign and gracious ink.

I'm not where I was.

I'm not where I'm going.

But I am where I need to be at this moment.

He has led me here. Now.

Soli Deo Gloria.

Worship

Living *Coram Deo*

You are not here to verify,
Instruct yourself, or inform curiosity
Or carry report. You are here to kneel.
—T. S. Eliot

They say it's all about the chase. I wasn't so sure. Yes, my excited heartbeat sounded audible enough to echo in the branches of the surrounding aspens. But I still couldn't feel my toes.

The unblemished blanket of new snow deepened the intense cold I felt. It also added to the thrill and a surge of adrenaline, since that bed of frozen flakes served as a blank canvas for a strange artistry: fresh elk tracks.

The November daylight was less than an hour old, and my twelve-year-old son was on his first elk hunt. Oh, and so was I. Yet we novices had, nevertheless, stumbled upon the recent footprints of a massive elk's early morning meandering. If you're impressed with our tracking ability, don't be. To be unable to see the tracks of a seven-hundred-pound animal in six inches of fresh snow would be beyond even my boundaries of ineptitude.

Despite barely being able to move his chapped lips, Joel was hardly controlling his excitement, struggling to keep it down to a quiet whisper. "Can you see him, Dad?!"

Even though I was clueless, my son was still young enough to think I might know what I was doing. I dismissed the temptation to offer a fabricated but nevertheless impressive answer that would've confirmed to Joel that this elk's unfortunate fate was sealed, now that he and his Daniel Boone of a dad were hunting it. Instead, I opted for a less exciting answer.

"No," I whispered.

But then my dad-ness kicked in, and I immediately followed that up with the sort of optimistic addendum that's supposed to come from a parent.

"Not yet."

And so our pursuit of the majestic animal continued. James Fennimore Cooper would have been proud. Dense trees. Frozen creekbeds. Uphill. Downhill. Sidehill. It didn't matter—we kept going. The elk's tracks continued over the Rocky Mountain terrain and our pursuit remained undaunted.

Midmorning arrived. Due to a wonderful invention called GPS, we found ourselves not too far from the time and place of a previously agreed upon rendezvous point with some of the other hunters who had allowed us to tag along on this trip. Though we could still easily see the tracks, I was beginning to realize we were probably hours behind the animal by now and losing ground by the minute. Plus, since my adrenaline was now back to a normal level—enabling me to reverse ridiculous notions from earlier in the morning that the arctic temperature wouldn't be that big of a deal—a hot drink seemed like a good idea. So, leaving the elk's trail, we opted for a quick check-in with whichever hunting companions might be in the area.

At the rendezvous point, we were greeted by another more-experienced-but-less-lucky hunter who had not been fortunate enough to stumble upon any tracks of his own. We then sipped some perfectly hot coffee and unfurled the excitement of our morning's pursuit.

As the steam from our beverages warmed us, we exchanged stories and waited for others to arrive. After a bit, two more appeared from the same direction Joel and I had been adventurously pursuing our prey. They revealed they had come across our tracks in the snow and had followed them for almost an hour.

Then they quickly got to the most important point. "Well, did you see him?"

"No." I said. "I think he was just too far ahead of us."

"Not the elk."

I was confused.

"The mountain lion."

Joel and I, wide-eyed, just stared. "Say again?"

"We came across your trail about an hour ago and saw that a lion was tracking you, so we followed."

It was time for a moment of silence. I didn't care how frigid the air was, a big inhale was appropriate at this point.

I've hiked and backpacked in Colorado for years and had known about the extremely elusive mountain lion. I also knew that, more often than outdoor enthusiasts in the Rockies would care to realize, a quiet but curious mountain lion will often watch them from higher terrain but then stealthily saunter on without the hikers ever knowing they had been observed. But for one to actually pursue a human's trail that closely would be highly unusual.

I thought they must be joking. "Are you serious?"

That led us on a hurried hike back to where we had left the elk's tracks and continued farther back up our trail. And there was the evidence. The elk's tracks in the snow. The overlay of our footprints on his. And then the truth on top: the unmistakable imprints of a large mountain lion's pursuing paws.

My Daniel Boone bravado suddenly departed, and I felt a temperature change on the back of my neck. We hunters had unknowingly been the hunted. The pursuers had been pursued.

"Uh, wow," I muttered.

"That's *awesome*!" marveled Joel.

We never saw the lion. Or the elk for that matter. But I did catch a glimpse of something going on in my life's journey.

And yours.

We pursuers are always being pursued.

～ ～ ～

Remember the woman Jesus encountered by that well in Samaria? She had been pursuing what she thought would ultimately fulfill her as a human being. The futility of her pursuit was evidenced by five ex-husbands in her rearview mirror.

I didn't finish the story earlier, so let's revisit it. She knew she was in pursuit of a husband and fulfillment, but what she didn't realize was that, in the midst of her pursuits, she was being pursued.

When Jesus got disturbingly personal in their conversation and pointed out that she'd been married five times and the guy she was currently living with wasn't her husband, I think she got a bit uncomfortable. So she did what I probably would have done—she tried to change the subject. Since Jesus was a Jew, she thought it would be safe and sufficiently stimulating to switch the topic to worship, which was a big point of distinction between her people, the Samaritans, and the Jews.[1]

But instead of switching the subject, she unknowingly brought the discussion to the bedrock that was beneath all the considerations about longings and satisfaction and husbands and living water. It was actually where Jesus had been taking the conversation from the beginning.

He targets the deep longings she has fervently tried to fulfill through powerless pursuits. But he also offers a vision of hope. As only the Son of God could do, he makes a prediction about her future journey as a human being and then validates the trustworthiness of his prediction by verifying to her that he, indeed, is the Messiah.

The prediction? It was not about a husband she would finally discover that would magically meet all her needs. It was about, of all things, her worship life. He speaks of a time soon when she will join a group of people who worship authentically, a group of "true worshipers" who "will worship the Father in spirit and truth, for they are the kind of worshipers the Father seeks" (John 4:23).

Unbeknown to her, this entire time they had been talking about *worship*.

~ ~ ~

But just to clarify, this woman didn't need to learn how to worship; she was already good at it. So am I. So are you. We are all born worshipers.

At the core of my identity as a human being is my proclivity and ability to worship. The fulfillment of my humanity is actually tied to my worship. An early form of the word *worship* was *worthship*. Worship is simply the act of attributing elevated worth to something or someone and demonstrating it through the devotion of my energy, resources, focus, time, and anticipation. There is no such thing as a human who *doesn't* worship. The issue, instead, revolves around *what* I worship. Is what I am elevating *worthy* of the worth I'm giving it? And that exposes a fatal tendency we all have, one that will undermine our humanity and definitely squelch Life: idolatry.

Far from being an antiquated practice of some extinct people who bowed before a deified statue, idolatry is alive and well in the twenty-first century. Idolatry is actually very proficient skill of mine. And yours. Remember our discussion about how we attach our God-sized longings to various pursuits that are less than capable of addressing those longings? In the process, we begin worshiping those pursuits. That's idolatry.

The list is long, but an idol is whatever, in a particular moment or season, I pursue above all else for returns like security, peace, meaning, self-esteem, satisfaction, or significance. An idol can be a possession, an experience, a habit. Even another person.

> We pursuers are always being pursued.

It can be something that's overtly sinful, or just a good thing that I elevate to an inappropriate place of importance. Power, money, possessions, careers, sex, fitness, leisure, success, appearance, drugs, relationships, reputation, education, titles, even sports teams and religion (and a lot of people get those last two confused). The list goes on and on. In fact, theologian John Calvin makes me uncomfortable with his frankness because I know he's accurate: he concluded that we are each a "perpetual factory of idols," continually devising new idols to worship—idols that, we presume, will provide what we need.[2] My constant invention of new idols and refurbishing of old ones become the Life-sapping cadence of my life.

Several summers ago, during a drought and food shortage along the West Coast, more than thirty brown pelicans from California crash-landed on asphalt and sidewalks in various parts of Arizona. The state's Game and Fish Department officials nursed the emaciated, bruised, and scraped-up pelicans back to health. They concluded that the dehydrated pelicans, due to mirages created by the sun's reflection on the hot and cool layers of air, mistook the pavement for water and attempted to land. Gliding in with their thirst to settle on water they had been desperately longing for, the pelicans experienced a jolting shock when pain came instead of relief.[3]

I know that feeling. It's familiar to all of us idol factories.

God refers to our propensity to exchange his glory for worthless idols[4] by using a metaphor of water and thirst. "My people have committed two sins: They have forsaken me, the spring of living water, and have dug their own cisterns, broken cisterns that cannot hold water" (Jeremiah 2:13). We build our own broken containers from dream vacations to long-sought promotions to sex sprees to substance abuse. We are deluded by the assumption we'll be able to use them to quench our soul's thirst. It's why Jesus offered the Samaritan woman what he called "living water." She had been trying to land her thirsty longings on the asphalt of failed marriage after failed marriage, and he was offering her the opportunity to dive into real water.

At its core, the issue is our *misdirected* worship. We weren't created to worship those things. As a human being, that's not the purpose for which I was originally made.

I listen again to Pascal's words about misdirected longings and relate them to my worship: "There was once in man a true happiness of which there now remain to him only the mark and empty trace, which he in vain tries to fill from all his surroundings.... But these are all inadequate, because the infinite abyss can only be filled by an infinite and immutable object, that is to say, only by God himself."[5]

A liberating reality for me to latch on to is that worship is central to being fulfilled as a human being, but it's got to be the worship of the God who created me, loves me, and wants to redeem me and my humanity.

Life with a capital L is impossible without a restoration of my worship in the right direction.

❧ ❧ ❧

Jesus is beckoning this woman back home. Back to water that can actually address her thirst. Back to her purpose. Back to true Life-giving worship. Back to Life.

He tells her that God has been, throughout all her idolatrous pursuits, pursuing her. As her gaze has been locked on either her rearview mirror, looking at the unmasked idols of failed marriages, or staring through the windshield at new ones filled with promise, she's never noticed the God above and beside her who was seeking her. For worship.

But he's not seeking a fan club. He is seeking men and women who will once again live their lives "for the praise of his glory" (Ephesians 1:12). With relentless love, he is seeking me to restore me for what I am hard-wired to do. To worship *him*.

What Jesus was offering her was not only a *proposition* to understand about worship but a *plot* that she could become a part of. He was inviting her return into the great story of his glory, which is our destiny as human beings.

And as I live my life glorifying and worshiping him, I return the other pursuits in my life to their appropriate size and capacity for fulfillment. As I'm worshiping and seeking him above all else, I can experience many of those former idols for what they can realistically offer me, and I can appreciate them for what they should've been in the first place: simple gifts from God. And I begin to enjoy my humanity as never before.

❧ ❧ ❧

Moving ahead four centuries after Jesus's conversation with the Samaritan woman, a theologian and scholar named Jerome translated the Bible from Hebrew and Greek into Latin. Known as the Vulgate, it became the dominant translation of the Bible for centuries and is still in use today. We've already talked about how Psalm 56:13 is a powerful statement regarding Life with a capital L: "For you have delivered me from death and my feet from stumbling, that I may walk before God in the light of life." Now here's something that has impacted me significantly: In the Vulgate, that phrase "before God" is translated, in Latin, as *coram Deo*. It means, literally, "in the presence," "before the eyes," or "in the face of God." *Coram Deo* is the way Life with a capital L is lived out.

Living *coram Deo* is not just an acknowledgment about God being ever-present during my days, but it's a decision I experience at the core of who I am as a human being.[6] It is a resolve to live all of my life in a God-centered way, aware that I'm constantly in his presence, with a purpose to live under his authority and to his glory.[7]

When I live *coram Deo*, I live a life of true worship. Jesus gave guidance to the woman by the well—and to you and me—about what true, God-directed worship is all about. It's to worship him "in spirit and truth" (John 4:23–24). It's to be made alive by his Spirit and to worship the God who has revealed himself to me in truth. It's to worship him while embracing the truth about *who he is,* which will involve humility, as well as about who he is *toward me* through Christ, which will involve intimacy.

To summarize, I think about it this way: *Worship is my active, all-of-life response to the worth of who he is and what he does.*

Ultimately, to live *coram Deo* involves humbly and intimately worshiping God on a daily basis. In humility, I will cultivate a high view of God, not living in the presence of a god I want—a heavenly genie who follows me around to dispense goodies—but the God who is. But because of his grace, it will also involve an intimate view of him, seeing him as my heavenly Father who has chosen to pursue me for a thriving, personal relationship that will glorify him as well as fulfill me.

True worship is not only a matter of going to church or corporate singing. It's an all-of-life response to the worth of his character by admiring him, the worth of his guidance by obeying him, and the worth of his agenda by following him.

True worship will mean engaging my mind and recognizing his worth in every nook and cranny of my life. I'll constantly be on the lookout for his fingerprints on my day and my story. I'll be aware of him and the story of his glory as well as my role in it. Letting his Word and Spirit illuminate the plot of worship being played out as I work and play, I'll look for ways to adore, obey, and follow him. I'll notice his worth. Not only will I be realizing life while I live it, I'll be realizing the Author of Life as well.

Poet Elizabeth Barrett Browning revealed some familiarity with the art of paying attention—being aware of the worth of God that's displayed in the everyday stuff of life—when she wrote,

Earth's crammed with heaven,
And every common bush afire with God:
But only he who sees, takes off his shoes,
The rest sit round it and pluck blackberries,
And daub their natural faces unaware.[8]

True worship isn't just a matter of the mind but the heart as well—it also means engaging my heart and resonating and agreeing with the relevance of his worth to my need. Jesus actually made a point of emphasizing that, when I think I'm worshiping, if my heart's unengaged, it's a vain waste of time.[9]

Man's chief end is to glorify God and to enjoy him forever. I can't enjoy him without my heart. In fact, John Piper has emphasized that reality in his paraphrase of the Westminster Shorter Catechism by saying our chief end is to glorify God *by* enjoying him forever.[10]

Duke University scholar William Willimon expressed his frustration over how we Americans are taking the heart out of our engagement with God. He sardonically conveyed his gratitude that, when it comes to Christian living and worship, the locus of influence seems to be shifting from North America, where we tend to just write rules, to "places like Africa and Latin America where people still know how to dance."[11]

What would you think about, in the midst of your day, taking a minute to do a little dance in response to the worth of God and what he's up to in your life? Who cares if anyone is watching? You're loved by the King of all creation, and he's up to some amazing things in your story, for his glory but also for your good. That is worth a big-time response. (Okay, if not a dance, at least a smile from the heart.)

True worship will also mean tossing aside my addiction to passivity pills and actively engaging my strength and behavior in my all-of-life response to God's worth. Worship is not a spectator sport. In both the Old and New Testaments, the Hebrew and Greek words we translate as "worship" involve physical postures and actions. Worship is not just an attitude—it's an activity. It will involve the way I spend my time and energy and money. Worship will be seen in the way I live my life, and it will happen in plenty of places besides church.

"Place of worship" is a phrase we see on city maps and tour guides, referring to a building or holy site. But when we're living Life with a capital L, when we're living *coram Deo*, everywhere is a place of worship—our office, factory, studio, kitchen, shop, classroom, ranch, farm, home, apartment, hotel, gym, athletic field, stadium, golf course, playground, hiking trail, beach, river, doctor's office, shopping mall, concert hall, theater, restaurant, pub, coffee bar, subway, airport, automobile, and, yes, even on a Harley. Everywhere I am is to be a place where I engage with God's worth.

Every activity of my life—my vocational calling, my recreation, my relationships, my education, my sacrificial service, and my communication of gospel hope to people whom God places in my life, even my intentional rest—every endeavor becomes a way of acknowledging God's worth in my life. Gerard Manley Hopkins, poet and priest, wrote,

> It is not only prayer that gives God glory but work. Smiting on an anvil, sawing a beam, whitewashing a wall, driving horses, sweeping, scouring, everything gives God some glory if being in his grace you do it as your duty. To go to communion worthily gives God great glory, but to take food in thankfulness and temperance gives him glory too. To lift up the hands in prayer gives God glory, but a man with a dungfork in his hand, a woman with a sloppail, give him glory too. He is so great that all things give him glory if you mean they should. So then, my [brothers and sisters], *live*.[12]

In every realm of our lives, there's a drought of Life water. We live in a "dry and weary land where there is no water," no other water but God (Psalm 63:1), and it is worship that will lead us to that water. When we begin to live *coram Deo,* those wilderness places become transformed by his "streams in the desert" (Isaiah 35:6). Our dehydrated souls find water through a deep and authentic embrace of his worth in every situation.

Then we start realizing his Life-giving nourishment is in every place and all of life. We also see that's been the case the whole time—that indeed *there is Life everywhere*—but we've just missed it because of our fervent but futile devotion to our idols. As John O'Donohue observed, "Sometimes the urgency of our hunger blinds us to the fact that we are already at the feast."[13]

〜 〜 〜

If I'm to learn to worship in "all of life," it will also and inevitably include doing so in difficult seasons of mystery and unanswered questions. The prophet Habakkuk modeled it well. "Though the fig tree does not bud and there are no grapes on the vines, though the olive crop fails and the fields produce no food, though there are no sheep in the pen and no cattle in the stalls, yet I will rejoice in the LORD, I will be joyful in God my Savior" (Habakkuk 3:17–18). His embrace of God's worth was not stifled by his own grim circumstances or unanswered questions.

That's easier said than done.

We can be tempted to think that worship is just a matter of honoring God when things are nice and our vision is clear, when the tides of turmoil or confusion are far away. If we let that misunderstanding mislead us, we'll permit difficulty and unanswered questions to squelch our worship and undermine our intimacy with God. In the process, a sobering reality and yet another devastating idol will be exposed: our tendency to worship answers more than we worship God.

Mystery is part of life. If there is no mystery, then I fully understand everything. If I fully understand everything, then either I've become God or taken a swan dive into a fairy tale.

Mystery is also a beautiful part of Life with a capital L. Our majestic and mysterious God, the One who has graciously initiated relationship with us, can indeed be intimately apprehended, but he can never be fully comprehended by a finite human being. Yes, we can have confidence about the major tenets of Christianity, such as God's revelation of himself in Scripture and the resurrection of Christ. But that doesn't mean mystery and unanswered questions are eliminated from our lives.

We can understand the plot but not necessarily every page. Understanding the forest doesn't mean being able to explain every tree.

But if we worship answers more than we worship God, if we idolize certainty in all arenas, we'll shrink God to fit within our fabricated, finite little boxes, and there he becomes something other than God. Our worship of

> Our "I don't knows" can and must be a place of worship.

him will become an empty, barren routine as our questions become barriers instead of bridges to his otherness and unconditional love. We'll employ trite and clichéd approaches to reality instead of a willingness to engage with the undeniable mystery that accompanies us on a daily basis. Peace will become something we try to obtain, not through intimacy with God, but from the attainment of answers (even if they are contrived) or by sticking our heads in the sand or the clouds and ignoring the difficult questions altogether. Propositions that include some semblance of certainty will be valued over and above the often-mysterious plot of his glory.

In our Life-suppressing superficiality, the true God who is indeed mysterious is replaced with a religious mascot who is containable and explainable.

During my college years, I spent some time at a study center in the Swiss Alps called L'Abri. It was in the small village of Huémoz, Switzerland, and led by an amazing couple, Francis and Edith Schaeffer. L'Abri is a French word that means "shelter," and it was indeed that. During stays of several weeks, it was a safe place for students from all over the world—believers and unbelievers—to honestly engage with big questions about life, truth, and the gospel.

I arrived at L'Abri on a Saturday. Two days later, Dr. and Mrs. Schaeffer returned to Huémoz from the Mayo Clinic in Minnesota, as he was in the early days of diagnosis and treatment of lymphoma, a deadly cancer that would ultimately claim his life in 1984.

Some of the most powerful moments for me during those days of study and reflection were during the evening discussion times, held in a small chapel perched on the mountainside. The room would be packed with several dozen chattering young people sitting on the floor. When Dr. Schaeffer would enter, respect for him would chase out the chatter, and the space would go silent. On the hearth of the enormous, glowing fireplace would be cushions where he would perch and then pour from a pot of tea. He would indicate he was ready with a one-word invitation.

"Questions?"

Honest, insightful inquiries would then come. Given where he was in his personal journey and battle with cancer, his responses were even more reflective. I was impacted by his insight regarding answerable questions as well as his authenticity about the unanswerable ones.

In one session, we had just finished a discussion about death and cancer when a Norwegian graduate student—an unbeliever but a genuine seeker—raised his hand. Dr. Schaeffer acknowledged him with a nod. Anders then asked a very brief but sincere and serious question. "Dr. Schaeffer, why God?" The widespread snickers among the rest of the students were awkwardly audible.

Dr. Schaeffer's disdain at the reaction in the room was swift and clear. "Quiet!" Silence quickly came. His frustration abated, he turned back to Anders, indicating he was about to address the young man's heartfelt question. Looking directly at Anders, Dr. Schaeffer's honest and soberly delivered answer was as short as the question.

"I don't know."

After a pause that conveyed he wasn't minimizing the question but, instead, had given an authentic response, he turned to the rest of the group and continued the session. "Next question."

A few days later, Anders embraced the gospel and submitted his life to Christ.

Knowing this had been a quest lasting several years, I asked him if there had been a pivotal, deciding factor for him. He affirmed there had been and referred to the evening of the previous week and Schaeffer's "I don't know" response. Anders said he connected with Dr. Schaeffer after the session for a follow-up, and Schaeffer's willingness to acknowledge our human limitations and embrace mystery was a key factor in moving Anders to accept the gospel. It pointed to a Christianity that was credible instead of one that glibly threw around ten-dollar answers to million-dollar questions while relying more on a denial of reality than an engagement with it.

The next time I saw Dr. Schaeffer was a couple of days later, during a worship service in the chapel. I'll admit I did more than glance at him as he sang and recited the Scripture readings. I watched and was moved deeply. Against the brutal backdrop of his own cancerous decline, I saw a man worshiping in the face of that reality. Instead of denial or empty ritual, I witnessed raw reverence.

Our "I don't knows" can and must be a place of worship. The "I don't knows" of our illnesses, our sinful choices, our pain, our jobs, our doubts, our relationships. There, the authenticity of our worship is deepened. There, the hollow ping of superficial religiosity is drowned out by the resounding strength that God provides as we embrace his worth and live *coram Deo* even in the midst of mystery and difficulty.

Let's go back to Habakkuk. What was at the core of his worship? In the very next sentence, he offers, "The Sovereign LORD is my strength; he makes my feet like the feet of a deer, he enables me to go on the heights" (Habakkuk 3:19). Instead of worshiping God because everything was easy and explainable, he chose to worship because God was giving him strength to live in the fallen and difficult terrain he found himself in. Habakkuk's worship of God in the mysterious darkness is what gave him strength to keep putting one foot in front of the other. Too often we pray that God would give us a path that will fit the ability of our feet, when instead he gives us feet to fit our path.[14]

We therefore press on in the face of mystery. And there we worship him in confident faith. Not because of his provision of all the answers, but in the strength he will provide as we take our next step through the perplexing puddles (as well as lakes) standing in our way. In those moments, our worship focuses not on our ease or ability to understand, but on the supreme worth of God's enoughness.

❧ ❧ ❧

Shortly after my eldest son graduated from high school, he and I traveled to France two weeks before he was to begin as a freshman cadet at the United States Air Force Academy. We had been reading up about the momentous events surrounding the Allied forces' D-day invasion of Normandy on June 6, 1944, and wanted to visit as many of the sites as we could. We concluded our final day at the Normandy American Cemetery and Memorial in Colleville-sur-Mer. Popularized in the opening and closing scenes of Steven Spielberg's film *Saving Private Ryan,* Colleville is a striking place of remembrance on the bluff overlooking the five-mile stretch of beach on the English Channel known simply by its code name during the invasion: Omaha.

The cemetery at Coleville contains the graves of 9,387 American soldiers, most of whom died in the D-day operations, and its Walls of the Missing memorial honors an additional 1,557 warriors. When you walk onto the solemn grounds, even though you are in northeast France, you are actually stepping onto 172 acres of American soil, granted as a perpetual territorial concession to the United States by the government of France. As a result, the American flag flies over the cemetery and is treated with the same honor it receives in the United States.

Aware that my son was about to enter the Air Force Academy, a friend who was a military officer helped me craft a surprise by arranging for Andrew to take down the flag or "retire the colors" at the end of the day.

As most Americans know, there are specific requirements regarding how we treat our flag to ensure honor and respect. Because of previous training he had experienced during high school, Andrew was aware of the precise details of properly folding and retiring the flag. So he humbly— and nervously—accepted the privilege.

> There is no such thing as a human who *doesn't* worship.

When the moment arrived late in the afternoon, visitors from around the world stopped wherever they were on the property and, out of deference, stood in silence as the US flag was lowered. With precise and purposeful movements, Andrew creased and tucked our nation's red, white, and blue symbol into a crisp triangular shape.

Standing in the midst of almost eleven thousand reminders of the oath he was about to take in just a couple of weeks—an oath that would convey his willingness, if required, to give his life for what that flag represented—he and I were both gripped by the formation of a memory that will be with us forever. Afterward, fighting back tears, the two of us walked among the sea of white crosses to reflect on what our hearts had just experienced.

As we stood there talking, we were politely interrupted by a group of ten British young men who turned out to be soldiers in training for a special forces unit in Great Britain. They were intrigued by something most Americans take for granted: the way Andrew had treated our flag. I backed away as he explained to the group of curious Brits the deliberate esteem he had just shown the US flag and why.

As a proud and sobered father, I listened to their exchange for a few minutes and then meandered farther away from them. As their voices faded, my thoughts transitioned from some British soldiers noticing my son's honor for his nation's flag to a far greater reality that was illustrated in what I had just observed. Staring out over the blue of the English Channel, a question stopped me in my tracks.

As my mind pondered, my heart was—and still is—quieted by the question: is my honor of *God* noticeable to others?

Years before I had noticed Dr. Schaeffer's worship during a chapel service in the Swiss Alps. But I had also noticed his all-of-life worship in the way he did his daily routine and interacted with students. In the ensuing years leading up to his death, I noticed his honor of God in the way he lived the remaining days of his life, right up to the point of hearing that he took his final breath on this earth while a recording of George Frideric Handel's *Messiah* played in the background. Talk about Life with a capital L—even in death.

Is my all-of-life worship of the worth of God something that intentionally comes out in the way I live my days? Is my engagement with God's value something that is noticeable in the way I work and relax, laugh and relate, share and serve, do my hobbies? Is it evident in the way I deal with mystery and difficulty? Is it conspicuous to others in a way that marks me, not as someone who is more overtly religious, but as a guy who is more fully human in the way I appreciate life and rely on God as I live my days? Does it show up in the way I talk with others about my relationship with Christ, giving a reason for the hope that I have?[15]

On that beautiful afternoon on the northern coast of France, my son didn't honor the flag in order to be noticed. He honored it because it represents principles, values, and realities he is willing to give his life for.

On an infinitely deeper level, may I live my life in the face of God, but not in order to be noticed by others (even though, unless I move to a deserted island, that will prove to be inevitable). Instead, may I live a life of worship because of an ever-growing sense of adoration for the One who alone can ultimately satisfy me. May that honor be evident in the way I begin my days, experience my days, and, yes, end my days.

May I, in the midst of all of my life's daily pursuits, be aware of the Lion of Judah who is continually pursuing me with relentless tenderness.[16]

May I humbly embrace the reality that, with every wayward step I take off the path, he lovingly tracks me still.

May I abandon my pursuit of mesmerizing mirages and embrace his grace and truth—grace that unshackles me from my ruthless idols and truth that unleashes me to enjoy his original purpose for me as a human being.

May I do each of my days in a way that honors the worth of the giver of Life, all the while appreciating and experiencing the Life that I am willing to give my life for.

May I daily live *coram Deo*.

Love

Giving Life Away

> She worked to live; then, also to live,
> for the heart too has its hunger, she loved.
> —Victor Hugo, *Les Misérables*

There is a difference between a pipe and a bucket. An impressively deep concept, I realize. Set a short pipe and a skinny bucket on their sides next to each other, and the cylindrical shape of the two objects might cause them to look similar, but the likeness ends there. One is blocked up at the end, the other one isn't. The result of that design distinction is pretty straightforward: what goes into a bucket stays in the bucket and what goes into a pipe flows through the pipe and ends up elsewhere.

At any given moment, every one of us is predominately more a bucket or a pipe.

I call it plumbing theology. It's necessary for Life and shows up in our relationships—both with God and each other—all the time. It's simple to understand, but it takes a lifetime to unpack.

❧ ❧ ❧

Speaking of relationships, at this point it might be helpful for you to know a bit about my relational résumé, which, I'll warn you, isn't very impressive. As we all know, when it comes to relationships, some of us are better than others. I am one of the others.

While being a person who loves meeting new people and hanging with close friends, I am still as much an introvert as I am an extrovert. That surprises many who meet me, because I love being with people. They don't see the introvert part right away. But I can be quite content holed up alone in a cabin in the mountains. That weird combination gives me an advantage in being able to relate with both kinds of people.

But there's also a disadvantage in that, somewhere along the line, I can disappoint both groups equally well. For example, introverts can get uncomfortable with my questions, and extroverts get frustrated that I don't spend enough time with them. Also, introverts can't figure out why I like going to a party, and extroverts get frustrated when I leave early.

Since I'm doing free therapy with you, I'll continue for another paragraph.

At six foot five and on the more comfortable end of the verbal communication spectrum, I'm told I can be a bit intimidating. Add to that the fact that I have a strong personality. (My family and friends would sarcastically offer "No kidding" to all of the above.) That all comes in handy plenty of times, but it also can cause problems. Shocker, I know. A drawback that saddens me is the way my personality vibe, when not tempered with some maturity, can inhibit my ability to see how much I hurt people when I'm being a knucklehead (it's actually when I'm being more of a bucket than a pipe, but now I'm getting ahead of myself). And when others react to being hurt by me, the combination of my personality and lack of authenticity in the moment can mask how vulnerable I feel deep down. The result is they tend to use a higher-caliber ammo than they need because they think my armor is thicker than it is. So, reeling in self-defense, I back away (and become even more of a bucket and less of a pipe, which I'll explain in a moment).

All that is to say, even though I'm in Remedial Relationships 101, I can tell you with deep confidence that, as we're regaining our humanity and figuring out Life with a capital L, relationships can be one of the most joyous Life givers and also one of the most painful Life inhibitors we encounter.

There are moments we are practically speechless at the gift of living in community and doing life with others—the joy of connectedness and the security of being known and supported are unrivaled delights of life. The reality that *there is Life everywhere* is nowhere more enjoyed than in the context of close relationships. But then—if you've been breathing on the planet more than a few months, you know this one's coming—there are those other moments in which we're so exasperated with the confusion, pain, and disappointment relationships can bring us that we're more comfortable just hanging with our dog. No wonder he's our best friend.

To figure out Life with a capital L, I've had to start figuring out relationships. Or is it, to figure out relationships, I've had to start figuring out Life? Regardless, my experience of Life with a capital L is directly tied to relationships. Interactions with others are where Life is either expanded or inhibited, either celebrated or crushed.

And to figure out relationships, I, of course, need to figure out love.

But to figure out love, I need to figure out plumbing theology.

❧ ❧ ❧

Remember the Scripture that was a central inspiration for Nikolai Yaroshenko's painting *There is Life Everywhere*? Feed on it again. "We know that we have passed from death to life, because we love our brothers. Anyone who does not love remains in death" (1 John 3:14).

If I'm not loving people (translation: a bucket), I might be alive, but I'm not enjoying that Life or living like it. But if I'm giving God's love away (translation: a pipe), it's an obvious indicator that I'm alive. Life with a capital L and love are inseparable.

When there's a love logjam somewhere in my journey (translation: my bucketness increases), it means a quick entry back into my prison cell of death. The converse is also true: one of the primary ways I leave my prison cell and head back out and start experiencing Life again is via the avenue of love (translation: I become more of a pipe again. Hopefully you're getting the hang of this).

Plumbing theology is simply a matter of receiving from God and then giving to others what I've received. It's throughout Scripture. "Be kind and compassionate to one another, forgiving each other, just as in Christ God forgave you. Be imitators of God, therefore, as dearly loved children and live a life of love, just as Christ loved us and gave himself up for us as a fragrant offering and sacrifice to God" (Ephesians 4:32–5:2). In other words, I'm to be a pipe of the love and forgiveness God has poured into me through Jesus.

Life with a capital L is impossible to experience without love. Does that mean I need to experience God's love or does it mean I need to experience love with other people?

Yes.

❦ ❦ ❦

It was the middle of the night, I think. At least it was dark as I looked out the jet's window. I'm not sure what my body clock's time was. I was on an international flight over the Atlantic and trying to stay awake. So I forced my eyes to keep watching the movie on the seatback screen in front of me. At first I paid attention to stay awake. Pretty soon I was paying attention to stay alive, as in Life with a capital L.

I was dealing with some unpleasant distance with a friend (if you're unsure how that could be happening, refer again to the earlier description of my relational skills). In short, I was feeling more alone because of the space between us, and it was due to more than the geographical chasm because of the trip I was on.

The movie? It was called *Shall We Dance?* (Men, I apologize. I promise the other movie I watched on the flight had plenty of explosions, gunfire, and screeching tires.) I wasn't very engaged until two of the main characters got into a discussion about relationships.

In response to a question about why people get married, Susan Sarandon's character, Beverly Clark, replied with an answer that grabbed me, not just regarding marriage but relationships and community in general. I made a couple of notes and then, shortly after I returned to the States, I rented the DVD (my wife was impressed) so I could write down the entire response. Before giving it to you, since Beverly's answer applies more broadly than just to marriage, I'll reframe the question. Why do we hunger for close relationships?

> Every one of us is predominately more a bucket or a pipe.

Her answer: "We need a witness to our lives. There's a billion people on the planet.… I mean, what does any one life really mean? But in a marriage, you're promising to care about everything. The good things, the bad things, the terrible things, the mundane things…all of it, all the time, every day. You're saying, 'Your life will not go unnoticed because I will notice it. Your life will not go un-witnessed, because *I will be your witness.*'"[1]

Hearing that, it hit me. At the core of the relational unsettledness I was experiencing with my friend was the ache that a key witness in my life was distant.

Our heart, the more awakened it becomes, cries out for witnesses to our life's journey. Not just a reluctant witness who yawns at the ebbs and flows of our story.

And not a critic witness who simply picks apart the multitude of ways we're screwing up as we're stumbling along. But a committed witness who is for us, providing loving truth and truthful love.

Just as important, if we're going to be fully human, our awakened heart will embrace the significance of the people around us as fellow images of God. As a result, we'll acknowledge their yearning that we be a witness to their lives as well.

To have witnesses and to be witnesses is a cry of our heart. Facebook friends aren't going to cut it.

~ ~ ~

There's a lack of love-flow in the world. But we still hunger and thirst for it. The longing to both receive and give love is innate to each of us. It's part of the DNA of our humanity. Unplugging the blockage of love in my journey is a central factor to fulfilling my longing for Life with a capital L.

But where is the logjam? Where is the obstruction in the plumbing of the passageways of my heart?

When it comes to love, a plumbing theologian could say we each have a large intake valve on top, where we receive the love of God and others, and an outflow valve on the bottom, which carries the love we give to others and the love we return to God. When there's an obstruction with our love, it's related to one of those two valves.

Before we pull those pieces apart, let's clarify what kind of love we're talking about. When John refers to love as a companion to Life with a capital L, he is not referring to a mere emotional love, which can be fundamentally selfish and only a response to what another person evokes in us. In the New Testament, there are several Greek words we translate as "love," including *phileo*, friendship love, and *eros*, erotic love (romantic love can be a combination of those two).

The Greek word we translate as "love" that Jesus and John used most often is *agape*. *Agape* is one of the key words in the New Testament, appearing about 250 times, yet it very rarely appears in classical Greek literature. In other words, *agape* is a distinctly Christian concept, a unique love. For me to learn Life with a capital L, I'm having to learn *agape*.

Instead of just being an emotional response to what's lovable in someone else, or conditional according to their conduct or perceived worth, *agape* love is a volitional, unconditional action. But it's not just a detached, external behavior either. It's a loving action that chooses to care from the heart (which, remember, is still different from mere emotion).

When Jesus tells us, "A new command I give you: Love one another. As I have loved you, so you must love one another" (John 13:34), he isn't launching a feel-good festival—you cannot command an emotion (unless you're in a drama class). He is inviting us into a lifestyle of *agape* that can only be experienced via plumbing theology. He is referring to his love for us but also to our embrace of his love. He's also referring to our calling—in our relationships with each other—to be pipes instead of buckets of that love.

～ ～ ～

Now, to really grasp plumbing theology, I'm learning that both my valves need to be working in tandem with one another. I can't be receiving love through my intake valve (from God and other people) without also engaging my outflow valve (loving God and people). If my outflow valve is plugged, it will affect the inflow valve. If I block up my experience of love with the inflow valve, it will impact the flow going from my outflow valve. Got it? Remember, it only takes a minute to understand, but it takes a lifetime to learn.

Now let's revisit that question I brought up a minute ago about blockage. A love logjam can occur in either of those valves, obstructing the love in my journey and, in the process, impeding my experience of Life with a capital L. To be fully human I must be fully loved and fully loving, so both valves need to be flowing freely.

The main valve is where it all starts: my reception of God's *agape* love for me. When I'm not opening myself up to God's love, it catapults me into a realm of expecting God-sized love from other people. That's not only the beginning of disappointment and isolation from others but from Life with a capital L as well.

I can't give to others what I don't have. All too often, the primary reason we're isolating ourselves by not loving others with *agape* or smothering them to gain their love is because we're missing the foundational love of God. If it's just a nice phrase—*the love of God*—but not an experienced reality, we're bankrupt in terms of what we have to give to those around us. I have to first receive God's *agape* before I can enjoy it and also before I can be a pipe of his love to someone else.

Years ago I played for a bar in the Lincoln Park neighborhood of Chicago. But thankfully for them, it wasn't music that I played. Some buddies and I, on a team representing the bar, played competitive darts in the winter and softball in the summer. (By the way, that's Chicago Sixteen-Inch Ball. No gloves. A hard ball. Real men. But I digress.)

> We're not enjoying Life or loving others as well as we could because we're not experiencing God's love as fully as we could.

Our dart league was on Monday nights, so during the fall season there was always *Monday Night Football* on the television in the background. One night, a buddy and I were sitting at the bar between matches, watching the game. While he had never been a church guy and wasn't yet a follower of Christ, he was nevertheless aware of my "God side," as he liked to call it. In response to a camera closeup of a fan holding a sign, he couldn't take it anymore because he had seen the same writing on signs numerous times at other games. He figured I'd have some sort of answer, so he blurted out, "What the heck is John three hundred and sixteen?!"

I laughed at both his exasperation and his honesty. I said, "It's a reference to a Bible verse—John's gospel. Third chapter. Sixteenth verse." With a grin, I stopped there.

He took the bait and probed more. "Well, what's it about?"

"God giving us Life with his love."

That was the foundation of some great conversations in the coming months. Once he figured out that God was not about making him religious but about restoring his humanity by loving him unconditionally and giving him Life, he finally said, "I'm in."

Jesus made the statement we know as John 3:16 in the context of a discussion with a religious leader about how we need a reboot to our humanity by becoming born again. Our humanity needs to be regenerated by God's spirit. Jesus then gives him—and us—the overall motivation, means, and outcome of this redemptive process in one of the most famous verses in all of Scripture.

"For God so loved the world that he gave his one and only Son, that whoever believes in him shall not perish but have eternal life" (John 3:16). By the term *eternal life*, you'll remember that Jesus is not only referring to heaven but a new context of living, of being human. Eternal life is Life with a capital L. It starts the moment I believe and continues, finally undiluted, in heaven. Compelled by *agape* love for us, Jesus gave himself in order that we could be born again—made alive.

God's Life is delivered through his love. The degree to which I grasp God's love for me will be the degree to which I experience his Life. If I don't grasp his love, I won't be able to fully experience his Life and fully engage with my humanity.

And therein lies an enormous blockage of love-flow.

We're not enjoying Life or loving others as well as we could because we're not experiencing God's love as fully as we could. We don't really grasp what John was talking about when he referred to the mind-blowing greatness of the *agape* love that the Father has lavished on us.[2] We might have dipped our toe in the water of his unconditional love, but we've never taken a swan dive. We don't *really* believe that he loves us with *agape*—love that is totally unconditional. That reality shows up in our tentative relationship with him and, consequently, our truncated relationships with each other.

❥ ❥ ❥

Last week, my wife and sons finally talked me into sitting down with them and joining American entertainment civilization by viewing an episode of the reality singing competition *The Voice*. This particular episode was one of several called "The Blind Auditions." The contestants, aspiring vocalists from around the country, stepped one by one onto a stage in Universal City, California. Under the spotlights, the budding singers could see the audience. But between them and the audience were four enormous red chairs, each facing the audience—not the stage—containing four celebrity musician judges: Blake, Usher, Shakira, and Adam. The contestant knew the celebrities were there but couldn't see any of them—only the backs of their chairs. Though the singer had been introduced to us, the television audience, he or she wasn't announced to the judges. They simply walked onstage and started singing.

The goal was for the contestant to sufficiently impress at least one of the judges so that he or she would, at some point before the song was completed, hit a button that swiveled his or her chair around to face the contestant in a dramatic moment of acceptance. Through that action, the judge was conveying "I like your ability enough to become your coach." If more than one judge hit his chair's button, the judges would compete with one another for the contestant's choice of who they wanted to have as their coach. I was hooked.

A brilliant twist to a traditional audition, it contained all the highs and lows you would expect. The ultimate high was, of course, when all four judges would swivel their chairs around to accept a contestant.

But it also contained the ultimate low when none of the judges turned his or her chair. The angst was there for the contestant and also for the viewer (it sure stressed me). Here is this person, immensely gifted, singing his heart out for an entire song to the backs of four chairs that never turn around to affirm him. After the song, the judges would all swivel toward the singer and try to encourage him, but the message had already been signed, sealed, and delivered: We don't believe in you enough to accept you and come alongside you.

I've got a question. Is your view of God being exposed right now? Mine was.

Many of us go through our lives thinking and acting like we've got to perform in just the right way to get God to turn his chair around toward us. We might have heard of the love of God, but that reality stays outside the real-world performance studio of our Mondays. We, exhaustedly, try to be good enough for God to love us. To embrace us. To accept us. We minimize the work of Christ and thereby maximize our feelings of rejection. *Surely he couldn't love me after what I've done. Surely I've not done enough to gain his favor.*

What I sheepishly find myself failing to remember is the thing I should never forget: because of the completed work of Jesus, God could not be more for me—and you—than he is at this very moment. "If God is for us, who can be against us?" (Romans 8:31).

After I've become a follower of Jesus, can I displease God through disobedience? Certainly. But I can *never* be out of his favor or beyond the reach of his acceptance. His Life-giving favor[3] has come to me through Christ's work on my behalf, not my behavior or performance.

I must continually remember that grace is the posture of a God who, through the completed work of Christ, lavishes me with his unmerited acceptance—and love.[4] A God whose love for me is unfailing and will never be shaken.[5] A God who holds me precious in his sight and honors me with his love.[6] A God who longs that I grasp how wide and long and high and deep his love is for me.[7] A God who accepts me and also wants more for me.[8] A God who wants to assure me that absolutely nothing—no sin, no circumstance, no failure, no opposition—will be able to separate me from his love.[9] A God who is continually with me, who is enough for me, who takes great delight in me, who rejoices over me with his own singing, and who, with his love, wants to quiet my clamoring heart that's continually coming up with empty reasons that he shouldn't love me.[10]

A God who turns his big red chair around the moment I step onto life's stage—*and does so before I ever sing a note.*

Brennan Manning, a deeply authentic man who grasped God's unconditional love in big-time ways, wrote a book titled *The Furious Longing of God.* It's about the yearning God has—that you and I would grasp his extravagant love for us. It is a love that seems too good to be true and therefore appears to be folly, a pipe dream. He reflects about his confidence that God will continue to raise up other "crazy writers to cry with me the French Easter liturgy: *L'amour de Dieu est folie! (The love of God is folly!)."*[11]

Oh, that I would be one of those crazy writers. For the sake of your Life. And mine.

Our lives are too short and God's love is too lavish for us to live as if we were spiritual orphans. May we instead live as the loved men and women that we are, and may we love as loved men and women, as pipes instead of buckets of God's *agape.*

❧ ❧ ❧

There's another part of our intake valve that can get obstructed. It's when we have problems receiving the love of people around us. When that happens, our outflow valve—our ability to love—gets messed with as well.

I'm discovering there are a couple of primary ways that our intake valve can get plugged: we either smother other people with our insecurity or cut ourselves off from them due to our woundedness.

Back to Universal Studios and *The Voice.* The studio of my life is set up opposite from the one in the television show. I walk onto my life's stage, and it's actually most of the *audience* who have their chairs turned away from me. The only one who is qualified to judge me has already spun his chair around to accept me, but the people in my life, when lacking *agape* (which, for all of us, is way more often than not), have their backs to me. Yearning for a witness to my life, I can spend my days desperately trying to get them to turn their chairs around and love me. If I change my song and performance a little bit for some, or a lot for others, they might turn around and give me their nod of acceptance. As a result, my relationships can become the proving ground of my worth, and instead of being places where I feast on *agape* as well as give it away, my relationships become seedbeds of insecurity.

My life then becomes driven to relieve the pain of continually looking at the backs of chairs. If I neglect going to God for the security-giving love only he can provide, ignoring the One who has already turned his chair toward me, I can get caught up doing ridiculous things to get other people to turn their chairs in my direction. My heart will then get weighed down by the compromises I end up making to get them to love me. I'll ironically smother their heart and squelch my own. If I don't stop that trend, I'll become increasingly insecure and someone other than who I really am. The other person may or may not turn their chair, but either way, instead of being a Life-giving dance of unconditional love, it becomes a death march of manipulation in both directions.

But perhaps an even greater pain is with those who, at one time, had their chairs turned toward us, but now, because of something we've done or their unexplainable change of heart or simply because of their own bucket tendencies, they have turned their chair back around and away from us.

Quiet rejection. Demeaning judgment. Crazy-making abuse. Poisonous slander. Brutal betrayal.

From spouses. Family members. Friends. People at work. People at church.

It is some of the worst pain we experience in our lives. As a friend wrote to me, "The most disappointing moments in my journey have been when I trusted godly people who I dared to believe loved me."

David, in the Psalms, speaks of this kind of hurt. "Even my close friend, whom I trusted, he who shared my bread, has lifted up his heel against me" (Psalm 41:9). "If an enemy were insulting me, I could endure it.... But it is you...my companion, my close friend, with whom I once enjoyed sweet fellowship...at the house of God" (Psalm 55:12–14).

The rejecter, abuser, or betrayer never sees the cause as being in them; it's always in you. And slander and gossip will have to enter the mix, because you must be demonized in order for them to justify their actions and change of allegiance. As Dan Allender observes, betrayal turns the past into a long series of questions and doubts (why did I trust him in the first place?) and isolates us in our pain.[12]

With the turn of each chair away from us, a layer of hurt is added to our heart and a love logjam is tragically formed. Out of our desire for protection from further wounding, we close our intake valve to human love a bit more. We then cut ourselves off from giving and receiving love from other people whose chairs are still toward us (ironically becoming a bucket ourselves in the process), because we now wonder if *they* can be trusted.

To dismantle the obstruction, I must take my pain to the One in the main chair that's unconditionally and always turned toward me. The One whose love is unfailing. The One who has himself suffered rejection and betrayal.[13] He helps me harvest the hurt. He helps me clarify that he, above all others, must be my primary audience. He uses the pain to lead me into deeper intimacy with him as well as others whom I can trust. He graciously exposes and refines some of my jagged edges that might have contributed, either a little or a lot, to the painful chair turn against me.

Though I might fear being hurt further, he leads me down a path of openness toward reconciliation. The other person may not be willing, but my heart will be free.

He directs me to combat the blitz of bitterness that is assaulting my heart and causing me to turn into a bucket and withhold my love from others. I realize, if I don't fight the tornado of bitterness, Life will be sucked from me and the toxic ache will gust into other relationships.[14] As someone said, "Bitterness is like drinking poison and expecting someone else to die."

So I embrace Christ's forgiveness of me in a fresh way and realize I must become a pipe of that forgiveness toward the person who turned their chair from me.[15] Yes, I will need to guard my heart and protect myself from people who continue to unrepentantly demonstrate painful chair-turning tendencies toward me, but I must resolve to open myself up to other pipes of God's *agape* and, in vulnerability and authenticity, let them love me in all my unhidden imperfection.

I need to be honest with you about a sobering reality in all this: the more we learn to engage our heart in our journey, the more vulnerable we'll become in love and relationships.

Difficulties in relationships didn't hurt as much when I wasn't as intentional about living from the heart. It's a high price to pay for having a more pliable heart, but it's a tuition that's worth it. As C. S. Lewis wrote,

> To love at all is to be vulnerable. Love anything, and your heart will certainly be wrung and possibly be broken. If you want to make sure of keeping it intact, you must give your heart to no one, not even to an animal. Wrap it

carefully round with hobbies and little luxuries; avoid all entanglements; lock
it up safe in the casket or coffin of your selfishness. But in that casket—safe,
dark, motionless, airless—it will change. It will not be broken; it will become
unbreakable, impenetrable, irredeemable.[16]

Yes, the more I'm paying attention to my heart, the more susceptible I'll be to
getting hurt, but also the more adept I'll be at guarding my heart from long-term
damage. And as my heart enlarges through the refining that relational pain uniquely
provides, my experience of love will expand in Life-giving ways that would otherwise
be impossible.

❥ ❥ ❥

The other possibility of a potential plug up of love is my outflow valve through which
I give God's love and Life away to others and reflect it back to him.

Yes, giving love away can become impeded from a lack of engagement with his
love, through woundedness from others, or simply through the disappointment of
people not fulfilling my expectations. But it can also get blocked due to pure self-
centeredness. That's when *we* become the one withholding love, the one turning our
chair away from another person in our life.

When we become more of a bucket of God's love than a pipe, refusing to give
his love and Life away, we become stagnant cesspools of selfishness. It sounds awful
because it is. We might disguise our self-centeredness in any number of ways, but the
stagnation quietly yet assuredly drains the Life from our journey and robs the people
around us of that Life they could be receiving from us.

While God's love for me is unconditional, my experience of his love is not. I
must keep giving his love away to keep experiencing it. The cycle is both powerful
and unavoidable: I stop loving others when I stop experiencing his love, but I also
stop experiencing his love when I stop loving others. "As I have loved you, so you
must love one another" (John 13:34). Buckets don't revel in the love of God, and not
giving his love away to others is both the result and the reason.

I can't hoard or stockpile God's love. When his acceptance and love ceases to be
a present-tense reality of my experience and instead becomes just a memory of something I once experienced—if at all—it ceases to be vibrant. He's still loving me as
much as always, but if I'm not giving it away, I'm not fully experiencing it's beauty and
vitality. A staleness toward God and a tiredness toward others enters the picture.

We're familiar with the "Best If Enjoyed By" labels on food packaging. If there were a label on God's love, it would be, "Best If Enjoyed NOW." Don't try to stockpile it. You'll never outgive God's supply. Enjoy it and give it away. In fact, enjoy it by giving it away. Enjoy Life as a pipe instead of missing it as a bucket.

When I see bucket tendencies popping up in me, it's not only because I'm not acting very loving. It's also because I'm not acting very loved. Yes, hurt people hurt people, but the opposite is also true: loved people love people.

When I determine to be a conduit instead of a container of the love of God, the diagnostic questions from the practical side of plumbing theology begin to flow. Am I giving others what God is giving me? Am I lovingly treating others as Christ lovingly treats me? Am I loving them by sacrificially serving their needs? Instead of only being concerned about having a witness to my life, am I also being an encouraging witness to others? As a fellow human being, am I—through my actions—conveying that I embrace their significance as a fellow image of God? Are my words Life giving? Instead of hoarding the resources of my time, energy, and money, am I being a generous pipe in God's hands? Am I extending to them the gospel that has given me Life? Am I bringing God's comfort, encouragement, and presence to them? Am I forgiving them in the way I've been forgiven? Am I extending grace to them—the same grace that's been extended to me? Instead of a selfish, stagnant container, am I being a conduit of Life for them?

> Yes, hurt people hurt people, but the opposite is also true: loved people love people.

Remember my less-than-stellar relational résumé? The degree to which it improves or not is directly related to how I am answering those questions.

Along with his command for us to love others as he has loved us, he introduces an indicator of whether we're actually doing so. "By this all men will know that you are my disciples, if you love one another" (John 13:35). As followers of Jesus, our love—our pipeness—is what should be noticeable to a watching world.

Our distinctive mark should be our love. Is that what we, as Christ's followers, are known for in our culture? Tragically, the answer is no. More often we're known for our boring religiosity, restrictive rules, ridiculous church politics, and judgmental posturing toward others, both within and outside the church.

Some Christians would counter that we should also be known for truth, and they would be correct. But when truth is given without God's love, it's not heard. And because we're delivering our truth to a watching world with our chairs turned away from them while yelling over our shoulder, people in our culture unsurprisingly dismiss us as the noisy buckets we too often are, clanging into each other while missing Life instead of celebrating it.

～ ～ ～

It was a December morning a little over two years after my dad had died. The two grandsons he had known were a lot bigger now, but still not too big to sit in my lap. A third grandson he had never met was just a few months old and still asleep upstairs.

Encased in their flannel pajamas, my two sons were piled on my easy chair with me in my study, playing with my laptop computer. They were making silly recordings of themselves, and I'd play them back for them to listen between their cackles. Some of the recordings I would save on my hard drive. In the process of saving one of the audio files, I typed a name starting with the letter *D,* and when it found its place in my file list, I saw the name of another recording from long ago.

"Dad—Voicemail Greeting."

I'd forgotten I had it.

Both my mom and dad have been beautiful, influential pipes in my life, consistently available with loving encouragement and care. I know, sadly, that's not a normal experience for a ton of people who had to deal with parents who bruised them with their bucket tendencies, so I don't take it for granted. But the fact, throughout my journey, that my mom's and dad's chairs have been consistently turned toward me in acceptance and love is still a gift I treasure.

With my dad, the last third of his life was his strongest in his relationship with God. An effective business leader, he began rising even earlier before work to devour Scripture on a daily basis. He opened his heart and grasped the love of God for him in ways he hadn't seen when he was younger. That awakening showed up in his relationship with me—he became a conduit to me of the grace and truth he was experiencing from God. He was the best man at my wedding and the first person I would call when I needed wisdom or encouragement. His sudden death had been a shock and deep loss for all of us, and though life has gone on as it always does, I still miss him incredibly.

So while my sons were continuing with their silliness, I stared at the name of an audio file.

In the week after his death, I had called my dad's office line just to hear his voice mail greeting. It was one of those quirky things we do as part of our grieving process. Because of the impact of just being able to hear his voice, I called it again and made a recording. I'd forgotten about it until, piled in an easy chair a couple of years later with two giggling sons, this computer screen was reminding me.

Without really thinking, I clicked on it. It was a voice I hadn't heard for way too long.

"This is George Heard. I'm not available to take your call right now..."

I'm not sure if it was his familiar welcoming tone or that phrase that reminded me how much I missed his availability, underscoring the painful reality that I could no longer call him at any time. But I couldn't move. My boys became silent, partly due to hearing this warm southern voice that mentioned their last name and partly because of the tears they saw welling up in their own dad's eyes.

In his book *Life Together,* Dietrich Bonhoeffer, while sitting in a prison cell, wrote about the reality that Christ-honoring, grace-centered relationships are "a gift of grace, a gift of the Kingdom of God that any day may be taken from us, that the time that still separates us from the utter loneliness may be brief indeed."[17] With my sons eavesdropping, I thanked God right there for the gift of my father's continual availability as a witness to my life over the years and prayed that I would be the same for them.

My dad's chair might be empty. But it is still turned toward me. And it is still dripping with the residue of love that could only be delivered by a pipe of God's Life.

And as I, in turn, am learning to give that *agape* away, I long to live a life of availability to the people of my story.

Not as a bucket, but a pipe.

Time

Life Is Daily

> We are always complaining that our days are few,
> and acting as though there would be no end of them.
>
> —Seneca

Golf will either reveal your foolishness right from the start or hone it enough to be publicly displayed in due time. Until you begin to play the game seriously. Then it gets worse.

That's when you begin to actually understand your foolishness.

My foolishness is evidenced by the fact that, long ago, I played to a single-digit handicap but now I play to a calculator handicap (which is one that requires computerized assistance at the end of the round to tabulate your score), yet I keep playing.

My foolishness is also evidenced by the contents of my garage. For every garden tool there are a dozen golf clubs. I cut down more weeds in one round of golf than an entire summer in my yard. But in the midst of all the weeds of folly, some seeds of wisdom can still take root.

For example, I've learned it's possible to determine whether a person is a beginner or advanced golfer just by watching him at the practice range. A novice will walk onto the practice tee with his bag of forty or so practice balls. Holding it about waist high, he empties the bag, and the balls plummet to the grass, ricocheting off each other to the four corners of the earth. After scurrying around and herding all the balls back into a neat little assemblage, he sets his bag of clubs down, each one awaiting its moment of glory. However, all but one club will end up disappointed, because only one will be chosen: the driver. The big kahuna. Why he brought the entire bag of clubs I have no idea, because none will see the light of day except for the big stick.

With the king of clubs in one hand and a small wooden tee in the other, he struts over to the huge batch of golf balls and salivates over the size of the pile. Best of all, he's not going to have to find or retrieve a single one of them himself. So since he can just flail away, no practice swings are necessary. He picks his first victim and perches it on the tee. With forearm muscles bulging, his viselike grip on the club initiates a colossal swing. The ball catapults off the tee, but instead of taking the scenic route up into the air, it scorches the grass. The number of decapitated worms isn't monitored by the Humane Society, perhaps because they grow back, but there are plenty.

Before the first ball even stops rolling, a second one is taken from the seemingly infinite pile and loaded onto the tee. Another mighty swing launches another ball, this one going in an entirely different direction than the first. Then another. And another. Observing the continuous motion from a distance, the image of a windmill comes to mind. Though beads of moisture are dripping from his forehead, no breaks are taken. Since there are so many balls to swing at, a few experiments are taken instead. *What if I held the club like this? What if I stood like this? Has anyone ever tried a behind-the-back swing?*

The frenzy of activity doesn't slow down until the size of the pile shrinks to a small number of balls. With just three or four remaining, a reality sinks in: *I better make these count.* So the amount of time between swings slows to a snail's pace as he tries to remember the instruction articles from every golf magazine he's ever read. He takes forever for the last shot since it will determine whether the pro tour is going to be a possibility. The result confirms probably not.

Let's shift to a low handicapper's practice session. It's quite different. After some wise stretching, the advanced golfer goes to the opposite end of the club spectrum to begin her session, picking a short pitching wedge. The first few golf balls are coaxed out of the bag with the blade of the club. A smooth tempo rotates her club in an arc that lofts the ball toward a predetermined target. After each shot, she pays attention to the ball's flight and discerns what, on the next swing, she should either reinforce or correct. With a deliberate routine, she works her way through most of the clubs in her bag, from short to long, finally finishing with the driver. The rhythm of her practice session is steady. The time she takes between her next-to-last ball and her final one is the same as the interval between her first two practice shots. The deliberate focus has been obvious.

So what's the distinguishing factor between these two practice sessions? The intentionality? Sure, but it goes deeper than that. Why was the advanced golfer more intentional? Ultimately, she began her session understanding something that the novice didn't realize until it was too late: the pile of practice balls was not unlimited. She knew there was only a finite number of golf balls to take a swing at.

Early on, the beginner acted as though he had an infinite amount, and he carelessly thrashed away while the pile was high. Focus and intentionality didn't enter the picture until there were only a couple of balls left. The advanced golfer was attentive from the beginning.

＊ ＊ ＊

Moses, the long-ago leader of Israel, was not a golfer as far as I know, but he understood a similar principle. In Psalm 90 he reflects on the unyielding quickness with which our days are absorbed into a lifetime. He was contemplating, in a short lifetime of seventy or—if we're healthy—eighty years whether there was some key that could help slow down the frenzied free fall of passing days. He tethered himself to a brilliant request before God: "Teach us to number our days aright, that we may gain a heart of wisdom" (verse 12). Instead of carelessly living as though he had an infinite number of days, he was resolving to approach each day as a gift, treated with a sense of relished appreciation, humility, and intentionality.

He saw that the way to deal with the shortness of his life was to actually embrace the brevity instead of denying it. As T. S. Eliot realized, "Only through time, time is conquered."[1] When I begin to consciously embrace brevity with a sense of purpose instead of panic, time becomes a launching pad of Life—a friend instead of an enemy.

When I was in college, I, of course, knew *rationally* that my days were limited. But *practically* I didn't think I needed to live accordingly. Most of us, when we're younger, know the comforting illusion that we have an infinite number of days in front of us. So we swing away, flailing through our days far more carelessly than the older version of ourselves, in retrospect, would be comfortable with.

But I'm now middle-aged. Just to look at that sentence seems like an out-of-body experience. I'm realizing with increasing conviction that there really is a fixed number of days attached to my life. For some approaching their later years, thinking about the limited days they yet have invokes notions of panicked frenzy or frozen fright. But whatever my age, Moses points out that my days, instead of being thieves that rob me of life twenty-four hours at a time, are God-given gifts through which I can taste Life more intensely.

A central part of being fully human is to wisely number my days according to the reality of why I'm on this planet, being aware of who I am and what I'm doing with my life and my days. That doesn't mean being overly serious but simply intentional. Numbering my days isn't just realizing there is a finite amount of them.

It's grabbing the Life out of them.

～ ～ ～

As I've tried to figure out this relationship of being fully alive and wisely embracing my days, Paul, alongside Moses, helps me see that Life is a gift to be experienced daily, not just every now and then.

He addresses a group of believers in the bustling, busy, and cosmopolitan first-century city of Ephesus. After speaking of the privilege Christ gives us of waking from our sleep and arising from the dead, he expands on how to experience that Life with a capital L: "Therefore be careful how you walk, not as unwise men but as wise, making the most of your time, because the days are evil" (Ephesians 5:15–16, NASB).

Now, by "careful," he is not meaning cautious or tentative. The Greek word he uses actually means "to see and perceive" or "to notice." Essentially, he's exhorting me to *pay attention* regarding the way I'm doing my days.

That's something I'm having to learn. I might be able to impressively hustle through a day and take care of a to-do list, but to actually pay attention is another matter. Leonardo da Vinci has never followed me around (even though there are days I feel like I'm old enough for that to have been the case), but he still exposes my lack of attentiveness through his penetrating insight: "The average human looks without seeing, listens without hearing, touches without feeling, eats without tasting, moves without physical awareness, inhales without awareness of odor or fragrance, and talks without thinking."

To wake up from our sleep is to become increasingly aware of who we are before God and this gift being of alive. To pay attention is a calling, requiring my active, deliberate engagement.

When my youngest son, Stephen, was just learning to talk, he shared some toddler wisdom that was grown-up sized. After I'd returned home after another full day at work, I collapsed in my chair in our family room. He bounded toward me and, with diaper-crinkling adeptness, climbed into my lap. I was still dealing with a couple of lingering items on my to-do list when he forced his way into my space and, firmly cradling my face by putting his two toddler-sized hands on my cheeks, made sure I had no choice but full eye contact. He then leaned forward just a few inches from my nose to deliver a father-changing speech that took an entire two words.

"Daddy here."

Was he merely making a statement about my new and appreciated presence in the house? The intensity of his eyes—which would've been humorous if his words hadn't been so piercing—conveyed that it was more than an acknowledgment of my geographical location. He was giving me an exhortation. An exhortation informed by something his developing awareness had picked up on in recent days: a distracted and unengaged daddy who was not practicing presence even though he was present. To frame it parallel with Paul's exhortation: "Daddy, be careful—pay attention—to how you occupy the space in this house. Be here and present with me. Now."

> Numbering my days isn't just realizing there is a finite amount of them. It's grabbing the Life out of them.

Too often during our days, we're not *here* even though we're here. We're not paying attention. We're not embracing, as Gerald May refers to it, "the sacrament of the present moment."[2] We're not noticing the significance of now. We're not living in the present tense, or what I prefer to call the *presence* tense.

It's the significance of being fully present. Of paying attention to how we can live and be fully human in this moment and situation.

It's realizing life—and Life—while we live it.

Right here. Right now.

❥ ❥ ❥

Paul points out that experiencing Life daily will also involve an insertion of some wisdom into the mix. It was an emphasis of Moses as well, who pointed out that wisdom would be the fruit of numbering his days. Or maybe that numbering his days would be the fruit of wisdom. Either way, they go together.

I number my days, not to become a panicked mathematician of my all-too-short lifespan, but as a wise—albeit finite—human being who is declaring that he wants to experience eternal Life in the context of each perishable day. Calvin Seerveld refers to "our utterly God-dependent fragility: we humans live literally on borrowed time. Even more so than fresh raspberries or fresh fish, humans are perishable goods."[3] We intuitively sense our temporal tempo of being perishable. So the powerful beauty of the Life Jesus gives us is a connection to an existence and reality that's not hemmed in by time. Even though my days are indeed perishable, I can still, in the midst of each delicate day, experience a quality of Life that's rooted in eternity. With the Life only Christ can provide, my day can become far more significant than I could otherwise dream.

And wisdom tells me that when I string together a bunch of those significant days, it will result in a lifetime of significance.

You could refer to it as Life math: very simply put, a lifetime is made up of individual days. In fact, that's all a lifetime is: the sum total of a number of days added together. It might be simple, but it's still a reality we're reticent to live by. Instead, we too often want our lives to be characterized by something that our individual days don't come close to resembling. But the truth of the matter is a bunch of wasted days added together won't make a significant life any more than a bunch of rotten or unripe grapes would be able to make a great wine. How I want my life to turn out had better be visible in my individual days, because the way I spend my days is the way I spend my life, period. To be careless with my days is to be careless with my life.

When encouraging his younger friend Timothy, Paul told him to "fight the good fight of the faith. Take hold of the eternal life to which you were called" (1 Timothy 6:12). Unless I've spent my individual days intentionally taking hold of Life with a capital L, I won't end up with a lifetime that's taken hold of that Life either.

❧ ❧ ❧

To number my days in a Life-giving way requires me to be intentional. As Paul said to the Ephesians, "making the most of your time, because the days are evil" (5:16, NASB). The days are not evil in and of themselves, but in a fallen world where death reigns, the natural inertia of each day will usher us away from Life unless we wise up and become very careful, paying attention and deliberately harvesting every opportunity for Life with a capital L.

To make the most of something involves a conscious effort on my part. Though I'm tempted to spend my days taking the path of least resistance, like a meandering drop of water on a windowpane, he's urging me to instead become intentional. He's urging me to redeem, to deliberately reclaim this day back from the Lifeless gravitational pull that otherwise will characterize my existence in a fallen world.

In the Greek language, there are two primary words that are often both translated as "time": *chronos* and *kairos. Chronos,* from which we get the word "chronology," is the simple, unavoidable passing of time and events. It's merely one minute added to another and another.

The second is *kairos.* It doesn't have a precise English equivalent, but it's referring to time as a special occasion or unique opportunity. While *chronos* is quantitative, *kairos* is qualitative. It's something that's momentous. It could be beautiful or tragic, but it connects us with the significance of being human. When Paul exhorts us to make "the most of your time," the word he's using is *kairos.*

Kairos is time infused with potential and possibilities as we steward both opportunities as well as difficulties. Surfers intuitively discern *kairos* when they're evaluating a wave whether to seize it or not. *Kairos* is what Shakespeare was referring to in the fourth act of *Julius Caesar,* when he wrote,

> There is a tide in the affairs of men
> Which, taken at the flood, leads on to fortune;
> Omitted, all the voyage of their life
> Is bound in shallows and in miseries.[4]

In Greek mythology, statues of the god Kairos depict a man with winged feet and bald except for a long lock of hair on his forehead—the reason being you could take hold of Kairos as he approached, but once he was passed, the opportunity was gone. My life has a lot more *kairos* moments than I realize. Often, whether I've seized them or missed them, they are still seen more clearly once they've passed. *Kairos* is a moment that must be embraced to the enlargement of my humanity if I do and to my regret if I don't.

Just going through life is *chronos.*

Life with a capital L is *kairos.*

It is a given that my life will be characterized by *chronos,* but the question is whether it will also be laced with *kairos.* That will have everything to do with how intentional I am about numbering my days under Christ's leadership.

❧ ❧ ❧

Sheer *chronos* devoid of any seized *kairos* will sap the Life out of us. And the day-in, day-out lack of Life will erode or crush our hearts.

C. S. Lewis penned a brilliant, imaginary dialogue called *The Screwtape Letters,* in which Screwtape, a senior devil, advises a younger devil named Wormwood. The devilish protégé has been assigned the task of undermining the journey of a human who has become a follower of Christ. Hear Screwtape's observations about how to numb the heart of this person assigned to Wormwood's antagonism.

> But, if [this human] can be kept alive, you have time itself for your ally.
> The long, dull monotonous years of middle-aged prosperity or middle-aged adversity are excellent campaigning weather. You see, it is so hard for these creatures to *persevere.*
>
> The routine of adversity, the gradual decay of youthful loves and youthful hopes, the quiet despair (hardly felt as pain) of ever overcoming the chronic temptations with which we have again and again defeated them, the drabness which we create in their lives and the inarticulate resentment with which we teach them to respond to it—all this provides admirable opportunities of wearing out a soul by attrition.[5]

The first time I read those words I was a young man alone on a train rumbling through the southeastern French countryside. I was midway through a pre-law degree, taking some time off to study the Bible at a few schools and study centers in England and on the Continent. I still have the book and just now took the tattered paperback off the shelf. As I stare at the worn page containing those words above, for a moment I went back to being a college student—flannel shirt, down vest, hiking boots, and next to me, a backpack containing all my belongings. Decades later, I now scrutinize the words and phrases I underlined while the rhythmic click of a train track underscored some reflective moments of my just-beginning journey: "dull," "monotonous," "adversity," "decay," "despair," "drabness," "resentment," "attrition." As a young man with a seemingly infinite number of days before me, those words seemed theoretical and distant.

At the time, I had an unspoken determination that I would try to elude those difficult words like a nimble little metal sphere in a pinball machine progressing down the incline while cleverly attempting to avoid the jolting bumpers and disappointing obstacles. I didn't fully accept the fact they are simply an unavoidable part of the *chronos* journey of a human on this fallen planet. I knew the likelihood that those things *could* come, but in my optimism, I wasn't fully engaging with the reality that they *would* come—at least to me. Sure, I'd already encountered plenty of painful and dull days, but I was hoping it was because I hadn't yet discovered the magic key that would exempt me from that stuff in the future. As I reflect on it now, I would describe it as thinking I could figure out how to just experience *kairos* (and only the pleasant kinds of *kairos* at that).

> To be careless with my days is to be careless with my life.

Some of my posture was due to a lack of distinction between *chronos* and *kairos* (even though I wasn't yet familiar with either word back then). To a younger person, everything is newer, so even a lot of *chronos*-type things, because they're newish, feel a bit like *kairos* (new degree, new job, new salary, new car, new city, new apartment, new friends). But once you've been around the track a few times, the *chronos* realities in your life lose their newness—the "been there, done that" card gets played. And what we once thought was *kairos,* we now realize was just *chronos.* That's when the incessant regularity of our days can begin to deafen and blind us to the privilege of being human, and unless we start recognizing and seizing the Life-giving *kairos* moments around us, we'll drown in the dullness and depravity of days in which only *chronos* is experienced.

Now, years later, I read the same page in Lewis's book and stare at the black ink from a pen held by my younger self that underlined "middle-aged," knowing that I am now that person being referred to. And I wince at the phrase "middle-aged adversity" because, as the days turned into decades, I've increasingly tasted it.

However, I've also discovered the severe mercy of God that inserts Life-giving *kairos* into the midst of fallen *chronos.* So I also read the words with a smile that quite adequately counters the wince. I read them as a man who is learning, sometimes more successfully than other times, to number my days and seize those *kairos* moments.

Sailors of old feared both the doldrums, as they called the haunting stillness of the sea, as well as hurricanes. There have been occasions when my soul has indeed almost succumbed to, as Lewis put it, *attrition*—brought about by the *chronos* combination of drab boredom as well as difficult storms, both incessantly lapping or crashing against the hull of my heart. Seasons when I've been so occupied with enduring the numbing or painful onslaught of *chronos* that I've missed the moments of *kairos* that are there as well. The result is predictable: I end up surviving instead of living. Existing in the *chronos* of my days instead of experiencing the *kairos* that's there also.

But through Paul's tutelage, I'm becoming increasingly able to recognize the rising tide of a Life-giving moment as it approaches. During days of potentially debilitating *chronos,* my gaze is lifted by his words about the grace-laden gift of being able to also intentionally embrace the *kairos* of Life that presents itself every day. I'm learning to pay attention to the daily reminders of *kairos* lurking behind more events in my life than I used to realize. In the midst of the despairing inertia of *chronos,* I'm learning to reclaim the privilege of being fully human.

∼ ∼ ∼

A while back I was reading an article by a wine writer who was both amused and impacted by the story a gentlemen had told him about the morning before his wedding. The groom, a collector of fine wines, had packed a couple of rare bottles he wanted to take to the resort where he was getting married. His fiancé noticed the bottles and, knowing how expensive they were, blurted out, "I thought we were saving these for a special occasion." He stared at her for a moment and then, smiling, said, "Honey, unless I'm missing something, I think our wedding would qualify for a 'special occasion.'" She stared at him and then burst out laughing, realizing her remark had spilled out without thinking.[6]

We find ourselves continually waiting for the special occasion that's always in the future, never now. To quote Pascal again, "So we never live, but we hope to live; and, as we are always preparing to be happy, it is inevitable we should never be so."[7] Or as John Lennon sang, "Life is what happens to you while you're busy making other plans."[8]

Bottom line, we all fall for the tomorrow trap. We procrastinate Life by missing the *kairos* in each day. Or, if we notice it, we don't embrace it.

Life with a capital L dives into every day as a storehouse of special occasions or, more accurately, significant occasions. Every day *kairos* is recognized but also seized. Some long moments, some short, but *kairos* nevertheless.

❧   ❧   ❧

Once we begin to get life's brevity, we can make the mistake of merely turning up the speed of the treadmill and carelessly gorging ourselves on *chronos* instead of carefully feasting on *kairos,* confusing excess for intentionality and quantity for quality. Instead of combating heart-killing *chronos* with Life-giving *kairos,* we opt for different, more titillating *chronos.*

I get tired of my old car that's still running fine, but instead of letting it transport me to a place where I can serve some people in great need (*kairos*), I buy a new one (exciting *chronos,* but *chronos* nevertheless). The result is that we mistake the numbing effects of excess for the fulfilling fruit of Life. And, ultimately, we've tasted no more significance than before.

Discernment is necessary. An ability to recognize the *kairos.* So Paul, as he continues his exhortation, puts it this way: "So then do not be foolish, but understand what the will of the Lord is. And do not get drunk with wine, for that is dissipation, but be filled with the Spirit" (Ephesians 5:17–18, NASB).

He tells me that, if I don't learn discernment, dissipation will be the result. Dissipation is what the frost of my breath does in a Rocky Mountain winter. I do a big exhale and see frozen vapor leaving my mouth. Then it dissipates. Vanishes. There's no evidence that my breath was even there.

Dissipation is the antithesis of being intentional, or it's being intentional about the wrong things. Paul brings up the visceral and potent illustration of drunkenness. When someone wakes from a drunken stupor, they have no idea what they've done or said. That period of time of their life's journey has vaporized, with nothing to show for it but the passage of precious time. Drunkenness is the epitome of dissipation.

I will never forget, years ago, the look I saw in a dying man's face. He was an elderly friend of a friend, and he was in the hospital with probably only a few days to live, and he knew it. He'd been a very successful businessman but was now semi-retired. He had heard me speak at a business luncheon months before, and through my friend, he asked if I could come see him. We had some small talk, and then he leaned forward from his hospital bed and took my hand and locked his gaze on me. I knew he was about to reveal why he had wanted me to come. At the luncheon, I had shared about my father, a successful corporate executive, whose last couple of decades were his strongest in terms of his walk with God. Dad had remained an effective business leader, but he had become a powerful spiritual leader also. He had finished well.

So I assumed this gentleman, who was looking at the diminished pile of his days and finally numbering them once he saw that only a few were remaining, wanted to talk about his spiritual journey. Or lack of one.

When he leaned forward, what was memorable was the look in his eyes. I can only describe it as terrified panic. The tone of his voice was consistent with the look in his eyes when he divulged what was assaulting his heart. I was starting to assume it was his fear of death. But the sentence he finally uttered revealed it wasn't just what was unknown ahead that was haunting him, but what was known behind him. Through a clinched jaw, he spoke nine words with a slow, staccato emphasis.

"I don't know what I've done with my life."

I continued to look into his eyes, conveying care but remaining silent. It was a *kairos* moment. I listened as he, an incredibly successful person in our culture's eyes, opened his bankrupt heart and honestly shared with me his story of supposed success that was actually a tragic tale of dissipation.

I was honored by his transparency as well as his vulnerability. I gently shared with him the hope of the grace of the gospel, even in the face of wasted days and years. I talked with him about *chronos* and *kairos*. Yes, he had missed a ton of *kairos* in his life for the sake of some impressive *chronos*. But I conveyed that the moment he and I were experiencing together was yet another *kairos* moment that he need not miss. He didn't. He seized it. He engaged his heart with God's forgiveness in the face of so much lost time. And we feasted on grace together.

～ ～ ～

"Make every second count," the adage goes. But the question is begged, "Make every second count *for what*?" How do I measure success for my life and, accordingly, my individual days?

Paul provides two keys of discernment that will help me avoid a dissipated life, and they are inseparable: "Understand what the will of the Lord is" and "Be filled with the Spirit" (Ephesians 5:17–18, NASB). To be filled with his Spirit is to be led by him. To be filled with his Spirit is to discern and fulfill his will. Earlier in his letter to the Ephesians, Paul points out that, in Christ, God has "made known to us the mystery of his will" (1:9). It's the mystery that—without Christ—we cannot fathom even though we nonetheless have eternity in our hearts.[9] With the Colossians, he spells it out when he talks about God's making known "the glorious riches of this mystery, which is Christ in you, the hope of glory" (Colossians 1:27).

Christ's Spirit inhabits me the moment I believe[10] and escorts me into the realm of Life with a capital L.[11] Like an engineless car that has finally received the engine that will enable it to do what it was meant to do, the fact that Christ is now in me is my hope for living my days according to his agenda and glory. As I walk under his Spirit's influence, he leads me in the direction of not only becoming healthier spiritually but also becoming more like the human being I was originally intended to be. Deeper spirituality enables deeper discernment about being more deeply human. That doesn't happen only in church but in factories, boardrooms, family rooms, classrooms, soup kitchens, shops, gyms, and concert halls.

With Christ in me, I learn, each day, in the rhythm of *chronos* and *kairos,* to seize the opportunities that will be the most God glorifying and Life giving. And once I've clarified, through Spirit-enabled discernment, what's important, I then go for it with everything I've got. Turning, with gusto and grace, each page he has entrusted to me in the story of his glory.

❧ ❧ ❧

I'm a big-time football fan. The two teams I most rely on for the fulfillment of my deepest longings, er, let's start that over. My two favorite teams are the Denver Broncos and the Auburn Tigers. When my boys were small, my wife, when picking out clothing colors for them on game days, pointed out the convenience of both team's colors being orange and blue. I just stared open-mouthed at her, hoping she wasn't thinking that I had picked the teams based on their similar colors. Anyway, among my teams' biggest rivals are the Oakland Raiders and the Alabama Crimson Tide.

So I'm a bit apologetic to reveal that a player I have been intrigued by is a quarterback who played for both Alabama and Oakland.

His playing career was winding down just as my spectating habits were heating up, but as a kid I was a fan of his leadership and athletic ability on the field at least. Known by his nickname, the Snake, Ken Stabler led Oakland to their first Super Bowl victory, and when he left the Raiders, he held team records for the most completions, passing yards, and touchdowns in the team's history.

One day after practice, as the story goes, an Oakland reporter who knew of Kenny's skill at quarterback and sense of humor but had doubts about his academic ability, thought he'd have some fun at Stabler's expense. While the quarterback was removing his ankle tape, the reporter read him some *kairos* prose from Jack London's poem "Credo."

> I would rather be ashes than dust! I would rather that my spark should burn out in a brilliant blaze than it should be stifled by dry-rot. I would rather be a superb meteor, every atom of me in magnificent glow, than a sleepy and permanent planet. The function of man is to live, not to exist. I shall not waste my days in trying to prolong them. I shall use my time.[12]

When he finished, the reporter asked, "Ken, what does that mean to you?" Underestimating the football player's intellectual acumen, he assumed he was going to get some version of "I have no clue." Instead, Stabler surprised him with an insightful grasp of what he'd just heard and conveyed it in a remarkably succinct way.

Without even looking up as he untied his cleats, the quarterback, with his southern drawl, replied with a nonchalant but definitive summary.

"Throw deep."

❧ ❧ ❧

Throwing deep. That's what Life with a capital L is all about. I don't know about Stabler's version of throwing deep in life, but I know about Moses's, Paul's, and Jesus's versions from what they've told us. For them, it wouldn't be to just turn up the excess of *chronos* but to relish in every available *kairos* moment.

Dropping back and throwing deep and celebrating my freedom. Engaging my heart. Relishing beauty. Receiving illumination. Entering the great story. Worshiping in all of life. Loving deeply. Stewarding the pain. Redeeming the time I have. Making the most of every moment or event in which *kairos* makes an appearance.

Throwing deep by doing my relationships authentically. Doing my vocation purposefully. Doing my recreation enthusiastically. Loving Christ passionately. Serving him earnestly. Running to him when I've failed and need grace and when I'm confused and need truth.

Throwing deep is paying attention, seizing each *kairos* moment I can. Seeing the *kairos* in a child's joke, a family member's tears, a friend's care, a stranger's need, a doctor's news, a church's intercession, a business's opportunity, a community's challenges, a culture's crisis.

It is embracing a potential teachable moment with my sons. Seizing a family time of intimacy, either through deep conversation or loud laughter. Moving through a window of change or impact at work. Savoring a special meal with friends. Realizing a need for rest and replenishment and taking a vacation. Relishing a sporting event. Engaging with a film in a way that propels me down a path of personal change. Embracing a moment of repentance before God. Letting a work of art catapult me toward a deeper appreciation for being created in the image of God. Pressing into a chance for growth during a season of pain, hurt, or disappointment. Paying attention to a *kairos* moment of decision, whether it will be made in pursuit of Christ's kingdom or my own convenience. Letting my commitment to Christ trump my desire for comfort. Taking a risk. Taking the road less traveled.

> We too often want our lives to be characterized by something that our individual days don't come close to resembling.

It is noticing when an unbelieving friend is finally ready to take a significant step toward faith and when a believing friend is in a crisis of faith. Realizing when a people group is most open to the gospel. Discerning when a ministry or business needs to be started or when one needs to be finished. Spotting a need with a person hampered by poverty and moving to fill it. Sponsoring an underprivileged child. Giving a Bible to someone who lacks one. Sensing when truth needs to be spoken with grace and when grace needs to be spoken in truth.

Being fully human is throwing deep with every day we've been given. It is discerning when it's time to weep and when it's time to laugh, when it's time to mourn and when it's time to dance.[13]

❧ ❧ ❧

At this moment in time, you and I stand before the pile of our remaining days. Yes, their number is set, but set by the One who has given us life and is restoring our humanity. The One who lavishes us with grace at the end of a wasted day and celebrates with us at the end of a day we've made the most of.

So instead of panicking that the pile is finite, may we number our days and relish the blessed opportunity we have, as restored human beings, to seize the Life out of every single one of them.

Throw deep.

Carpe diem.

Brokenness

Living with a Limp

> And I say without hesitation: "Bless you,
> prison, for having been in my life!"
> —ALEKSANDR SOLZHENITSYN

Even great performances aren't immune to ruin.

One of the many attractions of New York City is the immense assortment of live music seven days a week. Rock. Pop. Hip-hop. Rap. Electronic. Techno. Acoustic. Alternative. Indie. Classical. Country. Jazz. From concerts to clubs, you name it, they're playing it. It's a gigantic urban iPod.

Of the couple of jazz clubs I particularly enjoy whenever I'm in town, there is one I can't enter without thinking about an incident that took place there more than a decade ago.

The Village Vanguard, a preeminent venue known around the world to jazz fans, has been an anchor institution in the West Village for three quarters of a century. Outstanding jazz musicians from near and far have been launched and lauded in the intimate basement setting on Seventh Avenue. As is the case with many small jazz clubs, you usually know what artists are playing, but on rare occasions you might get a surprise bonus.

On a warm late-August Tuesday evening, David Hajdu, now a music critic for the *New Republic* and professor at Columbia University, found himself wandering around Greenwich Village and slipped into the Vanguard. The set had already started, and he found a seat at a table near the back.

A small combo of musicians was playing under the leadership of alto saxophonist Charles McPherson. During the second song, which Hajdu, writing about his evening in *The Atlantic,* described as a bit "languid,"[1] his restless eyes wandered to the trumpet player in the band who was off to the side of the stage. He was turned away from the audience as well as the rest of the band, but even with the partial view, he looked vaguely familiar.

During the next song, McPherson had the trumpeter come to center stage to take a brief solo. There the lights revealed his face, and Hajdu turned to the stranger next to him and whispered, "Is that Wynton Marsalis?"

"I seriously doubt it," the gentleman snapped.

You couldn't blame him. For the world-famous jazz trumpeter to be unbilled and playing backup in a small combo on a weeknight in Manhattan's dog days of late summer, it really would be unlikely.

But it was Marsalis.

Stylishly dressed in an Italian-cut suit, Wynton Marsalis oozed his typical elegance. But his style took a backseat to his skill, which quickly became obvious to everyone in the room. The entire fourth song was a solo showcase for trumpet, a 1930s ballad called "I Don't Stand a Ghost of a Chance with You."

Creative genius came on display, and people soon began exchanging discreet confirmations of both Marsalis's talent and his identity. His interpretation of the melancholy piece was masterful, at times his notes almost becoming trumpeted words. The audience was mesmerized. He came to the climax, an extended rendition of the title phrase, and allowed each note and syllable to linger. "I don't stand…a ghost…of…a…chance…"

Then, at the most dramatic point, with people literally hanging on every note—someone's cell phone went off. A little singsong melody of electronic beeps played and then hung obnoxiously in the air. Some groaned. Others giggled. Drinks were grabbed and the moment unraveled.

Marsalis paused and stood motionless with arched eyebrows. Hajdu, ever the journalist, grabbed his notepad. He scrawled two words: *MAGIC RUINED.*

No kidding.

❧ ❧ ❧

In our lives, a cell phone might be what interrupts the song of our journey, but instead of the ringtone disrupting us, it's the news we receive from the other end of the call.

Shattering news. A call from your doctor with a measured lack of information about a recent blood test, accompanied by a foreboding invitation, "If you could come to the office so we can go over some details." A spouse announcing that she's decided there's no hope and divorce papers have been filed. A friend forcing the words, "There's been an accident." Your boss telling you she wants to meet, mentioning something about downsizing. A friend sheepishly relaying plummeting news of slander about you. Your accountant conveying some disturbing updates about your assets—or what's left of them. A high school administrator delivering news that your daughter has been expelled. A loan officer calling about your mortgage, and the word *foreclosure* gets mentioned. An infertility specialist conveying test results that will lead, once again, to deep disappointment. A police officer saying your son is at the station. A trusted friend telling what you know to be a lie, providing a clue that betrayal is in the works. A college admissions official regretting to inform you, but informing you nevertheless, that you didn't get accepted.

> Life with a capital L actually unfolds *in the midst* of the land of the shadow of death.

It was just after 10:00 a.m. on a beautiful Orlando spring morning when my song was interrupted by a ringing phone. I answered and not only immediately recognized the voice of my wife, Arlene, but also the strain in her voice. She was at our pediatrician's office, having just taken our two-month-old son in for a regular checkup. Her voice trembling, she told me I needed to come right away. That was alarming enough, but I wasn't prepared for the designated meeting place. At that moment she was rushing to the emergency room at the Arnold Palmer Hospital for Children.

In the course of examining Joel, our doctor had noticed several symptoms that alarmed him so much that he'd opted for the ER as soon as possible. I arrived at the hospital at the same time as my wife and infant son. There, more tests revealed his electrolyte levels were off to the point of seriously threatening his life. Within minutes, our normally smiling but now terrified two-month-old was secured to a bed in intensive care with more monitors and tubes attached to him than I thought possible with such a small body. Disconcerting statements contributed to the blurred free fall in which we found ourselves.

"We're astounded he's still conscious."

"These levels are usually fatal, even with an adult."

"If you hadn't come in, it's doubtful he would have made it through the night."

"We need to get him stabilized before we talk this through with you."

It was later, during that talk, that the bomb was dropped.

"I realize this will be hard to hear, but we are doing everything we can to help your son make it through the night. That's our first priority, and hopefully he will. Then we'll start looking at causes and treatment."

Hopefully he will.

The amplifier in my heart turned up the volume of those three words so high they almost seemed distorted. My ears were ringing, my hands were sweating, and my voice was trembling as I tried to assemble some words of gratitude to the doctors for their care.

Because of the number of medical personnel rapidly moving in and out of the small room with an urgency suitable to the emergency, they asked if only one of us could be in there at a time. Arlene took the first watch during what was to become the most intense twenty-four hours of our lives. I headed to a waiting room down the hall that, thankfully, was empty. Immediately I was on the floor, face down.

With tears burning, lungs heaving, and heart racing, I tried to pray. Focus was illusive, and words even more so.

Instead of a silly ringtone interrupting my song, it was a grenade. Shrapnel from a fallen-world explosion was violently embedding itself in my heart.

I wasn't yet familiar with Nikolai Yaroshenko, nor had I seen his painting *There Is Life Everywhere*. But if I had, what was then racing through my heart on the carpet of that waiting room could be likened to an incredulous response to the concept. Really? *There is Life everywhere*? Here?

I'll fast-forward and let you know that Joel survived the night. A diagnosis and further treatments followed. It turned out to be an extremely rare condition related to his adrenal gland. He still bears a scar on his side from that long-ago surgery.

And I'm still living with a limp from that experience and many additional broken experiences since.[2]

But it is a limp that has introduced me to Life.

~ ~ ~

In the echo of explosions along our journey, it's tempting to forget that Life with a capital L actually unfolds *in the midst* of the land of the shadow of death.[3] It's a place where broken hopes and shattered dreams happen more often than we could ever be comfortable with.

When the delicate vase of serenity in our lives falls or gets pushed off its pedestal, the process of lunging for it is unsettling enough, even if the vase doesn't totally break. When the vase is jostled, it's disquieting enough to know we are vulnerable and not immune. But when the vase's fate goes beyond a mere chip or crack and violently smashes into countless pieces, we cry out with Job, "My days have passed, my plans are shattered, and so are the desires of my heart" (17:11).

In those shattered moments, Fantine, in the musical version of Victor Hugo's *Les Misérables,* provides a script for the lament, often unspoken, deep within us. Through her song "I Dreamed a Dream," she reflects about an optimistic time earlier in her life before she came face to face with a fallen world. It was a time when "hope was high" and life was "worth living." But then life happened. And her posture has changed. She finishes by concluding that her journey has become,

So different now from what it seemed,
Now life has killed the dream I dreamed.[4]

We've been there. But what can we do to move on with our journey?

The worst kind of pain is wasted pain so, in shattered moments, I'm at a crossroads. Over the coming weeks and months, my next steps will determine whether the trauma has been wasted or stewarded. When this *kairos* moment presents itself, will I seize it?

The decision is mine. Will I immediately receive God's care and eventually let both his healing and his refining run their course?

(I say "eventually" because, in the immediate aftermath of a broken experience, we need his presence not a prescription. The concussion from the blow first needs to subside. Standing in the midst of the wreckage, our need for God's embrace trumps our need for his instruction. Prescription, advice, instruction will have their time later. And those moments mirror what we need from each other as well: loving care and presence now, instruction—if ever—later. Please make a note of that if you come alongside me in my pain.)

God urges us to heave our ache and anxiety on him. He really does care for us. Eventually, in that process of receiving his love, our hearts are softened, and as Peter puts it, "in due time" he lifts us up and refines us.[5]

~ ~ ~

On my trip to Italy, after being robbed at the Milan train station, I delayed my itinerary by a day to file a police report, work on insurance claims, make sure the stored data on my computer devices hadn't been compromised, and purchase a few replacement items. Exhausted and exasperated, there was nothing else I could do about all my stolen items, so I took a taxi to the airport to rent an automobile to use over the next several weeks.

Malpensa Airport is outside Milan, so on our drive I noticed a road sign that had the word "Milano" with a thick red slash across it, from the upper right to bottom left. In the coming days, I saw those signs whenever I was driving out of a town, but this one was my first. I had a hunch what it meant, but I asked the cab driver anyway.

Straining his neck to make eye contact with me in his rearview mirror, he explained. *"Milano finito."*

"Thank goodness."

I don't think he understood my reply.

I've had plenty of crises in my life that were worse than that robbery, but it was still great to be leaving the place where it had happened. I was glad to be done. At least I thought I was done.

He dropped me off at the airport, and I went through the main terminal to the car rental desk. I picked up my keys and headed to the parking garage. Just before the exit, I noticed an engraved sign: *Stai per iniziare un viaggio.*

Translation: You are going to start a journey.

As I continued to my car, I thought about the sign and realized part of the journey I was beginning was the journey of stewarding the crisis I'd just experienced. As with any other painful interruption that's of any significance, I had a decision to make. Would it be *finito* or *viaggio*? Would I try to block it out and pretend it never happened, or would I journey with it and steward it—not coddling it in a pity party but seizing the *kairos* opportunity to learn from it? I consciously decided I would take the latter option. For me, the small but painful incident was over, but the journey wasn't.

A couple of weeks later, on the first day my family arrived to join me, we received word about the catastrophic wildfire in our neighborhood in Colorado. Though our house didn't burn, we knew that over three hundred others did, and for a time we thought ours had. During that shocking and stressful interval, we worked through the loss of our belongings.

Where did I go for insight? Because I had taken the *viaggio* instead of the *finito* option with my loss weeks earlier, I had essentially just come out of a real-life seminar about the sudden loss of belongings, and God had used it to refine and shape me. Were the contents of the briefcase the same as my house? Of course not. But it had been like a vaccination, inoculating me with a small dose of strength and perspective to equip me for the bigger crisis a couple of weeks later.

As we go through our journeys, the pain will be cumulative. Disappointment—large and small—will pile on top disappointment. But the question is whether the accumulation will serve to harden our hearts and make us more superficial in our approach to living, or will it strengthen our hearts, making us deeper human beings who are equipped to deal with reality instead of deny it.

You and I both have broken experiences. These are a nonnegotiable element of being human in a broken world; they are the periodic and painful reminders that things are not always as we want them to be. The variable comes in our response. When I encounter a broken experience, will I have a *finito* or *viaggio* approach to stewarding the difficulty that comes to me? At that moment will I seek to *escape* or *engage* the brokenness?

~ ~ ~

Those questions have led me to something I now refer to as pasture theology. The Bible refers to us as sheep (which, by the way, is not a compliment), and you could say we progress through seasons of our lives via numerous pastures of maturity. Increased maturity will be required to experience our humanity more fully and Life with a capital L more deeply. The growth in our maturity is like progressing from pasture to greener pasture, which is a fulfilling experience. That's the good news.

Now for the difficult part. Moving from one maturity pasture to the next is, most often, anything but a pleasant experience.

It requires going through a gate, which is usually a broken experience.

Potential gates can be enormous or nondescript, ranging from uniquely immobilizing tragedies (losing a home to a fire) to more ordinary reminders that the world is broken (losing a briefcase to a thief). They can occur over a day or a longer season. Gates can be constructed of debris from our own sin or simply from the shrapnel of a fallen world. Our own rebelliousness can create painful situations that end up being gates for us. Or a gate can be some fallen circumstance that God didn't author, but one out of which he can fashion a maturing gate, redeeming it for our good and his glory. A gate can be constructed by the sin or immaturity of other people that has generated some type of rejection or betrayal or abuse aimed at us. A gate can be a season of spiritual or relational drought, or it can be a loss of health, job, dreams, family, pride, possessions, hope, or comfort.

Regardless of the how it is built, a gate is a potential tool God can use as a vehicle of refining—a refining that needs to happen in order for us to grow. The gate, when engaged and walked through, shapes us for enjoying the new pasture of maturity God is bringing us to.

The reason Martin Luther once wrote "Affliction is the best book in my library" is also why Aleksandr Solzhenitsyn, in his memoir about being in a Soviet labor camp, wrote, "I nourished my soul there, and I say without hesitation: Bless you, prison, for having been in my life!" Affliction and prison aren't good in and of themselves, but God can bring good from them.

That's why James tells us, when we encounter a potential gate, to be joyful. (By the way, that doesn't mean a glib smile or a neurotic love of pain, but a gratitude that God is at work in our story.) "Consider it pure joy, my brothers, whenever you face trials of many kinds, because you know that the testing of your faith develops perseverance. Perseverance must finish its work so that you may be mature and complete, not lacking anything. If any of you lacks wisdom, he should ask God, who gives generously to all without finding fault, and it will be given to him" (James 1:2–5).

> When the magic is supposedly ruined in my life's song, it's not the end of the song.

We all want to get to the next pasture of maturity, but we'd prefer to painlessly hop the fence and not go through the gate. Yet it's the passage, a sort of birthing canal, that will refine and prepare us to be able to Live and thrive in the next pasture.

Let's say there is something in our character that needs to be worked on, but we resist God's refining and turn away from the gate. So we remain in the old pasture. Eventually, to say the least, it will become less than exciting to stay there. We then blame God for having to remain at the same level of maturity for so long. Yet the stagnation originates from our refusal to steward those broken experiences in our journey as best we can and pass through the awaiting gates.

Let me put the two options in the form of a couple of equations:

ESCAPE: Broken Experience + Resistant Posture =
Woundedness That Chokes Life

ENGAGE: Broken Experience + Pliable Posture =
Brokenness That Leads to Life

Paul illustrates the second equation by comparing us to clay pots. He then describes some of his experiences of brokenness. "We are hard pressed on every side, but not crushed; perplexed, but not in despair; persecuted, but not abandoned; struck down, but not destroyed. We always carry around in our body the death of Jesus, *so that the life of Jesus may also be revealed in our body*" (2 Corinthians 4:8–10). He's speaking of difficult gates he's pliably walked through so more of Christ's Life could be revealed in his story. Though agonizing at times, the brokenness didn't finish him off but instead escorted him into more Life in his experience and his ministry.

Gates can be excruciating. After encountering one, we sometimes feel that we'll never be able to take another step. But, as T. S. Eliot acknowledged, "In my end is my beginning."[6]

～ ～ ～

However, even though greater maturity and a deeper experience of Life is in the next pasture, we remain reluctant to walk through the gate of brokenness. We assess the difficulty of walking through that gate and compare it to the pain we're in now. But our current pain is easily medicated in the current pasture—through distraction, addiction, and our go-to idols of the moment. Our current pain is dulled. The pain of the gate, in comparison, seems too much, too intense. So, instead, we do a U-turn. We choose to stay in our current pasture, opting for medicating the pain through distracting idols. (But in those moments we eventually realize, in the words of Christopher Wright, "The worst thing about idols, as the Hebrew Scriptures so tirelessly point out, is that they are utterly useless when you need them most."[7])

Why do we do the U-turn? It's basically a case of sticker shock. You know the feeling when shopping for an item that you really wanted, and then you saw how much it cost and you changed your mind and moved away from the potential purchase in U-turn fashion? Maturity is often like that. Sure, we see some of the benefits of walking through that gate, but we back away because of what we sense it would cost us. As David Whyte observes, "We experience a form of internal sticker-shock, that the price of our vitality is the sum of all our fears, that the price of our passion and commitment involves the shattering of deep personal illusions of immunity and safety."[8]

Sure, we would like to become more mature and experience Life more deeply, but we'd like to do so without the brokenness that brings it about. In fact, to be honest, we'd like maturity to be gift-wrapped with immunity from difficulty. So we adjust our theology to allow for that deluded desire. You could refer to it as a sort of exemption theology (which is antithetical to pasture theology) in which we adopt a dangerously flawed perspective of God, viewing him and the gospel as a sort of force field, a protective bubble that is supposed to shield us from anything bad or difficult. Then, at the brokenness gates, we exchange the God we need (the One who can enable us to work through the difficulty) for an imaginary god we want (a god who doesn't want us to have to struggle).[9] We concoct rationalizations such as: *Surely this isn't something God could use in my life. Surely he wouldn't want me to have to deal with anything this difficult. Surely he doesn't want me to walk through this gate.* The U-turn is taken to help God out as well as us.

The result of such a flawed theology? When tough things happen, we think either God is failing to keep his promise or we've not yet figured out how to rub the genie bottle just right. Either way, the result looks like a sad combination of depression, anger, bitterness, and woundedness. Even more tragic than the pain, Life is choked from our journey.

There's a slight detail we're missing with our U-turn tendencies: the gospel is not a promise of immunity from hardship. Jesus couldn't have been clearer: "I have told you these things, so that in me you may have peace. In this world you will have trouble. But take heart! I have overcome the world" (John 16:33).

What is it about "you will have trouble" that we don't understand?

Jesus was explaining that we indeed live in a fallen world, and even as his followers, we will experience the same hardships as those around us. But in the midst of the difficulty, we can know that he will take the trouble and harness it for his purposes.

As we engage with his strength that overcomes, our hearts will be strengthened in the process. Augustine explained, "In the same fire, gold gleams and straw smolders."[10] He was referring to the reality that Christ's followers are not to suffer less, but differently. The reason? We can trust, whatever the difficulty, that it will be redeemed for his purposes.

~ ~ ~

So the question stands. In the face of the broken experience I'm in, will I submit to him and let him restore me to health and heal my wounds?[11] Will I, as Henri Nouwen put it, bring my broken experience under the "light of his blessing"? There, "what seemed intolerable becomes a challenge. What seemed a reason for depression becomes a source of purification. What seemed punishment becomes a gentle pruning. What seemed rejection becomes a way to a deeper communion."[12]

Choosing *viaggio*—to walk through that gate—will require trusting God to redeem the pain. It will also involve moving into a new arena of Life. Moving into a more robust maturity. Into a deeper embrace of what it means to walk with God as a fragile but fulfilled human being.

But first, after adjusting to the concussive blow of the broken experience, how do I then walk through it? Ironically, to move through this kind of gate will initially require stillness—but not the passive kind. If you get lost in the wilderness, survival wisdom says to do the opposite of what you are inclined to do, which is to panic and speed up your pace. Instead, slow down and build a fire. Settle your heart into the predicament and take an assessment.

As Psalm 46 advises, "though the earth give way and the mountains fall into the heart of the sea," instead of running, I should "be still, and know that" he is God and realize that he is my "refuge and strength, an ever-present help in trouble" (verses 2, 10, and 1). I first need to embrace the loving, mysterious enoughness of God in the midst of the storm.

I then begin to move through the gate—and that will be counterintuitive because it means to head into the pain. It's like turning the bow of my ship into the storm instead of trying to flee.

I just had the privilege of meeting Jerry Sittser, who went through an almost incomprehensible journey of loss and brokenness. In a single car accident, caused by a drunk driver colliding head-on with the minivan Jerry was driving, he lost his wife, his four-year-old daughter, and his mother. He writes openly about his grief in the transformational book *A Grace Disguised.*

In a conversation with his sister shortly after the accident, she conveyed the quickest way to reach the sun from the darkness is to head east, away from the setting sun. Jerry realized he had a choice. "Since I knew that darkness was inevitable and unavoidable, I decided from that point on to walk into the darkness rather than try to outrun it,…to allow myself to be transformed by my suffering rather than to think I could somehow avoid it. I chose to turn toward the pain, however falteringly, and to yield to the loss, though I had no idea at the time what that would mean."[13]

Walking into the pain is not only advisable but necessary.

It's also immensely challenging. I once was dealing with an excruciating decision that I processed with my family because it was going to affect them. Together we all came to the conclusion of the difficult path I needed to take, but I was still struggling. So we decided to pray about it together. During that time, my sixteen-year-old son, Stephen, prayed that God would "give me the nerve of Jesus." I had never heard anyone pray that and had no idea what he meant, so after we were done I asked him. He explained, "When Jesus was in Gethsemane and headed to the cross, he knew what he needed to do. It was the opposite of what he wanted to do, but he had the nerve to do it anyway."

Heading into the storm requires the nerve of Jesus. But he assures us of not only his nerve but his companionship as well.

So I gear up and dive into the pain. I ask the hard questions about God and life and me. I delve into what needs to be refined in me that may or may not be directly related to the gate I'm walking through. I determine what answers can be pursued now and what questions need to be filed away for later. I stare at the scalpel of God and trust his surgical precision.

I let him love me in the midst of the broken experience. As he's doing surgery on my heart in the midst of the storm, I must let him love me in the midst of the surgical process. In those painful times when I'm most tempted to think God's love has been delivered to the wrong address, that's when I can encounter his love the most.

~ ~ ~

Have you ever cried when you were alone? (If you're one of the tough guys, have you ever thought about crying when you were alone?)

No, you haven't. Nor have I.

Because neither of us has ever been ultimately alone.

David, when he was fearing for his life, prayed and acknowledged the incredible reality that none of us cry alone. "You have kept count of my tossings; put my tears in your bottle. Are they not in your book?" (Psalm 56:8, ESV).

It's a reality I'm simultaneously grateful for and humbled by: the infinite king of the universe is also mindful of me. And he cares. Constantly.

This astounding reality about his largeness and smallness, that he is both God and Father, both transcendent and immanent, is the reality behind a statement of deep gratitude in the midst of brokenness. It's from the sixteenth-century Heidelberg Catechism: "I trust him so much that I do not doubt he will provide whatever I need for body and soul, and he will turn to my good whatever adversity he sends me in this sad world. He is able to do this because he is almighty God; he desires to do this because he is a faithful Father."[14]

> Nothing will be left on the editing room floor of my journey. He'll ultimately redeem it all, wrestling beauty from the ashes for my good and his glory.

My tears are significant, and not only to me. They matter to the almighty God of all creation and my faithful Father. One of the most jolting verses in all of Scripture contains only two words: "Jesus wept" (John 11:35). John and others who were there witnessed the humanity of his tears and then also the divinity of his power. Jesus was at the tomb of his friend Lazarus, about to raise him from the dead. Even while knowing he was about to reclaim his friend from physical death, one of the most visceral evidences that the world is fallen, Jesus still wept over the painful and broken interruption of his friend's life. Fully human, he similarly enters into the pain of our lives—some small, some overwhelming—to, as fully God, both restore and care for us during the process of redemption.

We all learn—the impatient way—that God's timetable is not ours. The gap between whatever painful interruption we've experienced and his redemption of it might not be as short as the time between Lazarus's death and resurrection, but his care in the interim is the same.

When wine is aged, a primary objective is the softening of the bitter chemical compounds called tannins that are found in the skins, seeds, and stems of the grapes. The tannins, though bitter at first, are necessary for the structure and depth of the wine. When the aging has finished its work, the result is a beautiful refinement of that which was at first bitter.

When the psalmist referred to the vessel in which God collects our tears, the Hebrew word translated as "bottle" could just as appropriately be termed "wineskin."[15] The text doesn't mandate that we interpret the significance of the wineskin in this way, but Scripture's teaching about our maturing certainly allows for it. Could it be that God has collected every one of my bitter tears in his wineskin? Could it be that he is letting them age and soften under his restorative and redemptive guidance so that, one day, I will enjoy the mysterious fruit of this brokenness that is further maturing me? Could it be that this softening and deepening from my tears isn't yet finished, but he will continue to guide the process? James's words regarding the trials we have to encounter ring relevant: "The testing of your faith develops perseverance. Perseverance must finish its work so that you may be mature and complete, not lacking anything" (1:3–4).

I'm learning to grasp that God actually pays attention to my tears, but he also wants to redeem them. In the midst of broken experiences, I can be assured "that in all things God works for the good of those who love him, who have been called according to his purpose" (Romans 8:28). (It's important to note that, while this is a powerful truth, if I haven't digested it beforehand, it's difficult to do so in the midst of broken experiences. In that case it can come across almost as a catchall cliché. Instead, it's best learned in times of relative calm before encountering a storm.)

It's a powerful mast of reality to which I can lash myself in the midst of the storm: the broken experience I'm going through isn't good in and of itself, but God will bring good from it. With Job, whose dreams were also shattered in a storm, I can exult, "But he knows the way that I take; when he has tested me, I will come forth as gold" (23:10).

Nothing will be left on the editing room floor of my journey. He'll ultimately redeem it all, wrestling beauty from the ashes for my good and his glory.

The good he accomplishes might become clear soon or I might have to wait. But at some point on the other side of the gate experience of brokenness, we are assured that we'll be able to look back and see what J. R. R. Tolkien coined as a "eucatastrophe." Catastrophes are awful, but when you add the prefix "eu," which means "good," the result is a word that describes God's beautiful redemption and restoration of what initially only appeared to be awful.

❧ ❧ ❧

By the way, I didn't finish telling you about Wynton Marsalis at the Village Van-guard. Yes, the climactic and brilliant rendition of the song's climax was interrupted by a mobile device's silly ringtone. "I don't stand…a ghost…of…a…chance…" *Ring.*

People started chattering, the embarrassed owner of the cell phone scurried for the exit, and Marsalis stood frozen at the microphone. With the magic ruined.

Supposedly.

Yes, after the cell phone went off, the melody was messed up.

But not the song.

Marsalis didn't take the trumpet from his lips. After a silent pause, he resumed playing, note for note, the same silly tune of the cell phone. Then he repeated it.

Some responded with chuckles, and then the chatter quickly quieted down.

To the phone's ringtone Marsalis added some variations and key changes, his virtuosity back on display. The audience was, once again, spellbound.

He ended up in the same key of the interrupted song, mingling the inane tune of the mindless ringtone with the melancholy ballad, finally landing back where his earlier soaring rendition had been interrupted.

"…with…you."

An ovation thundered—greater than it would have been if the cell phone hadn't interrupted things.

Beauty from ashes is even better than mere beauty.

❧ ❧ ❧

I again descend the steep basement stairs of the Vanguard. I take my seat near the back, and as the soulful music starts, I am moved. Not because of the piece playing at that moment—it's too early in the set for that—but by the reality in my memory of Marsalis's long-ago masterful redemption of a 1930s jazz ballad in this place.

Recently, a portion of my life's song has been interrupted, yet once again. I am reeling, dealing with a strange combination of broken experiences—in my job, with some people, even my health.

MAGIC RUINED.

Not so fast.

What's tapping my heart is the reminder that, when the magic is supposedly ruined in my life's song, it's not the end of the song. The melody of my humanity might get interrupted with some unexpected ugliness, but it need not be ruined. In fact, greater magic can arise from the ashes, not by my cleverness or ingenious ability to climb out of the wreckage, but due to the mysterious and persistent grace of God as I become pliable before him. He enters into the sour notes of my life's interruption and merges it into the redemptive song he's composing with my journey.

"Beautiful," I quietly exhale, not because of the flawless song playing on the stage, but because of the less-than-perfect notes being played in my life. As David prayed, "Let the bones dance which thou hast broken" (Psalm 51:8, NEB). I've seen God redeem my pain before, and I'll see him do it again.

In "The Flower," poet George Herbert verbalizes what I've experienced on countless occasions:

Who would have thought my shrivell'd heart
Could have recover'd greenness?[16]

I will keep going through broken experiences. And I'll keep embracing them. As I remain pliable, they'll continue to change me, mature me, and lead me into more Life with a capital L. With each trip I take through a gate of brokenness, I become a little more authentic and humble and a little less superficial and defensive. In my relationships, I become a little more gracious and empathic, a little less judgmental and hardened. As a result of my brokenness, when truth comes along, my heart is less hard and more teachable. Instead of approaching life with a sense of entitlement, a spirit of gratitude inhabits the climate of my journey.

It's a weird thing, but the more familiar I become with brokenness, the more I learn to dance with my broken bones and the more Life I experience. Yes, there is Life *everywhere.*

After the show, I head back up the stairs and out onto Seventh Avenue and back into my journey.

I'm surprised by a blast of cold wind that slaps my face. It's unanticipated, but I decide it's more refreshing than chilling.

Smiling, I muse that the privilege of living is also unpredictable but beautiful.

And Living with a limp?

Even more so.

Heaven

Undiluted Life

> To enter heaven is to become more human than
> you ever succeeded in being on earth; to enter hell,
> is to be banished from humanity.
> —C. S. LEWIS

Eternity can make itself known even in a hectic moment. I hustled from my office, late for a lunch meeting after a conference call had gone past its scheduled time. So I almost didn't see her.

My office was part of a large suite that was also home to an attorney, a small software firm, and a start-up consulting group. The conference room, shared by all of us, had large double doors just off the reception area. When it was not in use, the open doors often attracted restless guests wandering from the waiting area.

Around the large table—the site of client meetings and a wide variety of brainstorming sessions—was a conversation piece in the form of bookcases that lined the walls. Actually it was the contents of the bookcases that drew one's attention. Instead of law journals or software manuals, the shelves contained over a thousand books of mine covering a wide variety of theological, biblical, spiritual, and leadership subjects. The collection provided an intriguing backdrop for business meetings, and it also would occasionally draw the attention of guests and clients.

On the way out to my appointment, while taking a shortcut through the conference room, out of the corner of my eye, I glimpsed a woman in her midthirties. She was in front of a bookcase and turned partly away from me. She held an open book in her hand. She wasn't standing, but sitting. In a wheelchair.

The sound of my movement through the room caught her attention. She turned and looked at me. I slowed to a respectful stop when I saw the glistening tears on her cheeks. Obviously, whatever she was reading had generated a powerful moment for her. My eyes and hers both instinctively shifted to the book in her hand, and I could see the cover and title.

Heaven: Your Real Home.

It is a substantive and contagiously hopeful book by Joni Eareckson Tada, a woman who has had a significant impact on many, including me. I had first heard of Joni when I was in college. I had been walking through a bookstore when her first book, *Joni: An Unforgettable Story,* caught my eye. Picking it up, I started to read the enthralling story of a teenager who dove into some unexpectedly shallow water in Chesapeake Bay and tragically suffered a fracture of her cervical vertebrae, permanently paralyzing her from the shoulders down. As I turned each page that afternoon long ago, I listened to a young woman tell her story of brokenness, honestly struggling with the brutal reality of a fallen world and also authentically engaging with the hope and Life of the gospel.

My attention was riveted. Instead of buying it, I ended up reading the entire book while standing there in the bookstore. (The budget of a college student, I guess. Years later I partnered with Joni on a project and laughingly confessed, assuring her that I eventually purchased a copy.)

Almost three decades after her accident, Joni—a prolific author and artist who holds her pencils between her teeth—had penned this book on heaven. It was now in my conference room in the hands of a woman in a wheelchair that was obviously not a temporary arrangement. I'm sure at some point, she had come to grips with the realization that this wheelchair was her home. But now she was reading a book that conveyed her real home was elsewhere.

She stared at the title for a moment, embarrassed that her tears had been witnessed, then looked back up at me. Realizing I had seen the title as well, she paused, and the corners of her mouth rose into an expression I will never forget.

It was a soft, almost sheepish smile framed by the tears on her cheeks, the moisture reflecting the room's usually bland fluorescent lights. But now the room was anything but bland—it was a holy place where time and eternity were conversing. A place where brokenness was tutored by wholeness regarding a dance that was yet to come.

The nonverbal exchange lasted only a few seconds. She didn't know me and I didn't know her. But I was deeply privileged to enter a moment with her that was simultaneously brief and unending. A *kairos* moment that was holy, other.

There was a lot that could have been said. Then, again, there was nothing more to say. With a smile and a quiet voice because I didn't want to interrupt the reverence of the room, I simply told her to take the book as my gift. She didn't speak but gave me a smile and a nod of thanks. I turned and left for my appointment as she returned to her hopeful longing for Home.

Now, years later, I don't remember anything about the lunch meeting I hurried into that day. But I do remember slowing down during an otherwise ordinary day, looking into a window of eternity, and sharing a glimpse of Home.

~ ~ ~

Is heaven real? Or is it simply an escapist illusion manufactured by weak people who can't deal with the flawed realities of an imperfect world? Peter Kreeft deduces that it's only escapism if it's not true. Only those who are certain heaven is imaginary can call it escapism. But if heaven is true, it's actually escapism to ignore it.[1]

The foundation for our belief in heaven is the same bedrock truth upon which the validity of Christianity rests: Christ's literal, historical, bodily resurrection from the dead. The Scriptures themselves acknowledge "if Christ has not been raised, our preaching is useless and so is your faith" (1 Corinthians 15:14). Plenty of sound and reasoned discussion is in print regarding the trustworthiness of Christ's resurrection, so there's no need to repeat that here.[2]

Suffice it to say that belief in Christ's resurrection is not a swan dive into lunacy but instead an embrace of a central and cogent tenant of our faith. Christ's resurrection confirmed who he claimed to be and the truth of what he taught. If he didn't rise from the dead, by Christianity's own admission, anyone who professes Christ is wasting their time, and the notion of heaven is sheer fantasy. But if he did, to follow him is more than reasonable (which is why, after the resurrection, his disciples gave their lives for him) and heaven is anything but make-believe.

Living Life with a capital L is a matter of living out the reality of Christ's resurrection from the dead every waking day. It's the reason I can trust him, because it validated his claims. But it's also—and this is vital to grasp—a preview of what will happen to me.

Hear him clearly: "I am the resurrection and the life. He who believes in me will live, even though he dies; and whoever lives and believes in me will never die" (John 11:25–26). Because I have received Christ's Life, I will be resurrected as well.

Life with a capital L is all about anticipating my resurrection and embracing its purpose—to get me Home.

~ ~ ~

Lauded as a blues guitar prodigy as a young teenager, Jonny Lang has been well known in rock and blues circles for the last couple of decades. His unique vocal range, combined with killer guitar abilities, has opened doors for him to share the stage with a diverse group of artists ranging from the Rolling Stones to Aerosmith and B. B. King to Sting.

A few months ago, I carved out an evening to hear him in concert at the historic Ogden Theater in Denver. It was an impressive show in which he didn't at all disappoint a very appreciative crowd. Midway through his set, Jonny quieted down after a number of floor-vibrating songs like "Turn Around" and "Blew Up the House" and began a reflective and hopeful piece called "That Great Day." Some are aware of the story of Jonny's conversion to follow Christ back in 2000, but others aren't. But in the next few minutes, everyone heard his hope.

As he began his soft guitar intro, the raucous crowd of over a thousand began to quiet down. But as his soulful lyrics entered both ears and hearts, the room became completely hushed.

He sang of a momentous day to come in which he would be part of a great gathering of generations of men and women who have been freed from their chains and forgiven of their sins: people who, upon seeing God's face, have their tears wiped away and are wholly and forever transformed. He concluded with the gripping statement, "Then we'll be together in Heaven forever, on that great day, on that great day."[3]

> On that Great Day, I'll experience a culmination of my humanity, not an annihilation of it.

There's nothing subtle about what he sang, and by the time Jonny finished this up-front liturgy of a Christ-companioned eternity, there was a silent attentiveness I'd never heard in a secular concert crowd.

He sang not so much to us as over us, almost like he was blanketing the audience with the hope-filled availability of heaven. I had heard the song numerous times before and loved it as much as ever, but what really captivated me during this particular performance was the response of the people. The combination of quietness, accented by some spontaneous cheers a couple of times during the song, and the eruption of an overwhelming ovation at the end seemed to betray the audience's hunger for such a hope.

Lang wasn't singing an escapist song, and the people weren't listening with escapist ears. The men and women in that auditorium, all with eternity in their hearts,[4] were recognizing something that's been familiar to them all their lives. Some were able to pinpoint what it was and others weren't.

It was the palpable sound of Home.

We're all wired with a homing beacon in our souls. It's that music we were born remembering. As Bob Dylan mused, "I was born very far from where I'm supposed to be, and so I'm on my way home."[5] Whether we actually understand where our Home is and whether we're headed in its direction might—depending on our journey—be in question, but each of us desires it.

C. S. Lewis's words make their way into deep parts of me:

> There have been times when I think we do not desire heaven; but more often
> I find myself wondering whether, in our heart of hearts, we have ever desired
> anything else… It is the secret signature of each soul, the incommunicable
> and unappeasable want, the thing we desired before we met our wives or
> made our friends or chose our work, and which we shall still desire on our
> deathbeds, when the mind no longer knows wife or friend or work.[6]

Home is constantly in the background. I might ignore, dismiss, or embrace it, but I can't deny it.

Since the day we were born, we've wanted to get there, but our homesickness is not as much a desire to go forward into something that's ahead as it is a desire to go back—to get back to the garden. Back to the paradise that was lost. We yearn to regain unfettered access to the tree of life so we can—without being encumbered by a fallen body and a fallen world—experience undiluted Life.

If I divorce my journey from that internal compass of eternity that's in my heart, if I deny that my ultimate destiny is a God-authored restoration to wholeness in heaven, the result will be a life of masked emptiness, resignation, and discontent. I'll be continually and hauntingly disappointed because I'll try to extract from this broken world a wholeness it cannot provide. How actively aware I am of that disappointment will depend on how much I numb it with idolatrous pursuits. But regardless of how fervently I chase my idols, I won't be able to shake the disillusionment.

Nor will I be able to outrun my fear of death. As best as I can, I will try to ignore the matter of my own death. In the words of skeptic-turned-believer Malcolm Muggeridge, "It is, of course, inevitable that in a materialist society like ours death should seem terrible, and even inadmissible. If Man is the very apex of creation, with nothing greater than himself in the universe; if his earthly life exhausts the whole content of his existence, then, clearly, his definitive end, his death, is too outrageous to be contemplated, and so is better ignored."[7]

But Life with a capital L changes the way I view death.

Far from being just an eviction from earth, my death either is an induction to undiluted Life or, without Christ, undiluted spiritual death that is no longer cushioned, as it presently is, by common grace. Instead of sequestering reality to the realm of only what I can see, hear, smell, taste, and touch, Life with a capital L involves an embrace of greater realities. Notions of heaven, eternity, and immortality enter the realm of my daily considerations, not as an escape, but as a compass. A compass that points to my destiny.

❦ ❦ ❦

Years ago some friends and I headed to Arizona for a golf weekend. It was also the weekend of the Masters golf tournament in Augusta, Georgia. So after a round of golf, we turned on the television. As we sat watching the telecast, Jack Nicklaus, the winner of six green jackets, was interviewed about how to win at Augusta.

He said the key to playing Augusta National is to play the course backward. Thankfully, he expounded further by explaining that you need to know where the holes are positioned on the greens. Once you know the pin locations, you back up from there to the best locations on the fairways from which you can approach the greens, and then you go back to the tee box and drive the ball to those locations on the fairways.

We looked at each other and laughed. When we had played that day, we had been doing the best we could to hit any sliver of a fairway we could, much less a specific predetermined spot. To land anywhere on a green was a cause for celebration. Sure, we realized the truth of what he was saying, but we also knew it would take a talented golfer to be able to play a course backward with that level of intentionality.

Life is to be lived backward. Unlike golf, talent is not the issue, but very much like golf, intentionality is. The better I'm able to live each day with the ultimate end of my earthly life in mind, the better.

And the more fulfilling. To just go out on a golf course and flail away with no pin in sight or mind would get old very quickly. Which is the way a lot of people feel about their lives.

A powerful distinction between insignificance and significance, between just existing and living, is an embrace of destiny. Am I going somewhere? Is there a goal? Is there a sense of completion ahead? If so, I can live each day backward with a purposeful intentionality that provides a sense of substantive hope. Anticipation and significance become part of my work and play. Otherwise, without an eternal destiny, I might be active (which could be a ploy to drown out the dreadful drumbeat of sheer existence), but it will merely and tragically be a life "full of sound and fury, signifying nothing."[8] A noisy and busy life is not necessarily a significant one.

> My death is an induction to undiluted life.

This journey of Life with a capital L—in which I've been returned to the trajectory of what it means to be fully human—is headed for a culmination. The Scriptures are clear for the follower of Christ: my destiny is immortal, undiluted Life. The implication of Christ's resurrection, and mine to follow, is spelled out by the apostle Paul: "For the trumpet will sound, the dead will be raised imperishable, and we will be changed. For the perishable must clothe itself with the imperishable, and the mortal with immortality. When the perishable has been clothed with the imperishable, and the mortal with immortality, then the saying that is written will come true: 'Death has been swallowed up in victory'" (1 Corinthians 15:52–54).

That immortal Life is what I'm headed for! That destiny is the backdrop of every event of every day. The apostle Paul, unveiling on a practical level why he does not lose heart in the midst of a journey that seems so often uphill, hones in on this sense of completion, on this goal of immortality: "Now we know that if the earthly tent we live in is destroyed, we have a building from God, an eternal house in heaven, not built by human hands. Meanwhile we groan, longing to be clothed with our heavenly dwelling, because when we are clothed, we will not be found naked. For while we are in this tent, we groan and are burdened, because we do not wish to be unclothed but to be clothed with our heavenly dwelling, *so that what is mortal may be swallowed up by life.* Now it is God who has made us for this very purpose and has given us the Spirit as a deposit, guaranteeing what is to come" (2 Corinthians 5:1–5).

Christ has "destroyed death and has brought life and immortality to light through the gospel" (2 Timothy 1:10). The day I trusted him, I received that Life and destiny. But since I was still in a fallen body, I quickly discovered the huge challenge of learning to live Life with a capital L while in a body with a lowercase b. That is part of the struggle of what the Bible calls *sanctification.* Becoming more fully human is a privilege I'm learning to unpack every day, but the beautiful and ultimate goal is to finally receive a resurrection-designed body that is more perfectly compatible with the Life I received the day I trusted Christ. The result will be perfectly full humanity and unencumbered Life with a capital L.

Perhaps you have the idea of heaven being an infinite neighborhood of clouds occupied by a multitude of former humans who are now immaterial Casper-the-Friendly-Ghost-type apparitions. While we're at it, let's continue with the popular perception and add the part about constantly playing harps and floating around and singing hymns all the time. All the time. Forever. And ever. Excited yet?

If you're concerned about boredom in heaven, let me go ahead and assure you, "No eye has seen, no ear has heard, no mind has conceived what God has prepared for those who love him" (1 Corinthians 2:9). Unending, changeless monotony will be infinitely far from what we'll experience in the timeless blessing of God's kingdom.

Bored, disembodied spirits are far from what we'll be after our transformation on the Great Day. The New Testament makes it clear that we, as followers of Christ, are eagerly awaiting "the redemption of our bodies" (Romans 8:23), that he "will transform our lowly bodies so that they will be like his glorious body" (Philippians 3:21), and "when he appears, we shall be like him" (1 John 3:2). The journey of becoming fully human will not be cut short by my death, but accelerated. I will be fully restored and conformed into Christ's perfect image of humanity. My transformation will be completed.[9] On that Great Day, I'll experience a culmination of my humanity, not an annihilation of it.

If I've been embracing Life with a capital L, what I've been learning on this earth about my spiritual life enabling—not inhibiting—my humanity will come to full fruition at my resurrection.

～ ～ ～

To embark on this journey of becoming fully human is to have an understanding of my destiny and to live my life backward from there.

Eternity invades our lives all the time. Moments of our daily lives are glimpses, touches of heaven itself. These heaven moments are like tethers that connect us in our physical daily lives to our eternal destiny. We have any number of heaven moments that hint to us what's to come on that Great Day.

For Paul, each day his groaning and decaying body served to remind him of his destiny—a destiny of being made whole by receiving a resurrected, glorious body.

Other heaven moments can be found in the created world you and I occupy each day. Creation is beautiful but still flawed. Our rebellion not only brought a fallen reality to us but to creation as well. From floods to famines, it groans. "For the creation was subjected to frustration, not by its own choice, but by the will of the one who subjected it, in hope that the creation itself will be liberated from its bondage to decay and brought into the glorious freedom of the children of God" (Romans 8:20–21). The destiny of creation is linked to ours: when our bodies become redeemed, creation will also become restored to its original splendor!

Last Christmas season, I was able to hear the Cecelia Chorus of New York perform Handel's *Messiah* in the historic Stern Auditorium of Carnegie Hall. Out of tradition, during the "Hallelujah" chorus, the audience stood and sang along. My seat was to the side and near the front, so with a slight turn, I was able to see many of the faces of both the performers onstage and the sold-out crowd of twenty-eight hundred. It was an experience I'll never forget: thousands of people singing in an urban metropolis of the world—whether they understood what they were singing or not—a verbatim proclamation of Revelation 11:15. My heart leapt as I heard,

The kingdom of this world
Is become the kingdom of our Lord,
And of His Christ, and of His Christ;
And He shall reign for ever and ever...

What made it so moving for me? Life with a capital L. When I'm living Life on a daily basis, I'm learning to embrace my destiny. I also consciously observe both the beauty and the flaws of this world. In doing so, I'm reminded and infused with hope that both creation and I are in store for a fulfilling restoration.

Yes, the kingdom of this world (earth) will become the kingdom of our Lord. The Bible is clear—earth itself, once paradise, will become paradise again. God's kingdom will be established on earth.

We're standing on it.

Over the centuries, thousands of Christ-taught petitions have been offered, "Your kingdom come, your will be done on earth as it is in heaven" (Matthew 6:10). On that Great Day, those prayers will be fully answered. The kingdom of this world will become the kingdom of our Lord! In a newly created order of a new heaven and earth,[10] it's not just humanity that is in store for a fulfilling restoration, but the entire cosmos.

The New Jerusalem, as a bride, will come from heaven to this new world.[11] As N. T. Wright exults, "It is not we who go to heaven, it is heaven that comes to earth."[12]

With Peter, we can live each day with a sense of anticipation: "But in keeping with his promise we are looking forward to a new heaven and a new earth, the home of righteousness" (2 Peter 3:13). Once again, the whole earth will become the kingdom of God—there will be no rebellious outposts to be found. Just as before the Fall, the glory of the Lord will once again cover the earth as completely as the waters cover the sea.[13]

As I live Life with a capital L, I will view creation as something very different from a disposable commodity. In anticipation of that Great Day, I will learn to be a caretaker, a steward of the earth, and each act of creation care will be an experience of my heavenly calling as well as a rehearsal of my destiny.

❧ ❧ ❧

Another tether to what's to come on that Great Day will be my longings—if I go deeper with them and allow them to connect me with heaven. Could that mean that my unfulfilled longings, instead of taunting me, become a gift?

As Proverbs tells us, "A longing fulfilled is a tree of life" (13:12). In the Garden of Eden, unfettered access to the tree of life meant the absence of unfulfilled longings. When we rebelled, we presumed we could fulfill our longings on our own—we didn't need God—and at the core of the consequent curse is the reality of unmet longings in our story.

What started in the garden will be completed in the New Jerusalem, where the tree of life will spread, perhaps like a grove of aspens, throughout the earth.[14] Through the resurrection of Christ, I can be assured that no God-authored longing will go unfulfilled in heaven.

In the meantime, some propose a quick-fix caricature of what Jesus offers and argue that all our longings are immediately satisfied when we believe the gospel. Others, understandably skeptical about that approach, opt for either ignoring their longings or at least divorcing their longings from their walk with God. None of these approaches are biblical or even logical. They ignore what can be referred to as the "already and not yet" reality of the gospel—when I have *already* received Christ's Life but have *not yet* been delivered from my fallen body and this fallen world.

Walking within that perspective, I realize that some of my longings, upon receiving Christ, are fulfilled now, but others won't be fulfilled this side of heaven. Yet in the hope of heaven, even those longings left unfulfilled are nevertheless addressed— some even lightened—because I realize they are not ignored by heaven's eyes.

Several years ago our family was driving through Wyoming. Beautiful country, but not exactly an epicenter of civilization, so gas stations were pretty scarce. One of my sons was at the wheel with a brand-new driver's license in his wallet and had not noticed the fuel gauge plummet toward a very undesirable reality. Soon the low-fuel light became an item of great family interest as we all groggily awoke from our naps and immediately acquired an acute longing for a gas station. Every sign along the highway was examined thoroughly, looking for any indication that our longing for fuel would not go unmet. The stress grew as the possibility of being stranded along the highway in the middle of nowhere, with no cell signal, increased in its likelihood.

And then, finally, we all saw it: a newly constructed, credible sign that assured us a gas station was ahead. We did the math and compared the miles-to-empty number on the dashboard with the sign's information about the number of miles to the gas station. We were going to be okay.

Everyone shared a satisfied sigh even though our longing was yet to be satisfied. How? Fuel had been credibly promised, so our longing was addressed even though it was not yet fulfilled.

Until the arrival of the new heaven and earth, I will have some unfulfilled longings, but that does not mean they are ignored by God. My unfulfilled longings can be a cause for despair, disillusionment, and abandonment to pleasure binges, or they can become an opportunity to intimately trust Christ and relate with the substantive hope to come. Living Life with a capital L is to rest in the reality that every longing is addressed in the reliable assurances of the resurrected Christ.

~ ~ ~

Another tether to heaven are my broken experiences and my pain—the unpleasant pages of my story. Creation is not all that's groaning in anticipation of the Great Day.

I am as well.

We are assured that, as God welcomes us Home, he will wipe every tear from our eyes. There will be no more death or mourning or crying or pain for the old order of things will have passed away.[15] As I live in confident hope of that day, my groaning, instead of becoming a source of despair or cynicism, can be the soil in which the seeds of hope bear fruit on a daily basis. Paul said, "I consider that our present sufferings are not worth comparing with the glory that will be revealed in us" (Romans 8:18). The suffering doesn't compare with the glory to come, but it can remind us of it.

My groaning, when brought into the light of my Life-laced destiny, can serve to remind me that my journey can be likened to a giant tapestry whose incredible beauty seen on one side comprises a jumbled and seemingly chaotic mass of threads on the opposite side. I often find myself feeling almost strangled by those chaotic strands of suffering on this other side of time in which I'm doing my days. When that's the case, exercising hope will mean anticipating—and even aching—for the Great Day when the tapestry of my story is flipped by his sovereign hand and he displays how he has indeed redeemed every thread for my good and his glory.[16]

~ ~ ~

I can also experience a tether to that Great Day through my obedience in every arena of my life, from vocation to recreation and all points in between. In a passage from 2 Corinthians, after we're assured of immortal life, we're told that "we must all appear before the judgment seat of Christ, that each one may receive what is due him for the things done while in the body, whether good or bad" (5:10). For the follower of Christ, that will not be a judgment of our sin—that has already been dealt with in Christ's substitutionary death—but rather a judgment of our obedience to his call in response to the salvation that has been lavished on us. We've already been graciously and irrevocably granted God's favor through Christ; our responsibility is now to please him.[17]

The more seriously I anticipate the certain arrival of the Great Day, the more passionately I'll pursue Christ's kingdom purposes.[18] My temporal actions have eternal consequences. The way I love God by loving others—serving the physical and spiritual needs of neighbors, the homeless, unreached people groups, clients, friends, and family and helping to shape my neighborhood as well as care for my culture—will follow me into eternity. If I live my life confining my days to whatever's convenient, wrapped up in the trivial pursuit of mundane goals, I will be missing Life with a capital L. And on that Great Day, once my eyes are opened to see the connection between time and eternity, some of the tears he will wipe away will be from my cries of regret.

❧ ❧ ❧

Five words in the final chapter of Revelation.[19] Five words that comprise one of the most powerful statements in all of Scripture. Five words that, when understood and anticipated, can transition a human being from existing to living.

"They will see his face."

In my journey on this earth, though I cannot see God, my greatest possible blessing is for his face to be graciously toward me.[20] But when I'm clothed in immortality, I—as *imago Dei*—will finally experience the *visio Dei,* the vision of the face of God.[21] In that moment, all my longings—for Life, for Home—will be brought to his feet. And my Christ-enabled gaze into the face of God will be the *summum bonum*—the highest good—of my entire existence.

"Now we see but a poor reflection as in a mirror; then we shall see face to face. Now I know in part; then I shall know fully, even as I am fully known" (1 Corinthians 13:12).

That Great Day, all the reflections and parts, the fragments and traces of Life that I have experienced in my journey, will pale in comparison with the whole. My existence will resonate with resolution.

In the meantime, until that Great Day when I will be clothed with my heavenly dwelling, God gives me—as a deposit—his Spirit who gives Life.[22] So every day of my journey, his Holy Spirit lavishes me with deposits of Life:

Extravagant grace.

Freedom to live.

A new and engaged heart.

Deeper enjoyment of beauty.

Illumination through his Word.

Involvement in the story of his glory.

Realigned worship.

Enablement to love well,

to steward my time and brokenness,

and to eagerly anticipate the resolution of heaven.

Yet on that Great Day I'll realize that all those experiences of Life with a capital L, as astounding as they are, have simply been scents, traces of Home. As I stand before God's face, it is then that I will be launched into Life undiluted, unencumbered, and eternal.

The journey of becoming fully human will finally be completed, and the journey of living as fully human will finally commence.

~ ~ ~

It was an extremely painful good-bye, but not a permanent one. More than a year ago, I was on my way to the airport when I got the call. It was from the wife of a dear friend, telling me that her husband's health had plummeted during the night. I had just been with Gerard two evenings earlier, when we and our wives had gathered in his home. He had been weak that evening, but I could now sense the fresh shock in Lisa's voice—that what he was now experiencing was much greater than the struggles of two days before. Or any struggle he had encountered his entire life.

Since receiving the news that he had pancreatic cancer, Gerard had waged an epic battle. In just a couple of months he would have reached the four-year mark since his diagnosis, an extraordinary achievement—he had outlived 95 percent of his fellow patients.

Just two months before this phone call with Lisa, she and Gerard, along with their three kids, had hurriedly packed their cars with whatever belongings they could think to collect as the historic Waldo Canyon Wildfire was screaming down the mountainside toward a neighborhood where both of us had enjoyed living for several years. Three days later, as I had driven through the smoldering, still closed-to-the-public streets with a couple of city officials, our SUV passed where my friends' house should have been. In disbelief, I checked and rechecked the scorched brass numbers on the curbside mailbox, the only structure still standing on the property. Their house was a heap of ash and conquered rubble.

"God, *really?*"

Gerard had later joked that losing his home to a wildfire was not that big of a deal compared with what he'd been through with cancer. I marveled at the heroic man God had shaped through his pliable perseverance through brokenness.

"Matt, they think this is it." Lisa's trembling words on the other end of the call, even though they seemed to come in slow motion, jolted me back to the present tense reality.

"I'll be right there." I hung up and called my assistant and asked her to change my flight to, well, I didn't know. I then altered my car's direction, and my heart's, and headed for the hospital instead of the airport.

As I entered his room in the intensive care unit, I was greeted by the pained but peaceful eyes of a friend literally in one last duel with death. After four years of courageously combating this cancerous enemy, he would finally lose the battle before the sun would set. He knew it. I knew it.

I walked over and gripped his hand.

His voice labored but bore no hint of despair. "I thought you had a flight this afternoon." I responded with a forced, faint smile and said that I wasn't going to make my flight. We both understood why.

He grinned and strained to deliver the final joke I would hear from him. "Hmm. Well, I'm not going to miss *my* flight."

And then he winked.

Yes, winked.

He knew he was heading Home.

❧ ❧ ❧

In those agonizing few hours as Gerard was shedding his temporal, earthly shell, he lost the battle.

But not the war.

During the fight, that hospital space was transformed into something far more than a sterile ICU room. It became a place in which death's conqueror displayed his triumph and hope. The awfulness of death and dying, and the pain of saying such a momentous and tragically premature good-bye, was not lost on any of us, including Gerard. Yet it was not just a place of death but also of Life.

Gerard had heard me use the phrase many times, and once, during an interval in the throes of his struggle that afternoon, he whispered in my ear, "Life with a capital L." Was it sarcasm? Not a chance. It was the deeper reality of what was going on in that room.

His use of the phrase took me for a quick moment to Nikolai Yaroshenko's painting: *There Is Life Everywhere.* And as I have on many occasions since seeing the piece, I again asked myself, "Is there really Life here— in this moment, in this place, in this circumstance?"

> A powerful distinction between insignificance and significance, between just existing and living, is an embrace of destiny.

Yes. There was. Gerard had modeled Life for me through excruciating circumstances that included the pain of cancer and the incinerating loss of a home. He was modeling it for me now.

When the beating of his heart stopped, his Life didn't. He is now more alive than I ever witnessed while knowing him. The Life that began when he received Christ as a twenty-five-year-old electrical engineer is now undiluted and unencumbered. His journey toward becoming fully human, according to what God originally intended, is now complete.

As I drove away that night, I wept tears of loss for us and of gladness for him. We were reeling in the shadow of this new and immensely painful reality of continuing our journeys without his physical companionship, but Gerard had left for that place Jesus was talking about when he explained he was heading there to get it ready for us.[23] It is a place that's unfallen and unmarred, and it would be the first place Gerard has ever been that was perfectly compatible with Life.

Let the undiluted Living begin.

❧ ❧ ❧

I'm about to hit Send on an e-mail, which will deliver this final chapter to my editor. Then I'll get in my car and head over to watch a young high school girl play a tennis match. I'm a big tennis fan, but that's not the only reason I'm excited to go. This is a girl who sent me a Father's Day greeting last year. With three sons, I'm very familiar with Father's Day notes from boys, but not having a daughter, I had never received one from a girl. It was uncharted and humbling territory. She sent it to me instead of her biological dad because, though she knows his location, she doesn't have his mailing address.

Grace—Gerard's daughter—is a beautiful reminder for me to embrace both the Life that's to come and also the Life that is.

From a younger woman in a tennis match to an older woman in a wheelchair, from a dad fighting in a hospital room to an adopted dad cheering by a tennis court, we all deal with the ebbs and flows of journeying in a fallen world.

But in the midst of the beauty as well as the brokenness, there can be Life.

Yes, *there is Life everywhere.*

Introduction: There Is Life Everywhere

The epigraph is taken from Robert Kurson, *Shadow Divers: The True Adventure of Two Americans Who Risked Everything to Solve One of the Last Mysteries of World War II* (New York: Random House, 2005), 22.

Chapter 1: Fully Human

The epigraph is taken from Frederick Buechner, *The Magnificent Defeat* (New York: HarperCollins, 1966), 118.

1. Thornton Wilder, *Our Town: A Play in Three Acts* (New York: Coward-McCann, 1938), 25.
2. Wilder, *Our Town*, 83.
3. Robert D. Abrahams, "The Night They Burned Shanghai," *Saturday Evening Post*, November 13, 1943, 91.
4. T. S. Eliot, "Choruses from the Rock," in *Collected Poems, 1901–1935* (New York: Harcourt, Brace and Company, 1936).
5. Wilder, *Our Town*, 58.
6. "Humanity," Merriam-Webster.com, http://merriam-webster.com/dictionary /humanity.
7. Genesis 1:27; Psalm 8:4–8; Psalm 139:14; 1 Corinthians 6:19–20.
8. Our humanity is not our "earthly nature" (Colossians 3:5). Our humanity is not our "flesh" that we are urged to fight against (Romans 8, ESV). Our humanity is not our "old self" (Colossians 3:9). It's not our humanity that's the problem but our selfish rebelliousness. God, referring to creation—which obviously included humanity—said it was very good (Genesis 1:31). Jesus became fully human (Hebrews 2:14–17) but was still without sin (Hebrews 4:15), so our humanity, in and of itself, isn't sinful. To say that my humanity is fallen (which it is) is not the same as saying it is evil any more than to say that the world, because it is fallen, is inherently evil. The world is in the process of being redeemed, as is our humanity.
9. John Murray, *The Collected Writings of John Murray*, vol. 2, *Select Lectures in Systematic Theology* (1976; repr., Edinburgh: Banner of Truth Trust, 2009), 17.
10. John 1:14; Hebrews 1:3; 2:14, 17.
11. Romans 8:29; 2 Corinthians 3:18.
12. John 3:5–8.

13. Yes, as Christ's followers, we should have the mind of Christ (1 Corinthians 2:16). Yes, we are supposed to set our mind on "things above, not on earthly things" (Colossians 3:2). Yes, "our citizenship is in heaven" (Philippians 3:20). But it's not an either/or scenario. To have Christ's mind is to engage with his purpose for my humanity. To fix my eyes on things above is to engage with the kingdom purposes Christ wants me to fulfill on this planet. To long for heaven is not to deny my humanity—my humanity will not cease in heaven but will instead be completed (see chapter 15, "Heaven: Undiluted Life"). To become more spiritual is certainly to become less sinful and worldly but not less human.

14. Matthew 11:19.

15. Which is part of the reason Christ is referred to as the "last Adam" or "second man" in 1 Corinthians 15:45, 47. See also Hebrews 2:14–17 and John 1:14.

16. Gregory of Nazianzus, "To Cledonius the Priest Against Apollinarius" (Letter 101), in *Nicene and Post-Nicene Fathers,* 2nd ser., vol. 7, ed. Philip Schaff and Henry Wace, trans. Charles Gordon Browne and James Edward Swallow (Buffalo, NY: Christian Literature, 1894), revised and edited by Kevin Knight, www .newadvent.org/fathers/3103a.htm.

17. 2 Corinthians 5:17.

18. Acts 13:22.

Chapter 2: The Hunger of Being Human

The epigraph is taken from George Eliot, *The Mill on the Floss,* bk. v (Edinburgh: Blackwood, 1860), 25.

1. Quoted in Christopher West, *Fill These Hearts: God, Sex, and the Universal Longing* (New York: Crown, 2012), 4. Also, for information about the golden record, see http://en.wikipedia.org/wiki/Contents_of_the_Voyager_Golden _Record.

2. Søren Kierkegaard, *Papers and Journals: A Selection* (New York: Penguin, 1996), 100.

3. C. S. Lewis, *The Weight of Glory: And Other Addresses* (1949, 1976, 1980; repr., New York: HarperCollins, 2001), 25.

4. John 4:10.

5. Lewis, *Weight of Glory,* 26.

Chapter 3: The Depths of Our Desire

The epigraph is taken from Fyodor Dostoyevsky, *White Nights and Other Stories* (New York: Macmillan, 1918).

1. Henry David Thoreau, *Walden, or, Life in the Woods* (1854; repr., Mineola, NY: Dover, 1999), 4.

2. John Eldredge, *Journey of Desire: Searching for the Life We've Only Dreamed Of* (Nashville: Thomas Nelson, 2000), 285.

3. Jim Carrey, Facebook, August 15, 2012, www.facebook.com/permalink.php?story_fbid=398572023538382&id=196914760370777.

4. John 4:14.

5. Blaise Pascal, *Pensées*, trans. W. F. Trotter (New York: Dutton, 1958), 138–139.

6. C. S. Lewis, *The Silver Chair* (New York: HarperCollins, 1953), 21–23.

Chapter 4: Life, Our Ultimate Longing

The epigraph is taken from Ephrem the Syrian, *Select Poems*, trans. Sebastian P. Brock and George A. Kiraz (Provo, UT: Brigham Young University Press, 2006), 19.

1. Tennessee Williams, *Collected Stories* (1985; repr., New York: New Directions, 1994), 20.

2. Williams, *Collected Stories*, 23.

3. Williams, *Collected Stories*, 25.

4. C. S. Lewis, *Poems*, ed. Walter Hooper (Orlando, FL: Harcourt, 1992), Kindle edition, part 2.

5. Wendell Berry, *A Timbered Choir: The Sabbath Poems, 1979–1997* (Berkeley, CA: Counterpoint, 1998).

6. John 4:14, 17:2.

7. John 17:3.

8. Hebrews 11:6.

Chapter 5: Grace, the Doorway to Life

1. Isak Dinesen, *Anecdotes of Destiny and Ehrengard* (New York: Vintage, 1993), 23–70.

2. In fact, *perisseúō* is from the same root as *perissos* ("abundant, to the full") in John 10:10.

3. Nancy Spiegelberg, "If Only I Had Known," in *Fanfare: A Celebration of Belief* (Portland, OR: Multnomah, 1981). Used with permission.

4. Anne Lamott, "Sincere Meditations," salon.com, May 27, 1999, www.salon.com/1999/05/27/sincerity.

5. Dinesen, *Anecdotes*, 23–70.

Chapter 6: Freedom

The epigraph is taken from J. R. R. Tolkien, "On Fairy-Stories," *Tales from the Perilous Realm* (New York: Houghton Mifflin Harcourt, 2008), Kindle edition, appendix.

1. Frederick Buechner, *Wishful Thinking: A Theological ABC* (New York: Harper & Row, 1973), 30.
2. John 8:31–36; Matthew 23:13–15.
3. Dietrich Bonhoeffer, *Letters and Papers from Prison*, ed. Christian Gremmels, Eberhard Bethge, Renate Bethge, and John W. de Gruchy, trans. Isabel Best (Minneapolis: Fortress, 2010), 188.
4. John Owen, *The Death of Death in the Death of Christ* (1852; repr., Edinburgh: Banner of Truth Trust, 1967).
5. *The Shawshank Redemption*, directed by Frank Darabont (Culver City, CA: Columbia Pictures, 1994), www.imdb.com/title/tt0111161/quotes.
6. Quoted in Carl Hulse, "Vote in House Offers a Shield in Obesity Suits," *New York Times*, March 11, 2004.
7. Hampton Sides, *Ghost Soldiers: The Epic Account of World War II's Greatest Rescue Mission* (New York: Anchor Books, 2002), Kindle edition, epilogue.
8. Sides, *Ghost Soldiers*, chapter 9.
9. Sides, *Ghost Soldiers*, chapter 12.
10. Sides, *Ghost Soldiers*, chapter 13.
11. 2 Corinthians 3:18.

Chapter 7: Heart

1. "Self Improvement," *Reader's Digest*, October 2001, www.timallen.com/actor/press_archive/readers_digest.php?xpt=1.
2. Victor Hugo, *Les Misérables*, trans. Isabel F. Hapgood (New York: Crowell, 1915), 53.
3. Blaise Pascal, *Pensées*, trans. W. F. Trotter (New York: Dutton, 1958), 277.
4. C. S. Lewis, *Poems*, ed. Walter Hooper (Orlando, FL: Harcourt, 1992), Kindle edition, part 2.
5. "The Voiceless," in *The Poems of Oliver Wendell Holmes* (New York: Thomas Y. Crowell, 1903), 430.
6. A variation of the story is told in *Frank Lloyd Wright: An Autobiography* (Petaluma, CA: Pomegranate Communications, 1943), prelude.

Chapter 8: Beauty

The epigraph is taken from St. John of the Cross, quoted in John O'Donohue, *Beauty: The Invisible Embrace* (New York: HarperCollins, 2004), 220.
1. Rollo May, *My Quest for Beauty* (Dallas: Saybrook, 1985), 72.
2. Elaine Scarry, *On Beauty and Being Just* (Princeton, NJ: Princeton University Press, 1999), 25–27.

3. O'Donohue, *Beauty*, 13.

4. John 14:6.

5. Philippians 4:7, 9.

6. Ellen Haroutunian, "A Baptism of Imagination: A Conversation with Peter Kreeft," *Mars Hill Review* 5 (Summer 1996): 56–73, www.leaderu.com/marshill /mhr05/kreeft1.html.

7. Jonathan Edwards, *The Works of Jonathan Edwards*, 2 vols. (London: William Ball, 1839), 1:125.

8. Jonathan Edwards, *Scientific and Philosophical Writings*, ed. Wallace E. Anderson (New Haven, CT: Yale University Press, 1980), 332.

9. For this concept of the Whole being represented in the fragments, I'm grateful to the writings of Hans Urs von Balthasar.

10. Fyodor Dostoyevsky, *The Brothers Karamazov* (New York: Random House, 1950), 202.

11. C. S. Lewis, *The Weight of Glory: And Other Addresses* (1949, 1976, 1980; repr., New York: HarperCollins, 2001), 30–31.

12. C. S. Lewis, *Till We Have Faces: A Myth Retold* (1956; repr., Grand Rapids: Eerdmans, 1971), 75.

13. James Oppenheim, "Bread and Roses," *American Magazine* 73 (December 1911): 214.

14. Luke 12:27.

15. Matthew 26:7.

16. Exodus 31:4.

Chapter 9: Illumination

1. Robert Frost, "Acquainted with the Night," from *The Poetry of Robert Frost*, ed. Edward Connery Lathem (New York: Holt, Rinehart and Winston, 1969), www.poetryfoundation.org/poem/177009.

2. Dante Alighieri, *The Divine Comedy*, trans. Clive James (New York: Norton, 2013), 3.

3. Emily Dickinson, "We Grow Accustomed to the Dark," in *The Poems of Emily Dickinson*, ed. R. W. Franklin (Cambridge, MA: Belknap Press, 1999), 198.

4. John 8:31–32.

5. Richard John Neuhaus, "Is There Life After Truth?" in *A Place for Truth: Leading Thinkers Explore Life's Hardest Questions*, ed. Dallas Willard (Downers Grove, IL: InterVarsity, 2010), 34, 23.

6. Søren Kierkegaard, *Provocations—Spiritual Writings of Kierkegaard* (New York: Orbis, 2002), 85.

7. Anne Lamott, *Help, Thanks, Wow: The Three Essential Prayers* (New York: Riverhead Books, 2012), 7.

8. Emile Cailliet, *Journey into Light* (Grand Rapids: Zondervan, 1968), 18.

Chapter 10: Story

The epigraph is taken from Annie Dillard, *Pilgrim at Tinker Creek* (New York: Bantam, 1974), 2.

1. Cloud Nothings, "Wasted Days," on *Attack on Memory,* Carpark Records, 2012, compact disc.

2. "David Foster Wallace on Life and Work," *Wall Street Journal,* September 19, 2008, http://online.wsj.com/news/articles/SB122178211966454607.

3. See All Comments: Sam at www.youtube.com/watch?v=vET9cvlGJQw.

4. John Logan and Brian Selznick, *Hugo,* directed by Martin Scorsese (Hollywood, CA: Paramount Pictures, 2011), DVD, www.moviequotesandmore.com/hugo -movie-quotes-1.html.

5. Walt Whitman, "O Me! O Life!" in *Leaves of Grass* (1892; repr., New York: Modern Library, 2000), 222.

6. Sting, "The Book of My Life," on *Sacred Love,* A&M Records, 2003, compact disc.

7. "*The Sound of Music*: Trivia," IMDB.com, www.imdb.com/title/tt0059742/trivia.

8. Genesis 2:17.

9. Romans 8:18–22.

10. Isaiah 40:5.

11. 1 Thessalonians 2:12; 1 Peter 5:10.

12. "Shorter Catechism," Orthodox Presbyterian Church, Question 1, http://opc.org /sc.html.1646.

13. Irenaeus, *Against Heresies,* 4.34.5–7.

14. Matthew 16:25.

15. Flannery O'Connor, *A Prayer Journal* (New York: Farrar, Straus and Giroux, 2013), Kindle edition, sixth entry.

16. David Brooks, *The Social Animal: The Hidden Source of Love, Character, and Achievement* (New York: Random House, 2011), 88.

17. C. S. Lewis, *Weight of Glory: And Other Addresses* (New York: HarperCollins, 2009), Kindle edition, "Is Theology Poetry?"

Chapter 11: Worship

The epigraph is taken from T. S. Eliot, "Little Gidding," in *Four Quartets* (1943; repr., Orlando, FL: Harcourt, 2014), 51–52.

1. John 4:20.

2. John Calvin, *Institutes of the Christian Religion* (1960; repr., Louisville, KY: Westminster, 2006), 108.

3. "Amusing, But Sad…Pelicans Mistake Asphalt for Lakes," Yehoodi.com, July 15, 2004, www.yehoodi.com/comment/66898/ amusing-but-sad-pelicans-mistake-asphalt-for-lakes.

4. Romans 1:23.

5. Blaise Pascal, *Pensées,* trans. W. F. Trotter (New York: Dutton, 1958), 138–139.

6. See Calvin Seerveld, *On Being Human: Imaging God in the Modern World* (Burlington, ON: Welch, 1988), 17.

7. See R. C. Sproul, *Before the Face of God: A Daily Guide for Living from the Book of Romans,* bk. 1 (Grand Rapids: Baker, 1992), 9.

8. Elizabeth Barrett Browning, *Aurora Leigh: And Other Poems* (New York: James Miller, 1872), 138.

9. Matthew 15:8–9.

10. John Piper, "One New Year's Resolution," Reflections on God's Word, December 29, 2013, http://feedonhim.wordpress.com/tag/john-piper.

11. William Willimon, "Messiness, Messiness, Is All I Long For…," Wordhavering, https://wordhavering.wordpress.com/tag/william-willimon.

12. Gerard Manley Hopkins, *Poems and Prose* (London: Penguin, 1963), 144, emphasis added.

13. John O'Donohue, *Beauty: The Invisible Embrace* (New York: HarperCollins, 2004), 227.

14. My thanks to Ray Vander Laan for this image.

15. 1 Peter 3:15.

16. My thanks to Brennan Manning for this phrase.

Chapter 12: Love

The epigraph is taken from Victor Hugo, *Les Misérables,* trans. Isabel F. Hapgood (New York: Crowell, 1915), 75.

1. Masayuki Suo and Audrey Wells, *Shall We Dance?,* directed by Peter Chelsom (New York: Miramax Films, 2004), Timestamp 50:50.

2. 1 John 3:1.

3. Proverbs 8:35; 2 Corinthians 6:2.

4. 1 John 4:9-10.

5. Isaiah 54:10.

6. Isaiah 43:4.

7. Ephesians 3:18.

8. Romans 15:7; Ephesians 3:20.

9. Romans 8:1, 39.

10. Zephaniah 3:17.

11. Brennan Manning, *The Furious Longing of God* (Colorado Springs: David C. Cook, 2009), 31.

12. Dan B. Allender, *The Healing Path: How the Hurts in Your Past Can Lead You to a More Abundant Life* (Colorado Springs: WaterBrook, 1999), 56.

13. Isaiah 53:3.

14. Hebrews 12:15.

15. Colossians 3:13.

16. C. S. Lewis, *The Four Loves* (1960; repr., Orlando, FL: Harcourt, 1988), 121.

17. Dietrich Bonhoeffer, *Life Together* (New York: HarperCollins, 1954), 20.

Chapter 13: Time

1. T. S. Eliot, "Burnt Norton," in *Four Quartets* (1943; repr., Orlando, FL: Harcourt, 2014), 16.

2. Gerald G. May, *The Awakened Heart: Opening Yourself to the Love You Need* (New York: HarperCollins, 1991), 71.

3. Calvin Seerveld, *On Being Human: Imaging God in the Modern World* (Burlington, ON: Welch, 1988), 37.

4. Shakespeare, *Julius Caesar, Great Books of the Western World,* vol. 1, *The Plays and Sonnets of William Shakespeare,* ed. William George Clarke and William Aldis Wright, act 4, sc. 3, lines 218–221.

5. C. S. Lewis, *The Screwtape Letters* (London: Bles, 1942), 142–43.

6. Matt Kramer, "The 'Special Occasion' Trap," *Wine Spectator,* April 30, 2012, 38.

7. Blaise Pascal, *Pensées,* trans. W. F. Trotter (New York: Dutton, 1958), 172.

8. John Lennon, "Beautiful Boy," on *Double Fantasy,* Geffen Records, 1980, $33^{1/3}$ rpm.

9. Ecclesiastes 3:11.

10. Romans 8:9; Titus 3:5.

11. John 6:63; Romans 8:11.

12. Jack London, *Jack London's Tales of Adventure,* ed. Irving Shepard (Garden City, NY: Hanover House, 1956), vii.

13. Ecclesiastes 3:1–8.

Chapter 14: Brokenness

The epigraph is taken from Aleksandr I. Solzhenitsyn, *The Gulag Archipelago, 1918–1956: An Experiment in Literary Investigation,* Parts III–IV, trans. Thomas P. Whitney (New York: Harper & Row, 1974), 616.

1. David Hajdu, "Wynton's Blues," *The Atlantic,* March 1, 2003, www.theatlantic.com/magazine/archive/2003/03/wyntons-blues/302684.

2. Thanks to Dan Allender for the phrase "living with a limp," *Leading with a Limp* (Colorado Springs: WaterBrook, 2008).

3. Matthew 4:16.

4. Alain Boubill and Herbert Kretzmer, "I Dreamed a Dream," *Les Misérables* (1980).

5. 1 Peter 1:7; 5:6–7.

6. T. S. Eliot, "East Coker," in *Four Quartets* (1943; repr., Orlando, FL: Harcourt, 2014), 23.

7. Christopher J. H. Wright, "Editorial: 'All Our Gods Have Failed,'" *Themelios* 18, no. 3 (1993): 3.

8. David Whyte, *The Heart Aroused: Poetry and the Preservation of the Soul in Corporate America* (New York: Currency Doubleday, 1994), 29.

9. My thanks to Pat Morley for the distinction that there is a god we want and a God we need, and they are not the same.

10. Augustine, *The City of God*, book 1, chapter 8.

11. Jeremiah 30:17.

12. Henri Nouwen, *Life of the Beloved: Spiritual Living in a Secular World* (New York: Crossroad, 1992), 79.

13. Gerald L. Sittser, *A Grace Disguised: How the Soul Grows Through Loss* (Grand Rapids: Zondervan, 1996), 42.

14. Heidelberg Catechism with Scripture Texts (Grand Rapids: CRC, 1989), Question 26.

15. Noted in the NIV's footnote for Psalm 56:8.

16. George Herbert, "The Flower," in *English Poetry: From Chaucer to Gray*, The Harvard Classics, 3 vols. (New York: Collier, 1909–14), 1:354.

Chapter 15: Heaven

The epigraph is taken from C. S. Lewis, *The Problem of Pain* (New York: Macmillan, 1944), 125.

1. Peter Kreeft, *Heaven: The Heart's Deepest Longing* (Cambridge, MA: Harper & Row, 1980), 168.

2. *The Case for the Resurrection: A First-Century Investigative Reporter Probes History's Pivotal Event* by Lee Strobel, *The Case for the Resurrection of Jesus* by Gary Habermas and Michael Licona, *Jesus' Resurrection: Fact or Figment?* edited by Paul Copan and Ronald K. Tacelli, *The Son Rises: The Historical Evidence for the Resurrection of Jesus* by William Lane Craig, and *The Resurrection of the Son of God* by N. T. Wright.

3. Jonny Lang, "That Great Day," on *Turn Around*, Almo Music Corp., Langy Tunes Music, 2006, compact disc.

4. Ecclesiastes 3:11.

5. *No Direction Home,* directed by Martin Scorsese (Hollywood, CA: Paramount Pictures, 2005).

6. Lewis, *The Problem of Pain,* 149, 151.

7. Malcolm Muggeridge, *Confessions of a Twentieth-Century Pilgrim* (San Francisco: Harper & Row, 1988), 144.

8. Shakespeare, *Macbeth, Great Books of the Western World,* vol. 2, *The Plays and Sonnets of William Shakespeare,* ed. William George Clarke and William Aldis Wright, act 5, sc. 5, lines 27–28.

9. Romans 8:29; 1 Corinthians 15:49.

10. Revelation 21:1; Isaiah 65:17.

11. Revelation 21:2.

12. N. T. Wright, *Surprised by Hope: Rethinking Heaven, the Resurrection, and the Mission of the Church* (New York: HarperCollins, 2008), 104.

13. Habakkuk 2:14.

14. Revelation 22:2.

15. Revelation 21:4.

16. Romans 8:28.

17. 2 Corinthians 5:9.

18. Matthew 6:33.

19. Revelation 22:4.

20. Numbers 6:24–26.

21. 1 John 3:2–3; Matthew 5:8.

22. 2 Corinthians 5:5; John 6:63.

23. John 14:2–3.

About the Author

MATT HEARD lives in Colorado Springs with his wife, Arlene, where they have relished the privilege of raising three amazing sons—Andrew, Joel, and Stephen.

A speaker, writer, and teacher, he has been involved in pastoral ministry for three decades. He is a graduate of Wheaton College and Reformed Theological Seminary and has pastored churches in Illinois, Michigan, and Colorado. Most recently he served as senior pastor of Woodmen Valley Chapel in Colorado Springs for twelve years. He has also been a leadership consultant and was the executive director of the Greater Orlando Leadership Foundation (now Lifework Leadership).

Matt enjoys skiing, fishing, and hunting in the Rocky Mountains. He appreciates great food, art, music, books, and movies. He's a sports nut, a passion that includes golf, scuba diving, and being a diehard fan. He also loves to ride—either a horse or his Harley.

And whether standing in front of people with a microphone or in a trout stream with a fly rod, whether sitting around a dinner table with friends or serving a need in his city, he—most of all—loves exploring and experiencing Christ's ultimate gift, Life with a capital L, and inviting other people into the journey.

To find out more or contact Matt, visit www.mattheard.org.